EQUESTRIAN TECHNIQUE

EQUESTRIAN TECHNIQUE

Tris Roberts

J.A. ALLEN
London

First published in Great Britain by
J.A. Allen & Co. Ltd
1 Lower Grosvenor Place
London SW1W 0EL

Some of the material contained in *Equestrian Technique*
has appeared in the author's previous work, *Basic Skills of Horse
Riding*, published by J.A. Allen in 1985 and now out of print.

British Library Cataloguing in Publication Data
A catalogue record for this book is available from the British Library.

Line drawings by Maggie Raynor
Book design by Sandie Boccacci

Typeset in 11/13 point Cheltenham by Setrite Typesetters, Hong Kong
Printed and bound by Dah Hua, Hong Kong

CONTENTS

PREFACE

My object in writing this book has been to explain, in clear, jargon-free language, just what it is that the rider needs to do in order to persuade his horse to perform a variety of manoeuvres. I provide detailed instructions, with explanations, for all the manoeuvres to be encountered either in everyday riding or in advanced dressage.

In preparation for this book, I conducted a wide-ranging search of the writings of the classical masters of equitation. This revealed a confusing variety of techniques, from which I selected those whose efficacy I could verify by personal experiment. The resulting set of tried-and-tested routines turned out, in the main, to be those based on the tradition of the Cadre Noir at Saumur, as represented in *Les Allures, le Cavalier*, by Yves Turquet de Beauregard, writing as L. de Sévy. My descriptions of these techniques were then checked for consistency with the practice of the Spanish Riding School in Vienna.

Much of the present text appeared earlier under the title *Basic Skills of Horse Riding*, where it survived the scrutiny of a number of contemporary masters. In the present version, which is addressed to the more serious student, rather than primarily to the beginner, certain sections have been considerably expanded, to provide a more detailed treatment.

Because I believe that the topics deserve the careful attention of all serious riders, I have added two appendices: one on the principles involved in the maintenance of balance, and one on the way the learning process works.

In a final appendix, I have added a number of short explanatory notes. Some of these are straightforward definitions; some are explanations of equestrian expressions where the meaning is not immediately clear from the words used; and some deal with terms borrowed from the science of mechanics that are often misused in the equestrian context.

ACKNOWLEDGEMENTS

I am grateful to the many pupils, both riders and horses, who have unwittingly helped in the preparation of this book. There are others, however, who have helped more directly.

It gives me particular pleasure to acknowledge my indebtedness to Mr Charles Harris, FIH, FBHS, FABRS, who encouraged me to go ahead when I first outlined to him my plan for the book. His detailed comments have led me to think deeply about how best to arrive at unambiguous clarity in the exposition of routines that really work. I regard his advice as especially authoritative in view of his long experience of classical equitation, which has included a number of years at the Spanish Riding School in Vienna. Nevertheless, he should not be taken as necessarily agreeing with everything in the book.

The photographs represent only a small proportion of those taken in the course of preparing this book and I wish to thank all those many friends, especially Miss Heather Carstairs and Miss Fiona Brown, who served so patiently as models. Many of the photographs finally selected were taken at the Mark Phillips Equestrian Centre at Gleneagles by kind permission of the Director of Training, Mr William Micklem, FBHS, and I am grateful to him and to his staff for their very helpful co-operation. The rein-tension training machine described in Chapter 5 was devised by me for the Centre and has been in use there for some time.

At all stages in the preparation of the book I have greatly appreciated the benefit of frequent and helpful discussions with Mr John D. Christie, who has also checked the proofs.

My thanks are due, too, to my publisher and his staff, especially my editor, Lesley Gowers, for advice and encouragement, for contributing many valuable suggestions for improving the text itself and for arranging for all the figures to be expertly redrawn by Maggie Raynor.

INTRODUCTION

The rider's control of the horse calls for a number of special skills, not the least important being the ability to make himself aware of what the horse is doing or is about to do. The development of the necessary skills comes only with practice, but the aspiring rider needs to know what sort of practice will be helpful. In this book I set out a sequence of stages by which full mastery can be achieved. The order of this sequence is dictated by the fact that each topic is, to some extent, dependent on others. In dealing with each topic in turn, we start with the needs and problems of the beginner and then go on into considerable detail before passing on to the next topic. In a continuous read-through, the novice may thus soon find himself faced with manoeuvres that are beyond his present competence. At a first reading it will accordingly be appropriate to skip ahead when this happens, and to turn to topics of more immediate application. A beginner's introduction to riding could be based on Chapters 1, 3, 4, and 8 alone, provided that the instructor is familiar with the material in the rest of the book.

In Britain, 'riding' usually means riding astride in what is sometimes called the 'English' style. The descriptions that follow have been written with this in mind, but it will be found that only minor modifications in technique are required either for riding side-saddle or for riding in 'Western' style.

Many riders will wish to tackle certain manoeuvres during the course of their training in an order different from that in which they are presented here. For example, many will wish to attempt jumps before venturing on lateral work. There is no serious disadvantage in this, since the reader can readily locate the sections that deal with any particular problems that might arise from not having worked systematically through the text.

The experienced rider, on the other hand, may find that some parts of the treatment cover too familiar ground. There is an advantage in perusing these parts, rather than skipping them, since the rehearsal, in a fresh account, of a topic usually taken for granted can sometimes help, and often in a quite unexpected way, in the resolution of long-standing points of difficulty.

It is instructive to look carefully at photographs of ridden horses in the light of the illustrations in this book. Such comparisons can prove very informative. Almost inevitably, when a photograph is taken, either the horse or the rider is not quite in the position one would regard as ideal. It is a good idea, when you are learning a new skill, to train your eye to detect errors in technique in others, since this can lead you to become aware of what you are doing yourself in comparable circumstances. This in turn can help you to improve your own technique.

The way I approach and handle the various topics is strongly influenced by ideas derived from my own research background in the fields of balance and locomotion. Indeed, the treatments of the transitions between the gaits and of the horse's preparation for the jump all come directly from my research. The treatment of the rider's balance is expanded in a separate appendix to include the physical principles on which successful balance depends, as revealed by experiment.

The learning process is central to equestrian studies since both horse and rider need to be trained. There are, however, many misunderstandings about learning in the current equestrian literature, reflecting the general confusion in the public mind about the nature of conditioned reflexes and the like. In my appendix on 'Learning and Teaching', I set out the distinctions between the various forms of 'conditioning', together with the relationships of these to habit-formation. I explain why habits, once formed, are so difficult to alter, and set out a technique by which this can be done. This is particularly relevant since undesirable habits are all too readily acquired by horse and rider alike. The importance of 'getting it right' from the very beginning cannot be too strongly emphasised. It is, in my view, a mistake to accept sloppy performance of a manoeuvre on the grounds that it can be tidied up later.

The book is aimed at the self-instruction of the rider, on the basis that self-instruction is by far the most effective technique for learning and, even in the presence of a formal instructor, the pupil must in fact teach himself. The movements of the horse often present problems to the rider of which the instructor may well be quite unaware. Consequently, the rider must learn to sit his horse in much the same way as one learns to ride a bicycle, learning from direct experience in a prepared situation rather than simply from the remarks made by an instructor. The function of the instructor is to manipulate the conditions in such a way as to give the pupil the best chance of learning for himself from his own sensations in the saddle. I draw attention to the sensations that the pupil should be particularly on the look-out for at each stage. The skilled instructor will have a large repertoire of routines which he can use to draw the attention of the pupil to those aspects of the learning situation that will best assist the pupil at each stage of his development. Even when excellent instructors are available, some students value the opportunity to study a written presentation at their leisure. In this way, they are able to sort out the various problems as they arise and can, as a result, more readily assimilate the instructions given to them in formal lessons.

The rider needs to pay special attention to the movements made by the horse in response to the rider's commands. It is by such movements that the horse signals his doubts, as well as his understanding. The horse is also learning, all the time. The skilled rider adjusts his commands to take account of the horse's signals, thus building up a rapport and establishing effective two-way communication between horse and rider. It is the successful communication between horse and rider, the feeling of 'being at one with one's mount', that provides a great deal of the exhilaration and satisfaction that can be derived from riding. It is probably the lack of attainment in this particular skill that is responsible for so many youngsters becoming bored with riding and giving it up after only a few years. Unfortunately, many teachers appear to treat learning to ride a horse as though it was like learning to drive a car, and the horse's contribution to the 'conversation' between horse and rider is totally neglected.

There is a certain mystique that has somehow grown up about 'dressage', and many instructors discourage their pupils from attempting certain manoeuvres until after they have 'earned the right' to do so by scoring suitably in an arbitrary series of tests. They refer to the manoeuvres as 'dressage movements', with the implication that they are something special, the exclusive province of the acknowledged expert. It is preferable to think of these movements primarily as suppling exercises for the horse. Then, instead of treating dressage competitions as an end in themselves, one comes to recognise them for what they really are, namely opportunities for riders to display how effective they have been in training their horses to move in elegant and supple obedience to the rider's commands.

In fact, the word 'dressage' is simply an ordinary French word for 'training' and there is no reason whatever why the non-competitive rider should not attempt any of the movements described in this book. He is entitled to the enjoyment and satisfaction that comes from successfully acquiring the relevant skills. Many of these skills have everyday applications. Negotiating gates involves the rein-back as well as turns from the halt. Starting the canter on the correct lead depends on a proper use of the unilateral leg aids that are best learned by practising turns from the halt. Successful jumping depends on skilled control of the speed over the ground, by judicious collection followed by controlled extension, and also on lateral adjustments to bring the horse to the obstacle along the best line of approach and with appropriate timing of the strides. The order in which the various topics are presented in this book reflects the way in which the successful performance of one manoeuvre depends on the rider possessing the skills previously acquired in practising some other manoeuvre.

Advice and instruction is offered to the rider at different stages of his development. For completeness, I start with the beginner. Where an assistant is needed, I address pupil and helper in turn, as well as setting out general principles for the benefit of both. When we come to the more advanced aspects of each topic, I address the more experienced rider who is seeking to improve his technique and to extend his repertoire. The reader can imagine himself in each implied role without difficulty.

The training of the horse follows smoothly if the rider knows what he is doing. Accordingly, in my view, the novice rider should learn his skills on an experienced horse, and the training of novice horses should be entrusted only to experienced riders. A novice rider on a novice horse is a potentially dangerous combination. Nevertheless, it is all too common to find in books on riding that instructions to the novice rider are inextricably intermingled with procedures for the training of novice horses.

This book aims to provide a comprehensive account of equestrian skills. It still remains true, however, that the fine polish essential for success in competition comes only from assiduous practice coupled with periodically submitting oneself to the informed scrutiny of an experienced and co-operative judge.

⌐1⌐ FIRST STEPS

Precautions

Many people are first introduced to riding by friends who already have some experience. Correspondingly, from time to time many riders find themselves acting as impromptu instructors to visitors and friends who have been invited to 'have a go'. Since successful progress is so dependent on making a good start, it is appropriate to begin a comprehensive book on equitation with a reminder of the sorts of things one might say to a friend who is being introduced to riding for the first time.

It is only fair to point out at the outset that accidents do happen, though not very often, and it is therefore sensible to take precautions. All the risks can be very greatly reduced by due attention to the proper training of both horse and rider. Putting a complete beginner up on an untrained or unreliable horse is just asking for trouble. All the early stages of learning to ride should take place only in a restricted and securely fenced area in which the instructor can at any time easily regain control of the horse as soon as the beginner shows any signs of getting into difficulties.

Here are a few elementary precautions that *everyone* should observe.

In practice, one can fall off a horse any number of times without actually hurting oneself at all, provided that the ground is fairly soft and one does not land on an obstruction such as a boulder or fence-post. The secret is to relax and curl up in the air so that one lands in a ball and rolls away. Since head injuries are by far the most serious of the common consequences of a riding accident, the importance of the hard hat cannot be overemphasised. Do not ride without one! I always wear mine. Several times it has saved me from injury. On one occasion, although my hat was smashed in a fall, I suffered no personal injury. Remember that the hat will be of no use to you if it comes off while you are in mid-air. Make sure that it fits properly and don't allow vanity to tempt you into dispensing with the chinstrap.

Appropriate footwear is also necessary. An ordinary town shoe is inadvisable because it can catch in the stirrup, making it difficult to disengage in an emergency. A shoe without a heel is also hazardous because your foot can slip right through the stirrup, leaving your leg trapped. At the same time you are deprived of the support of the stirrup if you should happen to need it to help you keep your balance.

The function of calf-length riding boots is to keep the rider's leg from being nipped between the stirrup leather and the saddle. One may be tempted to achieve the same result with ordinary wellingtons, but these usually have quite a deep tread on the sole compared with the smooth sole of the riding boot. A deep tread has two disadvantages. The stirrups tend to bounce against the projecting ridges of the tread so that it is difficult to get your feet back into the stirrups once they have slipped out. A more serious hazard is that the boot may jam in the stirrup and not pull free easily if you have a fall.

Do not wear anything that can flap about wildly in the wind. The flapping may catch the attention of the horse at an awkward moment. He may get the idea that something untoward is happening on his back and take fright. He may react suddenly and unexpectedly and this can upset your balance. He may also be given a fright by the sudden change in your apparent size and shape when you are putting on or taking off a jacket or other garment. Do not attempt this while in the saddle; always dismount first, and preferably have someone else hold your horse. If he were to take off with you in the saddle, while your arms are still entangled in the sleeves, you would have great difficulty in controlling him and you might easily find yourself involved in a serious accident.

With sensible precautions, there should be no trouble.

Mounting

It must be a dramatic experience for a horse, having for the first time accepted the pressure of the saddle on his back and the feel of the girth round his chest, suddenly to have the whole thing pulled violently to one side as the rider puts his foot in the stirrup to mount. Accordingly, it is better, if either horse or rider is a beginner, for the rider to be given a leg up. This is not nearly so easy as it looks. Both rider and assistant have to exert themselves, and their efforts need to be precisely synchronised. Some effort is needed to lift even a small child. Do not expect to lift a grown man with a flick of the wrist.

Before mounting, check that the bridle is correctly adjusted, that the girth buckles are about even on the two sides of the saddle, and that the girth is tight enough. Stand facing the saddle on the left side of the horse. Put your left hand on his withers and with the right hand draw the reins through the left hand to hold the bit square and firm in the horse's mouth. Do not pull too hard or he will go backwards. If he swings his head about, talk to him and pet him a little to get him settled. Do not rush things. Choose a quiet moment at which to mount.

For a leg up, the assistant stands facing the rider's left shoulder. He is going to lift the rider by the left ankle. The rider raises his left heel to bend the knee and to bring his lower leg to the horizontal, and puts his right hand on the centre of the saddle, the left being on the withers holding the reins. If a stick is carried, it goes in the left hand on the far side of the horse. Now we come to the difficult part. Rider and assistant have to synchronise their moves.

Figure 1.1 *Preparing to give a leg up. The assistant is ready to bring his elbows under the weight of the rider so that he can lift with his leg muscles rather than with his arms. Agreed signals are essential to ensure synchronisation of effort between rider and assistant.*

Figure 1.2 *Later stage in the leg up (started in Figure 1.1). You may be surprised how effective a lift can be achieved by proper synchronisation. The assistant is in the act of moving the rider's foot nearer to the saddle.*

The simplest way is to count 'one, two, three' out loud. The assistant puts his right hand under the rider's left ankle and the other hand under the middle of his shin (*Figure 1.1*). On 'one' and 'two' the rider sinks on the right leg with slightly bent knee and bounces up again. On 'three' he sinks, bounces, and springs upward to take his weight on his hands while he swings his right leg up and over the horse's back. Meanwhile he must stiffen his left knee to resist the upward push of the assistant against his ankle. He should try not to straighten his left knee too much because this would make his leg slip through the assistant's hands. The assistant times his lift from the count and prepares by bending his knees and elbows to get, as far as possible, underneath the rider's left leg. He has to lift the rider's weight a long way, right up to the point where the rider's left knee is about level with the top of the stirrup leather. He should keep the rider's knee close to the saddle, and when the rider swings his right leg over the back of the horse, the assistant should turn to bring the rider's ankle against the saddle also (*Figure 1.2*).

The rider must be careful not to land as a deadweight on the saddle. As he rises he leans forward, pivoting over the left forearm. The palm of the left hand is on the withers ready to take the weight. If the left elbow is held tightly against the body just in front of the rider's left hip, the weight can be taken entirely on this left forearm. The right arm is used simply for steadying. Then, as the right leg comes down into position beside the saddle, the rider's weight can be gently eased back into the saddle. Of course the right foot must be lifted high enough to avoid kicking the horse on the flank. If the horse is at all nervous, it may help to have a second assistant standing at his head, holding the reins close up behind the bit and fondling the horse's nose, talking to him, or giving him a couple of pony cubes to distract his attention.

In mounting with the stirrup you can choose either side, and you can choose to start facing forward or facing to the rear of the horse. Take first the most usual case of mounting from the left, facing to the rear. Prepare, as before, with your left hand on the withers and the reins drawn in to hold the bit square and steady. Have the whip, in the left hand, on the far side of the horse (*Figure 1.4*). Make sure your horse knows what you are going to do, by taking hold of the stirrup leather with your right hand and putting your weight on it. This will pull the saddle round to give the horse much the same sensations as he will get when you put your foot in the stirrup and start to get up. The point of giving this warning move with your weight on your right hand is that you will be in a secure posture if the horse reacts. If he were to start playing up when you are standing with one foot on the ground and the other in the stirrup you would be at a distinct disadvantage. You would need to keep a tight hold on the withers and to disengage your foot quickly from the stirrup, otherwise you could easily be thrown on your back under the horse's feet. This would be a terrifying experience both for you and for the horse; but you can avoid it if you watch what you are about.

If the horse swings his quarters away from you, shorten the right rein to pull his head round to the right. If he then leans against you to push you off balance while you are trying to get your foot up, give him a good punch in the ribs and speak sharply to him. Don't pull so hard on the reins. Assert yourself, but don't get angry. This will not help. The horse is trying to understand what you want him to do and he is doing his best by responding to all the various pulls and pushes that he can feel you making. Some of these are accidental. You may not even realise what you are doing to him, but he is not to know which of the pushes and pulls are accidental and which are deliberate commands. He responds to everything, and if you get excited, so does he. He may even come to enjoy the romp of dancing around with you, as though this is what you want him to do.

You will need to take particular care if your horse is for some reason especially eager to go forward. This may happen in the course of a ride. Suppose you have been cantering through a wood and have come to a gate for which you have had to dismount. Then, after negotiating the gate, you will be faced with the problem of getting back into the saddle. Meanwhile the horse will be eager to continue the exhilaration of the previous canter. If you are not careful, he may make off as soon as he feels your weight on the saddle even before you have managed to get your leg over him. At this point the reins will be in your left hand which is probably at the same time grimly hanging on to the mane. Your right hand will be clinging to the saddle to keep you from sliding off and you won't have a hand free with which to shorten rein. It will be hard to recover from this situation because the horse will be feeling unaccustomed bumpings from the saddle and this may well encourage him to gallop on.

To avoid all this, before attempting to mount, turn your horse to face some suitable solid obstacle. For example, put him with his nose hanging over the closed gate, facing the direction from which you have just come. The obstacle will hold back his urge to break away into a gallop and you can safely proceed with the business of mounting.

If your horse will not stand still when you put your weight on the stirrup leather with your right hand, you will need an assistant to hold his head and distract him with talk, with caresses, and with pony cubes. Keep trying until he gets used to the idea and stands quietly. Throughout all these preliminaries, your left hand remains on the withers and from time to time you may readjust the reins by pulling more of one rein or the other through your left hand with your right.

When you are ready to get up, and the horse is steady, turn sideways, facing toward the rear of the horse, and take hold of the stirrup leather with your right hand just at the top of the stirrup (*Figure 1.3*). Turn the stirrup toward you, lift your left foot and fit the stirrup over it with the tread against the ball of the foot. If you have any difficulty in reaching the stirrup, let it down a few holes. You need to be able to pull the stirrup toward you with your foot in it, otherwise you will never manage to get your weight over the stirrup.

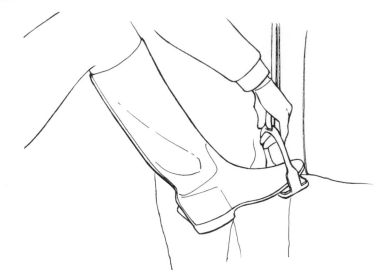

Figure 1.3 *Pulling the stirrup near you before mounting. This brings your weight nearer to the horse and makes mounting easier.*

Several things now happen in rapid succession. Pull the stirrup toward you with your foot in it, lean your shoulders in toward the horse, bounce once or twice on your right foot and then spring upward off your right foot to get your weight over the stirrup. As you begin to rise, quickly shift your right hand to reach over and grasp the far side of the seat of the saddle at the back edge of the flap, and use this handhold as a purchase, together with the left hand on the withers, to pull yourself up and forward over the saddle (*Figure 1.4*). Tuck your left elbow into your body, swing your right leg well up, and pivot over the left forearm until you are ready to lower your weight gently into the saddle. Throughout this manoeuvre try, if you can, to keep your left toe from digging into the horse's side. Your right hand comes free naturally as you let your weight down onto your seat.

An alternative routine, which definitely avoids digging your toe into the horse, is to start by turning forward instead of back. When you take hold of the top of the stirrup with your right hand, ready to put your left foot in it, turn forward, with your right shoulder against the horse. Keep your left hand on the withers even though you need to stretch a bit. Turn the stirrup toward you and put your left foot in it as before, but this time the toe will be pointing toward the horse's elbow. Pull the stirrup toward you with your foot in it, spring up as before, this time reaching with your right hand for the far side of the pommel. Swing up and over, and let yourself down gently into the saddle. Speak to the horse and take up the reins to prevent him from moving off.

Once you are in the saddle feel under the pommel with two fingers to make sure that the arch of the saddle is clear of the horse's backbone. Do not ride on a saddle that touches the horse's spine along the midline.

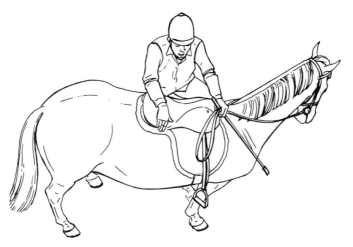

Figure 1.4 *Position of the hands just before mounting. Notice that the whip and spare rein are on the far side of the horse from the rider, hinting to the horse that he is not supposed to step to the side. Here the horse's head is turned toward the rider, discouraging him from moving toward the rider and overbalancing her as she prepares to mount. If the horse develops the habit of moving away, it may help to hold his head turned away from you.*

Adjusting stirrups

When the stirrup is hanging free the leather lies flat against the horse's side with the stirrup at right angles to its working position when the rider's foot is in it. You put your foot in from the outside, so that when your toe is pointing forward the twist of the leather will cause it to lie flat to follow the surface of your boot. If your foot goes into the stirrup the wrong way round, the twist of the leather will bring an edge to bear uncomfortably against your shin.

The tread of the stirrup should go under the ball of the foot and your heel should be a little lower than the sole of the foot. To get the feel of this position, take hold of the mane at the withers, or hold on to the pommel of the saddle, and stand up in the stirrups, with knees straight. Then, without bending either knees or hips, raise and lower yourself by moving your ankles (*Figure 1.5*). Rise on the ball of the foot and then relax the ankle to sink your heel as far as it will go. Do this several times to force your heel lower and lower each time. Now sit back again in the saddle.

When your heel is lower than the sole of the foot, the calf muscles are tensed and will form a bulge on the inside of the lower leg. Your leg has a hollow between this bulge and the knee. The side of the horse is rounded like a barrel and the hollow in the side of your leg between the calf muscles and the knee should fit snugly against the bulging side of the horse. This does not by itself govern the position of the leg because you can slide your leg up and down over

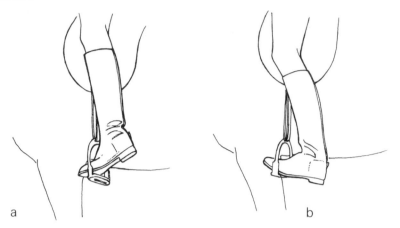

a   b

Figure 1.5 *Exercise to get the feel of the stirrup against the ball of the foot. Steady yourself against the withers; stand in the stirrups; then without bending at the knee, raise and lower yourself by bending only at the ankle.*

the horse's side while still keeping the hollow of your leg against the bulge of the horse. When you do this, however, you alter the position of your knee in relation to the saddle. If your saddle has knee rolls on it, as with a jumping saddle, you will find a hollow surrounded by these rolls. Your knee should nestle comfortably into this hollow. There are, thus, three things to think about when gauging the length of the stirrup leathers:

- The heel is to be lower than the sole of the foot, with the tread of the stirrup under the ball of the foot;
- The hollow of your leg below the knee is to fit over the bulge of the horse's side;
- Your knee is to fit snugly into its nest in the knee rolls of the saddle.

To judge whether the two leathers have been adjusted to equal lengths, stand in the stirrups with your knees straight. Check that the saddle is not displaced to one side by looking to see that the pommel is centrally placed over the withers. You may be able to move the saddle to one side or the other by putting more weight on one stirrup or the other while you bounce up and down on your ankles.

When you wish to adjust the stirrup leathers, do not take your foot out of the stirrup. Lift your knee sideways away from the saddle and grasp the free end of the stirrup leather, placing your thumb on top next to the tongue of the buckle (*Figure 1.6*). Relax the pressure of your foot on the stirrup and pull the leather upward and outward. This will pull the buckle away from the bar. Relax the pull of your hand slightly to allow the leather to dip down between your hand and the stirrup bar. This will loosen the buckle and you can manipulate the tongue of the buckle with your forefinger. To lengthen the leather, push down gently with the foot, meanwhile relaxing slightly with your arm. The buckle will slide away from the bar. To shorten, raise your hand while relaxing your ankle. The buckle will slide toward the bar. Feel for the desired hole in the leather with your thumb and work the tongue into the hole using your forefinger and a slight increase in the pressure of your foot while lowering your hand. When the buckle is positioned to your liking, shift your grip to that part of the leather running down from the buckle to the stirrup. Pull up on this while relaxing your foot. Then, keeping your fingers well away from the buckle, put pressure on the foot while still holding up the outer part of the leather with your hand. The inner part of the leather will slide over the bar to bring the buckle hard up against the bar with a click. Smooth away the free end of the leather, tucking it into the keeper on the saddle-flap, if you have one, and adjust the other side similarly. Once you have mastered this routine, you will be able to adjust your stirrups at any time without having to stop or to ask for assistance.

It is usual to ride with a longer leather for dressage than for jumping. Some riding schools advocate riding as 'long' as possible for hacking and for general school work, instructing their pupils to shorten up by two holes for jumping. The idea of this is to stretch the pupil's hip joints. I prefer to use the safe jumping length for all occasions, with special periods of riding without stirrups to exercise the hip joint. This plan makes it easy to take advantage of any casual opportunities for jumping that may arise during a hack. It also provides more security for the rider if the horse should unexpectedly be startled by anything.

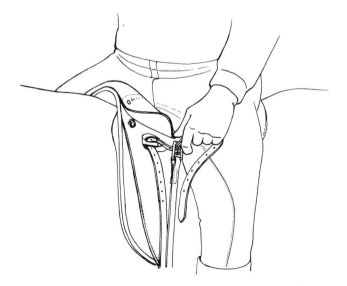

Figure 1.6 *Adjusting the length of the stirrup leathers. Keep your toe in the stirrup and work the buckle along the stirrup leather by moving hand and toe up or down together.*

Checking the girth from the saddle

The tightness of the girth often changes when your weight comes into the saddle. This may be because the saddle changes shape slightly, or just because it comes to fit more snugly onto a different place on the horse's back. Another factor is that many horses take a deep breath just when you are trying to tighten the girth. Then they relax once you are up, and the girth goes slack. To check

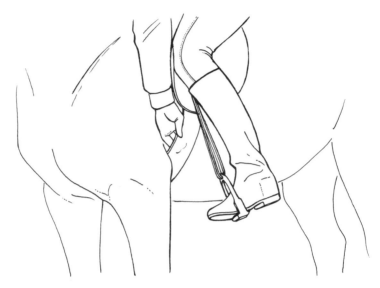

Figure 1.7 *Checking the tightness of the girth.*

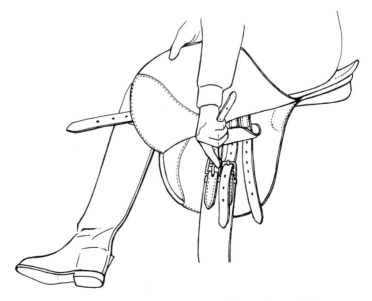

Figure 1.8 *Adjusting the girth from the saddle.*

the girth from the saddle, lean forward and feel the girth just below the bottom edge of the saddle-flap (*Figure 1.7*). You should be able to slide thumb and two fingers in easily, but you should not be able to pull the girth more than one or two centimetres away from the horse's side. To adjust the girth, move one leg forward, without taking the foot out of the stirrup, and lift the saddle-flap so that you can get your hand on the girth straps. Place your thumb on the protruding tongue of the buckle and feel for this tongue underneath with the forefinger (*Figure 1.8*). Use the other fingers to take a firm grip on the girth strap. Pull upward on the strap and use the thumb and forefinger to manoeuvre the tongue of the buckle into the next hole. Your thumb finds the hole and your forefinger feels where the tongue of the buckle has got to so that you know whether to pull harder or to let down the tension to allow the tongue into the hole.

If your girth has a second buckle, or if you are using two webbing girths each with a single buckle, both buckles will need to be adjusted, using the same technique for each. Check that the buckles are at about the same level on the two sides of the horse.

The safe position for the beginner

The procedures for mounting and checking stirrups and girth soon come to be virtually automatic. I have described them in detail so that you can help a friend who is getting into the saddle for the first time.

The beginner suddenly finds himself unusually far from the ground and may feel some apprehension. I usually go through the following routine to establish confidence. You, as instructor, hold your hand above the horse's withers and have the mounted pupil hold on to your hand to balance himself. The pupil then stands in the stirrups with knees straight and adjusts his body until he is in balance and not exerting much force on your hand. The pupil then moves his weight up and down using the ankles only and without bending either at the knees or at the hips (*Figure 1.5*). This allows him to feel the close fit of the legs against the side of the horse. The pupil now lowers his seat gently into the saddle, bending at the knees and hips. You next move your hand slowly forward, telling the pupil to follow by bending forward at the hips and stretching his hands forward, but all the while keeping his lower leg hanging straight down. Keep going until the pupil's chest is against the horse's withers (*Figure 1.9*) and his hands are almost round the horse's neck, elbows well in front of his knees. Have the horse walk on a few paces with the pupil still in this position. Emphasise that he is to keep his lower leg straight down. Then rock him gently from side to side at the shoulder to demonstrate that he is quite secure so long as his feet hang straight down. He will be much less stable if he allows his heels to come back. Demonstrate this also. Then let the pupil relax back into the normal position in the saddle.

The beginner should be encouraged to keep his knees close against the saddle at all times, with his lower legs hanging straight down except when he

Figure 1.9   *The safe position for the beginner. The rider is much less stable if he allows his feet to move back behind the vertical.*

is using them to make a deliberate signal. He should be warned not to attempt to wrap his lower legs round the horse in the mistaken hope of improving his security.

When you are a beginner you may not at first appreciate the importance of moving your feet well forward if you should start to get into difficulties. This may not feel natural. Indeed the most natural thing is to curl up when anxious. If you bend your knees as part of this reaction, this will bring your feet back. There are two disadvantages in this. In the first place, with your feet back rather than forward, you will be less secure in the saddle, as you can feel when the instructor pushes against your shoulder. In the second place, the horse may react to the feel of your heels against his sides. The contact of the rider's lower leg with the side of the horse is a very effective signal, and the horse may interpret a strong contact here as an emphatic command. He will take the contact of your feet behind the girth as a command to go forward more vigorously, and he may respond by doing something, such as breaking into a gallop, which may not be at all what you intend! The resulting increased bouncing will just make it more difficult for you to keep your balance. So on no account let your feet slip backward. You can hang on to the mane, or to the neck-strap if there is one, to avoid getting left behind, but this will not save you from falling forward. The horse's neck is very narrow and there is not much that you can get a purchase on once you start to topple. That is why you need to push your feet well forward. If, at the same time, you turn your heels away from the horse, this will bring your knees tight against the saddle where they will be of most use in helping you to keep your balance. If your knee contact is well forward of your seat, you are much less likely to topple forward. So, far and away the most important thing to remember if you have the misfortune to feel that things are beginning to get out of hand is to *get your feet well forward with your heels away from the horse*.

After the instructor has made this point clear to his pupil, he will be ready to lead him on with a leading rein or to work either on the lunge or with long reins.

Communication

As soon as the horse begins to go forward, the rider will feel the saddle moving under him. At the same time, the horse will be feeling, through the saddle, the way the rider's body-weight is moving about on his back. This interaction by feel is the basis for an important channel of communication through which the rider can influence the horse, and the beginner's first task is to get used to making himself aware of what the horse is doing, by paying attention to details of the feel of the horse moving under him. In this book, I have tried to indicate what sensations the rider can expect to encounter during various manoeuvres and what sorts of things he should feel for in order to establish a rapport and keep up a 'conversation' with his horse.

Indeed, the basic problem in getting your horse to do what you want is one of communication. He needs to understand you and you need to be aware of his doubts and problems. There should be a continual exchange of signals. Once you know what to look for you will come to realise that the horse is all the time 'talking' to you with little signs and gestures. Keep up the conversation by talking back, not only with your voice, but also with every part of you, your attitude, your mood, your tone of voice and, particularly, your contact with his body.

Some principles of learning and teaching
(This topic is taken up again in more detail in Appendix 2.)

Remember that all stages of your interaction with the horse count for him as a learning situation. His main aim in life is survival. For a large herbivore which in the wild would make a succulent meal for a predator, the price of survival is a constant vigilance. The situation in which the horse finds himself is thus continually being reassessed, second by second, to determine whether a state of alarm is appropriate.

In general terms, he has three 'states' to choose from. In addition to 'alarm' there is 'placidity', in which he may graze, sleep, or just stand about, and there is 'play'. At any moment he has to be able to switch instantly to the alarm state. He is particularly good at remembering situations in which the alarm state has been appropriate at some moment in his previous history. If he comes to associate something you do with an alarm state, you will have to be very patient in re-educating him.

In contrast, he is not very good at remembering what he himself happened to do at a particular time. He may not realise that an alarm has been set off by his own action. He just tends in the future to avoid getting himself into the sort of situation in which he felt the alarm. He does, however, recognise situations where he has not been alarmed and he will tend to move into situations where he has previously been rewarded, such as with food or with caresses.

The process of modifying behaviour by systematic reward is an important part of any teaching situation. Remember that the horse is learning all the time. A reassuring caress is just as much a reward as a morsel of food. It happens to be true that any behaviour that is followed by some kind of reward is more likely to be repeated than actions that are not systematically rewarded. The effect is often small, but it is usually cumulative. In man the positive effects of reward are often large and dramatic. A single trial may suffice, if it succeeds, while failures, even painful failures, are often not taken too seriously. The opposite is true for the horse. Alarm situations are learned, almost indelibly, at a single trial, whereas changes in behaviour induced by positive rewards build up only very slowly.

A curious feature of the domesticated horse, and one which distinguishes him from many other animals, is an apparent propensity to tolerate and co-operate with man, particularly when the horse is in the 'play' state. He is prepared to accept, as a valid and apparently satisfying reward, the caresses of his human companion's hand and the encouraging tone of his voice. He seems eager to try to understand what his human companion would like him to do. With other humans we can communicate by language, though this is not our only means of influencing one another. The horse does not understand our spoken language so it is up to us to develop a special language which he will understand.

Do not underestimate the role of telepathy here. There is no doubt that the horse can sense your mood and sometimes you can sense his. Be on the alert for this because if you respond appropriately this can help to build up a bond between you. Apart from this you must exercise patience, repetition of rewards, and scrupulous avoidance of anything likely to alarm the horse. This is not to say that you may never use a rebuke, just that the rebukes you administer must be like those accepted between horses in establishing the hierarchy of dominance within a herd. Your rebuke must not look like an attack by a predator.

Handling the rein

It is through the rein that the rider influences the feel of the bit in the horse's mouth. You train the horse to pay attention to the bit. He in his turn moves the bit about in his mouth and reacts against the pull of the reins. You can, to some extent, feel what he is doing, so the reins provide a channel of communication in both directions between horse and rider. Unfortunately the portion of rein hanging between your hand and the bit has appreciable weight and, if you are not careful, it can swing about and produce unwanted effects on the bit. To

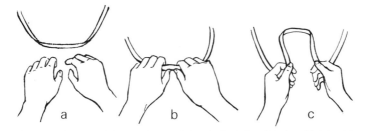

Figure 1.10 *Taking hold of the rein. (a) Reach forward as to a keyboard. (b) Take hold with three fingers of each hand. (c) Separate the hands and turn the thumbs uppermost.*

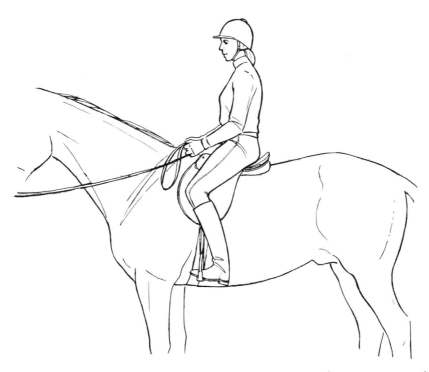

Figure 1.11 *A reasonable rest position on a general-purpose or a jumping saddle. The seat-bones are in the lowest part of the dip in the saddle; the back is upright and the rider looks ahead in the direction of the horse's ears. The upper arm hangs freely with the elbow by the rider's side. The hand is over the withers at such a height that the rein appears from the side to run in a straight line from the rider's elbow. The stirrup leathers are vertical, with the heel below the toe and the stirrup against the ball of the foot. On a dressage saddle, with the stirrup bars nearer to the dip in the saddle and the rider's legs rather straighter, the heel would come nearer to a vertical line down through the rider's shoulder and hip (see Figure 9.4).*

the horse, any change in the feel of the bit in the mouth will be equally important, and he will react to a 'signal' which you may have allowed to pass along the rein accidentally. You may not be aware of having done anything to the reins. Meanwhile the horse may behave as if you have been shouting at him. It is for this reason that you need to give a good deal of thought to the way you handle the reins.

Start with the rein lying over the horse's neck just in front of the withers. Bring the hands forward with the knuckles upward, thumbs toward one another, as though reaching for the keyboard of a piano (*Figure 1.10*) and lay hold of the rein with three fingers of each hand. Separate the hands to take up the slack in the rein. Grip the rein lightly between thumb and forefinger in each hand, turn the hands to bring the thumbs uppermost and bring the hands to about 12–15 centimetres apart. The hands should come to rest just above the withers and in front of the pommel of the saddle (*Figure 1.11*). The rein running to the horse's mouth passes between the fourth and fifth fingers. The loose, spare loop of rein lies forward over the forefingers. The fingers are curled in a half-clenched fist (*Figure 1.12*). The position of the hands is such that, from the side, the line of the rein passes straight from the bit to the rider's elbow.

The rider's upper arm hangs vertically from the shoulder, with the elbow just clear of his waist. The aim is to keep the same light pressure on the bit all the time. This is called 'contact'. However, the horse does not usually keep his head still, so the rider has to be ready at any time for his hands to make the necessary compensating movements, as otherwise the rein will occasionally go slack and then pull tight with a snap.

The jerk on the bit when the rein snaps tight after flopping free counts to the horse as a shouted command to stop, such as you might use in an emergency. Of course, if the jerk is repeated at every step, the urgency of the command rapidly fades. The horse learns to disregard it, except as a continual nuisance. The consequence is that he pays less attention to the command to stop when you really need it, and also he may show little inclination to go forward freely when you want him to do so.

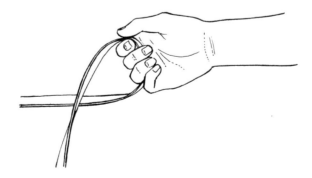

Figure 1.12   *The normal grip of the fingers on the rein.*

There are several movements that can be used to keep the reins from going slack. The most obvious is the forward and backward movement of the elbow as the upper arm swings from the shoulder. This movement should be accompanied by adjustments of the angle at the elbow to keep the forearm moving along the same line, like a piston. Then there are the horizontal movements of the forearm and of the hands swinging in toward your body, separately or together. The forearm swings, like a gate on its hinges, about the vertical line of the upper arm. The hand swings, again like a gate on its hinges, about the wrist, which is held with its axis vertical, thumb uppermost.

By using these movements in various combinations, and also by moving the shoulders to lean forward or back, a considerable range of movement of the horse's mouth can be compensated for without needing to shift the position of the hands on the rein. If the horse makes an even larger forward movement with his head, then you must let the rein slide through your fingers. Take up the slack again as soon as you get a chance.

Shortening rein

The simplest movement for shortening rein to take up slack is just to separate the hands while sliding them along the reins. This is effective only when your hands are near the buckle joining the two reins at the centre. To take up more slack you need to draw the rein through each hand in turn, and to do this quickly you have to use both hands. One pulls while the other slides. The pulling hand has to do two things at once. It has to pull the rein through the sliding hand, but it must not let go of its own rein. The trick is to close the hand firmly on the rein to grip it in several places (*Figure 1.13*): between thumb

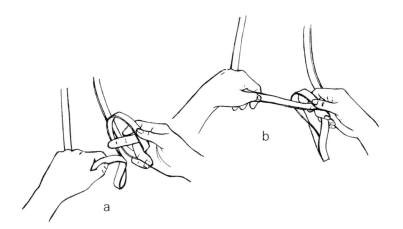

Figure 1.13 *Shortening rein without disturbing the contact with the horse's mouth. Hook a finger of the right hand into the loose rein lying over the forefinger of the left hand. Slide the left hand down the rein toward the horse's mouth. Resume the grip and repeat with the other hand.*

and forefinger, between the ring finger and the little finger, and between the ring finger and the palm. The ends of the first and second fingers can then be lifted a little to form a claw, without loosening the grip of the other fingers on the rein. By turning the hands toward one another with the back of the hand upward, the loose rein lying over the forefinger of the hand that is to slide can be hooked into the claw of the other hand. The claw closes on this rein while the sliding hand relaxes its grip and is then moved quickly toward the horse's mouth without at any stage losing its contact with the rein. The sliding hand then resumes its grip and the hands exchange roles to move what was previously the pulling hand down the rein in its turn. It may be necessary to repeat the manoeuvre a few times to find the best position for the hands on the reins.

There are some situations in which it is not convenient to use both hands. For example, if one is sitting forward at the gallop with hands low down on the horse's shoulders, the horse's neck is between your hands, and the two-handed manoeuvre is not possible. Shortening the rein in these conditions must be achieved by each hand on its own. This is done by inching the rein through the

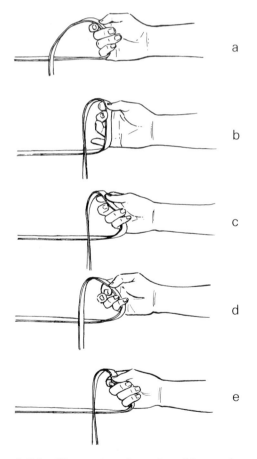

Figure 1.14 *Shortening the rein with one hand only.*

fingers. Grip with thumb and forefinger, relaxing the other fingers (*Figure 1.14*). Separate the fingers to slide the third and fourth fingers along the rein away from the forefinger. Grip with the third and fourth fingers, relax the thumb and slide the forefinger along the rein to close the spaces between the fingers. Then take up the pressure again with the thumb and move the thumb and forefinger to pull the rein through the other fingers. Repeat the whole sequence several times. Usually you will be able to move the rein only a little way through the hand at each step, but with a little practice you will find it easier. It is certainly a most useful manoeuvre.

Taking a contact

The positions of the fingers when holding the rein are very like the positions taken up on the handle of a suitcase. You should not, however, pull too hard on the rein. Nor, on the other hand, should you ever allow the rein to go completely slack, for then you will have no chance of feeling what the horse is doing to the bit, and he in his turn will not be able to feel what you are doing with your hands. For any communication to be possible, there must be some tension in the rein, and to maintain this tension you have to be continually adjusting the rein in your hand, allowing a little to slide through and then taking it up again, as well as moving your hands to compensate for the movements of the horse's head. What you need is a delicate control of the fingers such as you might use to hold a small bird, using just enough firmness not to let the bird escape and at the same time being very careful not to crush it. Remember that the horse feels the bit in his mouth pressing on his lips and tongue with exactly the same force as the rein exerts against your fingers.

It is important for both horse and rider to distinguish between 'leaning on the rein' and 'feeling' it. Keep some tension all the time, as otherwise the rein can snap taut unexpectedly, but you should not need to carry the whole weight of the horse's head. If the horse is in some doubt about what is happening to the rein, he may throw his weight against the bit to try to pull the rein free and thus escape from being pestered by the confusion of signals in his mouth. It is a mistake for the rider to fight back by just pulling harder. What he has to do is to convince the horse that the movements of the bit mean something. The steady pull doesn't mean anything in itself. It is the *changes in pull* that matter.

To appreciate this point, try the following experiment. Bring the tips of the fingers of one hand against the palm of the other. Hold still for a moment, and observe that you soon feel hardly anything, even if you are pressing quite hard. Now move some of your fingertips ever so slightly. The movement is instantly noticeable. There is nothing particularly mysterious about this. It is a well-known fact of sensory physiology that tactile sense organs soon adapt to steady conditions and that they are much more effectively excited by changing stimuli.

It is easier to learn how to adjust the tension in the reins if you have some way of knowing in advance what it is going to feel like when you are handling

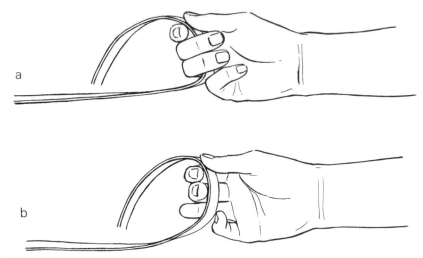

Figure 1.15 *Using the fingers to give the 'alerting' signal with the rein. The fingers curl and uncurl in rapid succession, alternating between the two positions illustrated. The grip of the thumb and forefinger prevents the rein from sliding and maintains a steady tension as a background to the fluctuations in tension produced by the movement of the fingers. The effect is to make the bit feel interesting in the horse's mouth so that he pays attention to it.*

the reins correctly. One way to approach this is to try out the feel of a few known tensions. You can do this at home. You will need a strap about the same width as the reins, and a few manageable objects of known weight in the range from 1 kg to 5 kg. A bucket and a brick will do very well. The bucket will weigh about 1 kg empty, and about 4 kg with the brick in it.

Hang the bucket from the strap and take the strap in one hand with the same grip as you would use on the rein (*Figure 1.12*). Let your hand hang down so that the pull of the strap comes against the second and third fingers. With the bucket empty, the pressure of thumb and forefinger is enough to prevent the strap from slipping, and it is easy to jiggle the bucket up and down using the other fingers (*Figure 1.15*). This is the sort of tension to aim at for routine use. If you have less tension than this the rein is apt to go slack accidentally and then to snap taut again to give an unwanted jerk to the horse's mouth.

Now put the brick into the bucket and take the strap in your hand as before to see what this sort of tension feels like. You will find it is now much more difficult to jiggle the bucket up and down with the fingers because the whole hand is engaged in the task of holding on to the strap. You may need as much tension as this, or even a little more sometimes, for certain special situations, such as to restrain an over-eager horse from rushing at a fence. But if you find you need such a tension for more than a few seconds at a time you should do something about it.

If you were to relax your arm completely while sitting in the saddle, the hand would hang vertically down from the shoulder. Now imagine the hand drawn forward by the rein (*Figure 1.11*), still with the arm completely relaxed. The rein will need to pull against the weight of the hand and forearm to bring the hand forward from the vertical position. If you grip the rein with the normal grip (*Figure 1.12*) you will be able to feel how much tension is needed to support the weight of your hand. Do not hold your hand out deliberately. Let your shoulder, elbow and wrist go quite slack and just hold on to the rein with thumb and forefinger alone. If the horse now moves his head, your hand will go with it.

When you are actually riding it is not appropriate to let your muscles go completely slack. It is better to aim for a somewhat springy condition with supple joints. Any stiffness is to be avoided, but your joints should not be so loose as to be floppy. The normal rein tension is just a little more than that needed to support the weight of the hand and forearm. You provide this slight extra tension by bearing down gently with the elbow while still allowing the hand to be carried by the rein. Make yourself aware of the feel of the rein against your fingers. Be attentive to what the horse is doing to the bit. If you make the bit interesting to him he will move his mouth forward to restore the contact whenever you let your hand go forward. You maintain his interest by sending messages along the rein with your fingers.

The messages that you want to send along the rein to the bit consist of small changes in the tension. It is much easier to send such messages if they are superimposed on a light tension than if there is a strong pull going on all the time. Your first message after mounting is to tell the horse that you are ready to move off. For this you use the 'alerting' signal.

Alerting the horse

While you are settling yourself in the saddle after mounting and while you are adjusting girth and stirrups, the horse should stand quite quietly. If he does not, speak to him, calling 'Stand!', and give a brief pull on the reins. Be careful not to bang his sides too much with the stirrups or with your legs, as he will take this as an encouragement to move on. If he is very restless, lift your heels well away from his sides and turn your toes in. This will feel 'pigeon-toed' and will bring your knees firmly onto the saddle. Give repeated brief pulls on the reins, keeping your hands as low as possible, rubbing his neck to calm him. Keep on talking to him, calling sternly 'Stand!', and 'Hold!', or 'Wait now!'. A steady pull is of no use. He may throw his head up, or start to walk backwards, or he may rear. Lean forward, rub his neck, and give repeated brief pulls on the rein. If he does not settle quite quickly it may help to walk on a few strides, halt and try again.

In the more usual situation, the horse will stand calmly and wait for you to give the signal that you are ready. You take up the reins and adjust your grip so that, with your elbow hanging beside your hip, the rein is just taut from your hands to the bit. Now, keeping your grip with thumb and forefinger, and without changing the position of your hand, you make a series of rapidly repeated movements with the other fingers, curling and uncurling them against the rein (*Figure 1.15*) to send along it a series of small pulls that have the effect of tickling the horse's mouth with the bit. If you watch the horse's head while you are jiggling the rein, you will see him prick up his ears and lift his head slightly. At the same time he will start to move the bit about in his mouth with tongue and lips. You may hear the bit clicking against the rings. All these are signs of alertness, indicating that the horse is attending to the bit. You are now both ready to move on.

The command to move forward is given with the legs, but it is not understood unless the horse has been warned, by the alerting signal, that the command is coming. Before this he has been asked to ignore quite large movements of your legs while you are making your adjustments to girth and stirrups, and you have discouraged him from responding to your legs by pulling the rein whenever he attempts to move forward. You are now suddenly going to change the significance of the feelings that the horse gets from the movements of the saddle and of your legs against his side. You have taught him that a pull on the reins means 'Stop!', and that he should ignore the movements of your legs. Now you wish him to alter his responses. To do this you need a new set of signals.

Driving the saddle forward

While you are sitting in the saddle you are never quite still. Tiny movements of your head or shoulders, the movements of breathing and everything else, all are reflected in small subtle changes in the feel of the saddle against the horse's back. If you make a deliberate effort to relax your back, the horse will feel it. Similarly, when you brace your back, after first relaxing, the horse will feel it even if you do not at the same time do anything deliberate with your legs.

There are many different ways of bracing the back. It may, for example, be hollowed, or it may be rounded, and you can alter the pressure against your individual seat-bones, putting more weight on one side or on the other. For the 'move on' command, what you want is a bracing action that pushes the saddle forward. You do this by moving your pelvis as though to sit on your 'tail', or to tuck your tail in under you. If you practise this at home, sitting on a stool with your feet off the floor, you will find it is quite easy to make the stool slide forward. This is the movement you need in the saddle, though it does not need to be too exaggerated.

As you brace your back, the pressure of your legs against the saddle will alter. You emphasise this effect slightly by first moving the lower legs on both sides a couple of centimetres sideways from their rest position, keeping your knee on the saddle, and then closing the legs again against the horse during the bracing of the back.

Walking on

The command to move on is made up of a number of components carried out in sequence. Sit quietly in the saddle, keeping your legs still so that the horse will realise that the adjustment stage is over. Take up the reins and make the alerting signal by tickling the bit. Open your lower legs slightly and then, all at the same time, brace your back to slide the saddle forward, close your legs, and ease the tension in the rein. Each component plays its part in encouraging the horse to move off. The preliminary preparation is essential. The horse must be 'listening' for your command, so you must indicate that you have finished fussing about with the stirrups or with your clothing, and you must get him to wake up and be attentive.

It is not necessary to bring the heels back, indeed it is preferable not to do so. The leg pressure should be applied over the girth with the foot in its normal position. A slight clenching of the calf muscles is really all that should be necessary. One often sees youngsters trying to start their ponies by kicking their heels backwards with all their might and at the same time waving the reins about. It is not surprising that their poor ponies do not know what to do. The 'heel back' is part of a command to turn, but the horse does not know which way to turn, as the commands are given on both sides at the same time. The rider is trying to get the pony to move on, but the jerks on the reins mean 'Stop!'. To make matters worse, a youngster will often resort, in frustration, to beating his pony with the whip, often still holding the rein in the whip hand so that each blow of the whip is accompanied by a jerk on the bit.

Effects of jerks

A jerk on the rein produces a bang on the mouth, whether the jerk is deliberate or accidental. The horse hardly needs to be taught that a brief pull on the rein means 'Slow up' or 'Stop'. But a jerk is something much more severe, a real 'shout', with an element of punishment in it. Repeated jerks are both confusing and distressing. The horse tries desperately to escape from the attack on his mouth. He throws his head about, opens his mouth, pulls wildly at the reins and may plunge all over the place. Great tact will be needed to calm him. It is accordingly most important for the rider to develop techniques of handling the reins that avoid jerks so far as possible. The occasional deliberate jerk will then have a useful effect. In contrast, repeated jerks without special significance come to obscure all the signals one wishes to convey along the rein and the horse tends to stop 'listening' to the rein and just goes on persistently fighting against it.

The situation to aim for is one in which both horse and rider contribute to maintaining a steady light tension in the rein. The rider allows the muscles of his hand and arm to act like very soft springs. Any movement of the horse's mouth is followed smoothly by the rider's hand, without allowing the tension in the rein to rise and without ever letting the rein go slack. The horse, for his part, learns not to lean too heavily against the bit and he also seeks to regain contact when the rein begins to go slack.

To teach the horse not to lean on the bit, you give when he pulls. This has the effect that, when the horse moves his mouth forward in an attempt to pull the rein free, he does not, in fact, achieve any change in the feel of the bit in his mouth. If his head movement fails to produce the desired effect, he gradually gives up making it. As soon as he brings his nose back in, you follow in with your hand, keeping the contact. Occasionally you can indicate to him that you don't want him to poke his nose out, by giving a brief pull on the reins just as he starts his head movement. You can also give one or two brief jerks if he persists in holding his head out and down for more than a moment or two. If he starts to graze, don't attempt to lift his head up by a long strong pull on the reins. Just nudge the reins and use your legs to ask him to walk on. He can't walk on and graze at the same time.

If he gets into the annoying habit of repeatedly lungeing downward and forward with his head, you must avoid letting him have the satisfaction of pulling you off balance because this rewards his misbehaviour. He is trying to pull the rein free, and if you topple forward he will have succeeded in his objective of relieving the pull of the bit on his mouth. If you are quick enough to catch the moment when he is just starting this lungeing movement, you can discourage him by a brief pull on the reins. Another strategy is to grip the reins very firmly and to bring each hand across his neck to block the forward movement of the rein. When he throws his head down, he pulls your fists hard into the top of his neck. As well as helping you to avoid overbalancing forward, this will make the reins feel to him quite solid and unyielding. If you can manage it so that he never succeeds in snatching the rein from you, but always finds the rein solidly blocked when he tries this trick, he will eventually decide there is no profit in it and will give it up.

When you have got into the way of making the bit interesting to the horse by tickling with the reins, he will come to seek this interesting sensation. He will 'feel' for the bit by a gentle forward movement of his head. If, at the same time, you have allowed your hand to move forward a little, he will step forward to try to bring himself closer to the bit. Of course, his step does not have this effect, because as he steps forward he carries you forward at the same time. But he is not to know this, since you reward his forward movement by yourself resuming the gentle pressure on the bit. In this way you teach the horse to go forward when you move your hand forward, even though the logical effect of your hand movement would appear to be to reduce your contact with the horse's mouth.

Emergency stop

After mounting and setting the horse in motion the next important manoeuvre that you need to master is how to stop. In this context it is wise to remember that only the most vicious and unfriendly horses will deliberately try to throw you off. This means that if you take up the right position in the saddle, namely the 'safe position' illustrated in *Figure 1.9*, you can survive any but the most violent movements that the horse is likely to make. Keep this in mind and don't panic.

Most important: *keep your heels away from the horse*. Many beginners, when they get apprehensive, try to hold on by wrapping their legs round the belly of the horse. This reaction, which is apparently instinctive, has two serious disadvantages. It brings the knee away from the saddle, making the rider much less secure in his seat, and it brings the rider's heels against the horse's side. The pressure of the heels against the belly feels to the horse like an urgent command to gallop, and this is just what he is likely to do. Meanwhile the apprehensive rider goes all stiff in the body and rattles about in the saddle. Because the knees are not against the saddle the rider's centre of gravity doesn't stay in place over the midline of the horse. Then every time the rider's weight comes down in the saddle, that is to say, at each stride of the horse's progress, the impact tends to throw the rider further and further off balance until he eventually falls off.

To avoid all this, concentrate on pushing your heels well away from the horse. Push them forward a bit, rather than back. This will bring your knees firmly against the saddle, which is just where you want them. If both knees are firmly against the saddle, your weight will be in the right place, over the mid-line of the horse. Think of keeping the centre-line of your chest over the centre-line of the horse's neck. If the horse is not galloping on wildly, a few brief pulls on the rein will tell him to slow down and stop. Don't attempt to stop him by sheer force. The reins do not work like the brakes of a car, where the harder you press on the brake pedal the more effective the brakes will be. With the horse, a strong pull on the reins just encourages him to pull harder against you and the effect is to deprive you of any chance to 'speak' to him through the bit. Instead of pulling like mad it is better to give with the reins, letting your hands go well forward, round his neck if need be, and then gradually you can take up a light contact. When you have managed this you can start to signal to the horse with brief pulls. If he does not seem to be responding to this and it feels to you that you are being run away with, the rule is: 'steer for the open spaces, and turn your horse into a circle'. Gradually make the circles smaller and smaller. Also try turning the horse first to one side, then to the other, all the time concentrating on keeping your heels well away from him. Eventually he will run out of steam and you can get him back under control – and enjoy the exhilaration in retrospect.

It is really a sign of serious bad management for a beginner to be run away with. The beginner should never be offered a ride on a horse if there is any doubt about the horse's response to the 'stop' command. Furthermore, the first thing to teach a beginner, once he is in the saddle, is how to stop, and he should practise this repeatedly. Another principle is: when you first get up on a horse that is strange to you, set about practising the stops right away, even after only a few strides. In this way you build up your own confidence, and you also tell the horse that you know what you are doing, and that you do not mean to allow yourself to be trifled with.

The essential parts of the command to stop are: heels away from the horse, knees in, sink in the saddle if you can, think about stopping, and apply a few brief pulls on the rein. The horse will feel you relaxing into the saddle ready for the stop, and it is surprising how effective a little telepathy can be. After some practice, he will stop for you in response to the feel of the saddle alone as you relax your spine and bring your knees more firmly against the saddle. The voice command of 'Whoa!' can also be effective, but only if the horse has first been taught this in association with the signals of saddle and reins.

Lunge and side rein

The risk of a beginner suffering a runaway is, of course, very much reduced if the instructor retains control of the horse with a lunge rein. The beginner can then accustom himself to the horse's motion without any fear.

At first, the beginner's reins should be attached to a headcollar or to the side rings of a lungeing cavesson instead of to the bit (*Photo 1.1*). In this way the horse is saved the problem of interpreting the violent movements of the bit that can be caused accidentally by inexpert handling of the reins. Side reins can be fitted to discourage the horse from wandering if he is not used to keeping out to the full length of the lunge rein.

The beginner should practise the leg movements needed for the 'walk on' command and should get used to keeping his heels away from the horse once it is in motion. He should also pay attention to relaxing his spine slightly, so that the shoulders and pelvis can move independently. The pelvis has to be allowed to rock from side to side with the movements of the saddle that are inevitable while the horse is walking. Meanwhile the shoulders and upper part of the rider's body have to remain in balance over the horse's midline. The arm exercises which I shall describe later are intended to help the rider to learn how to balance himself in the saddle. They also help to make the rider's balance independent of the rein.

The first stage, however, is to get the beginner to relax at the knee. So long as he keeps his heels away from the horse, the knee will be pressed into the saddle. Then, without moving his knee from its position on the saddle he should swing his lower legs about, forward and back, together and independently, and in and out sideways. From time to time he should halt, stand in the stirrups using a hand to maintain balance, and rise and fall on the ankles alone, keeping knee and hip straight, as described earlier. The aim of this exercise is to train the rider to keep his heel below the line of the stirrup so that he will get the full benefit of the effect of the bent ankle on the firmness of his grip with his knees.

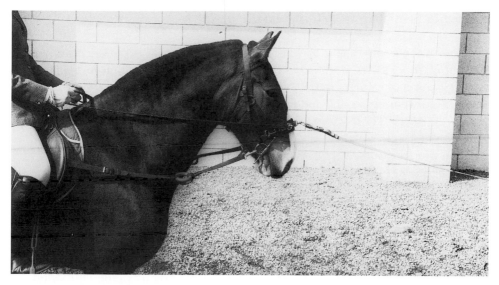

Photo 1.1   *Lungeing cavesson. The lunge rein is attached to the centre ring while the beginner's reins are attached to the side rings. Side-reins attached to the bit serve to discourage the horse from wandering. With this arrangement there is no risk that the horse will suffer any accidental jabs on the mouth.*

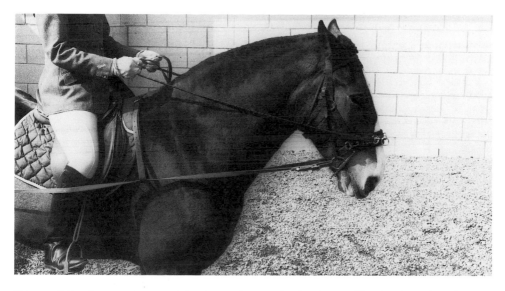

Photo 1.2   *Long reins used in the training of a beginner. The beginner's reins are attached to the side rings of the cavesson, to avoid accidental jabs on the horse's mouth. The instructor walks behind so that the horse is not tempted to attend more to the instructor than to the rider. The long reins provide security against the horse taking off out of control. Note the looped strap preventing the long reins from becoming entangled with the rider's feet.*

Movements of the horse at walk

As soon as the horse begins to walk on, the beginner will experience unfamiliar sensations from the movement of the saddle. Indeed, even before that he will have felt some movement in the saddle because no horse ever stands absolutely still. The movements of the saddle are caused by changes in the activity of the horse's muscles. These changes are of two kinds. When a muscle is active it feels harder to the touch. It is not so easily deformed when you squeeze it, as you can see for yourself by feeling your biceps while you alternately tense and relax the muscles of the arm. The saddle rests on the muscles of the horse's back, so that when these muscles become tense or relax, the saddle sinks in to a lesser or greater extent. The muscles of the two sides of the back may change independently, leading to a rocking of the saddle from side to side.

The other way the horse's muscles affect the position of the saddle is a consequence of the way the muscles act to keep the animal's weight from collapsing onto the ground. One may think of the body as being supported on the bony skeleton, which is made up of stiff, virtually incompressible, rods. However, the bones are not rigidly coupled to one another and the flexibility of the joints makes it quite impossible for the bony skeleton to stand up by itself. Each joint needs to be stiffened by the pull of the tendons that pass from one bone to another across each joint, like the rigging of a ship. In most cases there is a muscle involved as well as a tendon. Muscles and tendons are all springy and they stretch when they are pulled upon; but whereas the springiness of a tendon is a constant characteristic of that tendon, the muscles can have their springiness altered by messages from the animal's nervous system.

When we look at the hind limb of a horse from the side we see that the joints between the bones are arranged in a sort of zig-zag, so that the weight of the body would collapse the leg against the ground if the muscles were not working at each joint to keep it from folding. I have spoken of the muscles as springy, but the body does not bounce up and down all the time like a weight supported on simple springs. The reason for this is that muscles have a sort of 'shock-absorber mechanism' built into them. A muscle will develop more tension if it is being stretched than it can when it is shortening. The effect is just like that of the combined action of the shock absorbers and springs of a car, though the actual mechanism is quite different.

When a horse is standing still the combined thrusts of its legs pushing against the ground must exactly balance the effect of gravity. If the limbs do not push hard enough, the body will fall; and if the limbs push harder than just enough, the body will be thrown upwards. If the body is moving, there are other factors we must take into account. Extra force is needed to set the mass of the body into motion, and once it is moving we need other forces to bring it to rest or to change the direction in which it is moving.

As well as pushing with the legs against the ground there are other effects that must be achieved by muscular action. Imagine trying to set up a table without fastening the legs to the top. Although the table-legs are quite stiff, they will not carry the weight of the table-top unless they are prevented from tilting over. It is essential to stiffen the angles between the legs and the top. In the same way, the horse's legs have to be prevented from slewing round as well as being made stiff enough to carry the weight.

The varying thrusts of the legs tend to produce twistings of the trunk and these in turn have to be resisted by the muscles of the back. You can feel corresponding changes in the muscles of your own back when you put your weight first on one leg alone and then on the other. By adjusting the actions of these trunk muscles one can move the body about without taking the feet off the ground. You will see the horse doing this while grazing, as he moves his head to reach for fresh areas of grass to crop.

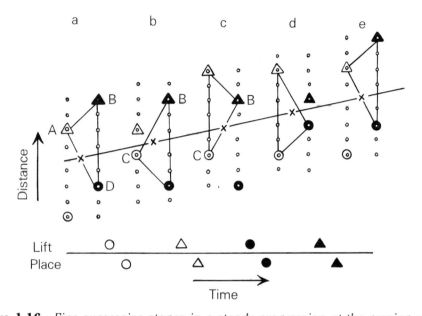

Figure 1.16 *Five successive stages in a steady progression at the grazing walk. In each stage the relative positions of the feet are indicated by the following symbols (which are also used in later diagrams): Triangle = forefoot; Circle = hindfoot; Open symbol = left side; Filled symbol = right side. x = position of the centre of gravity. The small circles indicate four possible positions for each foot: (1) Full ahead, i.e. just arrived on the ground; (2) Half ahead, i.e. this foot has been on the ground for one, and only one, segment of the forward progression; (3) Half trailing, i.e. even after one more segment of forward progression there will be no urgency about lifting this leg; (4) Trailing, i.e. about to be lifted. The head is toward the top of the page in each case. Below: The moments of lifting and placing. When the left hindfoot is lifted, the body is supported on the triangular support ABD. During the movements of the left forefoot and right hindfoot the centre of gravity passes across the line CB. The body is stable at all times, there being always at least three feet on the ground.*

The slow movement of the body of the grazing horse involves changes in the amount of support provided by each of the legs. From time to time one of the legs is completely unloaded so that the thrusting muscles can be relaxed. Other muscles are then brought into play to fold up the leg, lift the foot, swing the leg forward into a new position, and then to let the foot down again onto the ground. The thrusting muscles are then brought back into play to provide limb support to the trunk in a new direction. If you continue to watch, you will notice that the horse always lifts his feet in the same sequence: left hind, left fore, right hind, right fore, and so on. When each leg is in the air, the trunk is safely supported on the other three legs and there is no danger of overbalancing (*Figure 1.16*).

You will sometimes see a horse dozing with the weight very unevenly distributed between the hindlegs. One leg may be bent with just the tip of the hoof resting on the ground (*Figure 1.17*). The haunches then appear markedly unsymmetrical, the resting side being carried very much lower than the weight-bearing side. There are similar, though less pronounced, differences to be seen between the forelegs, and you can feel these when the horse is walking along. If you rest your hand on the side of the withers just beside the backbone you can feel the shoulderblade pushing upwards at each step when the weight comes onto that leg. Then as the horse moves forward over the weight-bearing leg, you will see the point of the shoulder, down at the level of the chest,

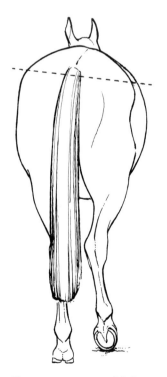

Figure 1.17   *Resting a leg. The quarters are higher on the weight-bearing side.*

moving backward toward you. When the foreleg is swinging forward, the shoulderblade can be felt to sink away from the backbone. The chest is displaced sideways at each step. It bulges toward the swinging leg because the muscles are more relaxed on that side.

As you sit in the saddle at the walk you will feel the effects of these changes in the horse's body. The saddle rocks from side to side and at the same time surges forward and backward over the horse's back. The surges arise from the fact that the legs do not push straight upward. When the axis of a leg is tilted forward, from the foot, as it is toward the end of the support phase of the stride, it tends to topple forward and thus pushes the trunk forward. When each foot is set down after a swing phase, it props against the trunk and checks the forward motion. The sideways rocking of the saddle comes from the rolling motion of the horse's body as the support thrusts alternate between the limbs of the two sides.

The sequence of leg movements

To understand what is going on, feel the way your own pelvis moves when you are walking with long strides. As you move over the supporting leg and while the other leg is swinging forward, you will feel your body first rising and then

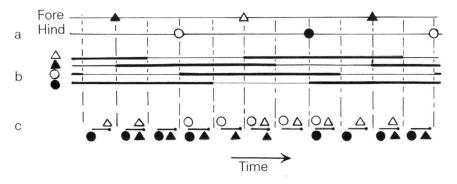

Figure 1.18 *Timing diagram for the walk. **(a)** footfalls of the forelimbs and hindlimbs; **(b)** durations of the support phases (heavy lines) and of the swing phases (faint); **(c)** patterns of support, with the head to the right in each case. (Symbols as in Figure 1.16.) The cycle is arbitrarily divided into eight epochs at the moments of lifting and placing of the feet. Each support pattern shown applies to the whole of the corresponding epoch. The pair of forelegs and the pair of hind-legs each move like the legs of a man walking, each foot of a pair being lifted only after the opposite foot has come to the ground. The two pairs are out of step, the hindlegs moving earlier than the forelegs, so that sometimes there are only two feet on the ground. At the trot the feet spend relatively less time on the ground. Forelegs and hindlegs move like the legs of a man running, this time they are almost exactly out of step. Consequently, at the trot there are two phases in each stride where all four feet are off the ground (see Figure 3.2).*

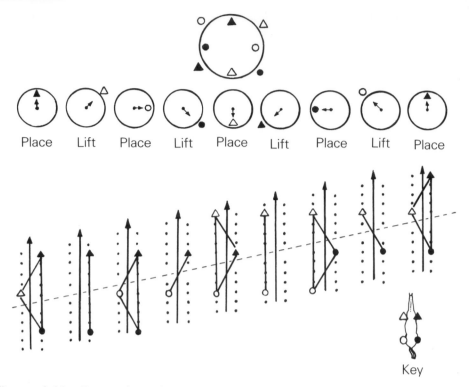

Place   Lift   Place   Lift   Place   Lift   Place   Lift   Place

Key

Figure 1.19 *Succession of support patterns at the walk.* Above: *moments of lifting and placing arranged like the hour-markings on a clockface to show the repetitive nature of the cycle. Symbol inside the circle = moment of placing; symbol outside = moment of lifting.* Below: *support patterns at successive stages.*

falling forward. During the forward-falling phase, the supporting leg gives an extra push, when you straighten the ankle and push the hip down on that side. The swinging leg gives a little after touchdown, providing a flexible and springy support to absorb the momentum of the falling trunk. The centre of gravity of the trunk is lifted up over the forward leg by two mechanisms. It first rises passively like a pole-vaulter, and then it is actively lifted by straightening the leg. During the strong thrust of the supporting leg, the hip on that side is first pushed passively upward by the initial impact, and then it is later brought level again by the activity of the back muscles. The hip on the side of the swinging leg is actively lifted while the free leg is passing the supporting leg and during the development of extra thrust by the supporting leg at take-off. The hip is then moved forward and downward to extend the swinging leg ready for landing.

The ordinary, or 'medium', walk of the horse is slightly different from the grazing walk. When grazing, the horse slowly moves his trunk forward over stationary feet, with occasional steps by one leg at a time. Between the steps there is a pause with all four feet on the ground (*Figure 1.16*). When he walks

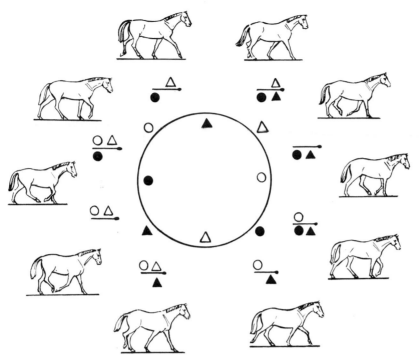

Figure 1.20 *The cycle of movements at the walk. The support patterns shown in Figures 1.18 and 1.19 together with corresponding side views, are here set out in appropriate positions around the clockface of Figure 1.19. The outline drawings are taken from* Descriptive Zoopraxography, or the Science of Animal Locomotion Made Popular *by Eadweard Muybridge (1893).*

on without grazing, he first lifts his head, then he takes a sequence of steps without any pauses between the movements of the individual legs. Indeed, he starts to move the next leg before the previously stepping leg has touched down (*Figures 1.18, 1.19 and 1.20*) so that there are moments in the cycle during which the body is supported only by a single pair of legs. One consequence of this is that each leg now has to develop a greater thrust, at least half the body weight, instead of only a quarter when standing still, or a third when one leg is being swung forward.

You can perhaps visualise the movements of the walking horse by thinking of two men striding along one behind the other, out of step by a quarter of a cycle (*Figure 1.18*). Look at the forelegs first (triangles). Each foreleg swings forward in turn, but only after the leg of the opposite side has already come to the ground to take over the support of the body. Thus, in *Figure 1.18b*, the left foreleg (open triangle) continues to support the body until the right foreleg (filled triangle) has been placed on the ground. The hindlegs (circles) also execute a walking sequence like that of a walking man, each hindfoot coming to the ground before the opposite hindfoot is lifted. Because the swings of the forelegs are out of step with the hindlegs, there are times when two legs are both swinging forward at the same time, leaving the body supported only on the other two, as indicated at the bottom of the figure.

Figure 1.19 shows the sequence of support patterns in the ordinary walk, for comparison with the grazing walk illustrated in *Figure 1.16*. The moments of lifting and placing of the individual legs are arranged round a clockface to emphasise the repetitive nature of the walking cycle. *Figure 1.20* combines this clockface layout with the side views of a walking horse at different moments in the progression.

The forces developed against the trunk by each of the legs follow a sequence like that described above for the human walk. Because the thrusts at the shoulders are not synchronised with those at the hips, the trunk is set into complicated twisting motions. As a result, the saddle executes oscillations of all possible kinds: swaying from side to side, surging forward and back, and vertical movements of rising and falling. Three sorts of rotary motion also occur: rolling from side to side about the longitudinal axis, pitching in the fore-and-aft plane, and yawing from side to side about a vertical axis.

The body of the rider is not rigidly fastened to the saddle. As the horse's body moves, so the rider's weight is continually being moved about by the movements of the saddle. Every so often, when the movement of the saddle changes direction, the rider's seat comes up against some part of the saddle with a jolt. The skilled rider absorbs these jolts by the flexibility of his spine. The horse also feels the jolts transmitted to his back from the saddle. In this way the horse can distinguish at once between carrying a rider on his back and carrying an inert load. He can also readily distinguish the involuntary swayings and jerkings of a beginner from the smooth movements of the skilled rider.

Movements of the horse's head

In addition to the complicated movements of the saddle, the rider has to contend with the movements of the horse's head. These head movements affect the reins, and if the rider is not careful the horse will feel the bit moving in his mouth in ways that do not reflect the intention of the rider. The horse does not know that the rider has not initiated these movements of the bit, and consequently may well become confused.

The head of the horse is relatively very heavy because, although it contains air spaces in the nasal cavities and elsewhere, it also contains the large masses of ivory forming the grinding teeth. This heavy weight on the end of the long neck forms a massive pendulum which needs large forces to set it into motion and to change its speed or direction of movement. The muscles that pull on the neck to move the head also pull on the trunk. In this way, the horse can use the momentum of its very heavy head to assist in moving other parts of the body.

For example, when the horse lifts his head the muscular effort involved has the indirect effect of tending to lift the hindquarters, because the support at the shoulders acts as the fulcrum of a lever. When the horse is walking briskly you will see that he lifts his head each time he needs to bring one of his hindlegs forward. As well as lifting the head and neck up and down, he may nod his head alone, pivoting at the base of the skull, just behind the ears. In consequence the rider feels the reins moving forward and back quite a long way. It is very important that he should learn to let his hands follow this movement smoothly. The necessary movement of his hands will be quite different from the movements of his shoulders that result from his being moved about by the saddle. The rider's arms have, therefore, to be very flexible. They have to give easily when the rein is drawn forward and they must be brought smoothly back again a moment later to take up the slack when the horse's mouth moves in again toward his chest.

Arm exercises at walk

The smooth control of the rein is perhaps the most difficult thing that the beginner has to master. It is for this reason that I advocate that, when the beginner is having his first lessons with reins and stirrups and with the horse on the lunge, the reins should be attached to the rings at the side of a cavesson or of a headcollar rather than to the bit itself. The rider can then get used to the movement of the horse's head without accidentally jerking the bit in the mouth.

When you are a beginner you may at first instinctively try to use the reins as an aid to balance. This should not be allowed to become a habit. It is as well to start without holding the reins at all, concentrating on learning the proper position for the feet and practising the suppleness of the back that will allow you to move with the saddle rather than being moved about by it.

When you have begun to keep your back supple and have learned to swing the lower leg without moving the knee off the saddle, you can try some more adventurous moves. Hold both arms out sideways as far as they will go, palms upward. Then, keeping the elbows up and out, swing the arms forward at the elbow to bring the hands in front of the shoulders. Swing the arms out again to their full extent, again turning them palm upward. Repeat several times. This exercise helps to lift and expand the chest, and it lifts the shoulder-blades away from the pelvis.

Leg aids

Now combine the arm movements with movements of the legs. Pay attention to the sideways rolling of the saddle at each step. Notice that the saddle follows the movements of the horse's shoulders. When the left foreleg is on the ground you will see the point of the left shoulder moving back toward you. At the same time the saddle tips up slightly on the right side and down on the left. Emphasise this tilting by lifting your right leg sideways at this time, moving the foot about 5 centimetres away from the girth, but keeping the knee firmly pressed against the saddle. Then, as the weight comes onto the horse's right foreleg, bring your own right leg in against the horse's side and put a little more weight on your right knee. Take care that your foot does not move backward as you bring it in. It should remain on the girth. Make corresponding movements with your left leg also until your knees and pelvis are rocking from side to side in time with the movements of the horse's shoulders.

The alternating contact of your legs with the sides of the horse will have the effect of encouraging him to walk on. For this reason these movements are called the 'leg aids for the walk'. If your leg movements are too exaggerated, the horse may break into a trot; so if you are not ready for this, be careful not to give him too much of a thump with your leg. The combination of arm exercises with leg movements and rocking sideways in the saddle will help you to relax your spine until your shoulders can move independently of the movements of your pelvis. It also helps you to dispense with the rein as an emergency hand-hold.

Rein exercises at walk

You are now in a position to take up the rein and to get yourself used to the movements of the horse's head. At first have the reins attached to the cavesson or to the headcollar with the horse on the lunge. Later you can try the same exercises with the rein in its normal position attached to the bit. You will probably find that it is very hard to concentrate on what is happening to the rein without your arm getting unacceptably tense. It helps to have something else to think about and for this I recommend changing hands.

Changing hands

The aim of this exercise is to achieve such flexibility in the arm that the rein feels as though it is kept taut by the weight of your hand alone. The arm pivots freely without any pull being exerted at the shoulder. With your hands in the rest position, just above and slightly in front of the pommel of the saddle and with about 12−15 centimetres between your thumbs, you will see that your forearm is not quite in line with the rein. If you swing your hands inward toward your body, keeping the thumbs on top, this will pull on the rein. If you swing your hands outward until the forearms point to the sides of the horse's mouth, the rein will go slack. You can use this sideways swinging of forearm and wrist, together with some forward and backward movement of the elbow, to allow the rein to come and go with the movements of the horse's head.

To practise this without thinking about it, keep changing the reins from one hand to the other and back again. The technique for getting both reins into one hand is as follows. Suppose you want to get both reins into the right hand. Roll your hands over to bring the thumbs toward one another and get ready to cross your hands to bring the left hand behind the right. Open the fingers of the right

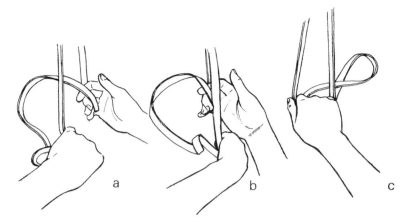

a   b   c

Figure 1.21 *Taking both reins into one hand. Keeping control of the rein by curling the fingers, open the right hand and lay the left rein into it behind the rein that is already there.*

hand slightly, keeping a grip on the edge of the right rein with the second and third fingers and lifting the thumb (*Figure 1.21*). Then pass your left hand across behind and to the right of the right hand, laying the left rein into the fingers of the right hand on top of the rein that is already there. Close the fingers and thumb of the right hand and let go with the left. You now have the two reins in the right hand, the two parts that go forward to the bit being separated by the width of your hand, so that you can steer as necessary, simply by rotating the hand horizontally at the wrist. To separate the reins again, take hold of the left rein with the left hand just where it passes from the right hand toward the bit, and allow the loose central part of the left rein to slide out of your right hand without letting go of the right rein.

Lightening the hand

In the rein exercise to lighten the hand on the rein, you repeatedly perform the following sequence of moves. Start with the reins in both hands as normal. Put both reins in the right hand. Hold the left hand out to the side fully extended from the shoulder, palm upward. Take the reins into the two hands and separate them. Put both reins in the left hand. Put the right hand out sideways from the shoulder. Separate the reins into the two hands. Put both reins into the right hand, left arm out. Separate the reins again, and so on. Throughout all these moves, the rein is to be kept just taut, the hands coming and going with the movements of the horse's head at every stride, and your legs swinging on and off the horse in time with the rolling movements of the saddle.

After you have been given a chance to get the feel of this exercise with the rein attached to the headcollar, the reins may be shifted to their proper place on the bit. You can now tell whether you are being successful in your handling of the rein because any jerk on the bit is likely to make the horse slow down and you will have to work harder with your legs to keep going.

Long reining

At this stage you can change over from the lunge to the long reins with these fastened to the rings of the bit. The regular reins should at first stay on the headcollar or on the side-rings of the cavesson (*Photo 1.2*). When the long reins are used in place of the lunge, the horse is no longer prompted by watching the instructor or by feeling the signals passed to him by way of the lunge rein. Control of speed over the ground becomes dependent on the rider's seat aids and leg aids, with the long reins held in reserve so that the instructor can control any tendency for the horse to run away. When the beginner has attained confidence with this arrangement, the regular reins can be shifted to their proper place on the bit with the long reins also still in place beside them.

You, the rider, are now supposed to be in control of the horse. Your instructor is there just to make sure that the horse does not make off in response to some unintended stimulus from your legs, and to give you confidence. You can now practise 'Walk on' and 'Stop'. You can also make the horse go faster or slower by adjusting the urgency of your leg movements and by adding occasional brief pulls to the steady tension you maintain on the rein.

Your first aim as a rider should be to develop a supple springiness in all the joints of your body, and particularly in your back, in order to absorb the motion of the saddle without jolting. You should also try to achieve independence in your lower leg so that, with your knees against the saddle, your lower legs are relieved of the need to hold on to the horse to preserve your balance, and can be devoted entirely to their proper task of signalling to the horse. Remember that security in the saddle depends on balance rather than on grip.

A general suppleness in the body makes it easier to ensure that your hands maintain a continual gentle contact with the horse's mouth with no accidental jerks, or unintended increases in tension. You can then turn your attention to exploring the effects of each of the aids, singly and in combination. After you have established the significance of each of your various signals when you make them with distinct and definite movements, you will be able to start to use rather smaller signalling movements until, eventually, your signals become imperceptible to the onlooker.

Action of the 'aids'

If someone tickles you in the ribs when you are lying down, this makes you lift your knee and bring your elbow down to cover the place where you are being tickled. The effect of your leg on the horse's side is rather similar. You will see from *Figure 1.18* that when one foreleg is past the halfway stage in its support phase, the horse is ready to lift his hindleg on the same side. You apply your leg to the horse's side during the support phase of the foreleg. This makes him bring that leg back more briskly, thus pushing the body forward, and it makes him lift the hindleg a little earlier. The combined effect is to speed up the walk.

Another way to speed up the walk is to encourage the nodding action of the horse's head. You do this by rhythmical adjustments of the tension in the rein. You pull a little when the horse is bringing his nose in, and you relax the rein a little extra when his nose is moving forward. As well as these rhythmic actions of the rein on the horse's head, which have the effect of increasing the vigour of the steps, you can also use the reins to adjust the speed over the ground. So long as the horse is contributing to the role of the rein as a signalling system, by gently seeking to maintain the contact, then a slight reduction in the pressure of the bit will tell him to move forward and take longer strides, especially if at the same time you are active with your leg aids. Similarly, a slight increase in rein tension will tell him to take shorter strides.

The effects of the rein on the speed over the ground can be independent of the effects on the vigour of the stepping action produced by encouraging the horse to nod his head. But to get these two valuable kinds of rein aids to work, you must first persuade your horse to abandon the habit of playing at tug-of-war with you, and you must develop a sufficiently springy control of your hands to avoid the accidental jerks on the reins that inevitably follow those moments when you have allowed the rein to go slack.

With the horse on the long reins, you can practise adjusting the speed of the horse over the ground and you can also attend to the 'character' of the horse's stepping action, distinguishing between a lazy, slouching action and a more lively, alert action in which the legs are picked up more briskly and raised higher at each step.

Steering

When you want the horse to move straight ahead, make sure that the pressure exerted by the rein is equal on the two sides of the bit. Also, apply your leg aids symmetrically, at the level of the girth, and keep your weight centrally placed in the saddle. To change direction you alter the symmetry of all three kinds of signal.

To turn right, you first move your right hand back toward you by about a centimetre or so. The horse feels the bit move in his mouth and he will shift his head to bring the bit back to a position where it feels the same to the lips on the two sides. Do not attempt to pull the horse's head round as though you are turning the steering wheel of a car. Just give a sufficient signal to tell him to move his head. As soon as you can just see his eye on the right side you have gone far enough and you can resume a symmetrical pressure on the two reins. You do not need any more head movement than that which just brings his eye into view. The purpose is simply to indicate that a turn is coming and that it is going to be to the right.

The main command to turn is given with the leg. The effect of the squeeze of your lower leg against the horse's side is to increase the vigour of the activity of the legs of that side and, in particular, to tell the horse to lift the hindleg on that side. To make a turn to the right, you need more activity in the legs of the horse's left side. You indicate this to the horse by applying the left leg aid a little behind the girth, while the leg aid on the right remains as before directly over the girth. One effect of the asymmetry of your legs will be to alter the distribution of pressures between your seat and the saddle. As your left leg goes back to give the leg aid for the right turn, the whole of the saddle twists very slightly to the right. You can emphasise this rotation of the saddle by shifting your weight to put more weight on the right knee. It is the combination of the changing feel of the saddle together with the new unsymmetrical position of the leg pressures that is effective in telling the horse to make the turn. He will actually turn quite readily, without the need for any rein signal, in response to the leg aids accompanied by small shiftings of the rider's weight.

During early training, with the horse on the long reins, the rider may exaggerate each of the components of the aids for turning, first to one side and then to the other, so as to get the feel of what is required and of the way the horse responds. When the rider can manage the steering, and can demonstrate the effectiveness of his commands to stop, the long reins can be dispensed with and the rider can practise on his own. Gradually the intensity of his signalling movements should be reduced until he is able to give effective commands to the horse without his aids being conspicuous to the onlooker.

By the time the rider is ready for competitive dressage work, the aids should be virtually invisible. The rein aids are almost imperceptible nudges executed by the fingers alone and applied during the steady contact with the horse's mouth. For the leg aids, all that is needed is a small movement of the foot inside the boot, to alter the pressure against the stirrup. This has two effects: it alters the tenseness of the calf muscle, which the horse can feel because the rider's calf is resting against the horse's side; and it alters the tension in the stirrup leather. The leather does not hang absolutely straight down from the bar on the saddle because the horizontal distance between the bars is less than the width of the horse's body. Accordingly, when the tension in the stirrup leather is increased, it presses harder against the flap of the saddle. The horse can feel this change of pressure, just as he can feel the change in the feel of the saddle when the rider puts more weight on one knee than on the other. Eventually, both horse and rider develop the habit of 'listening' intently to one another by feel so that they can each respond to even the smallest hint of an indication by the other.

Just as the rider practises the movements that he must make to help his horse to understand his wishes, so he should be on the look-out to feel for the changes in the horse's muscles that accompany the horse's movements. For the horse to move any leg, he has first to shift his weight onto the other legs. The horse may also make use of the changes in the momentum of his head as he swings his head about, sideways as well as up and down. The horse is continually on the alert for signs of approaching danger and you can tell when something catches his attention by the way his ears are suddenly aimed in a new direction. By paying attention to the movements of the horse's ears and head, and to the changes in the feel of the horse's muscles as conveyed to him through the saddle, the rider can learn a great deal about the horse's intentions. In this way he can avoid being taken by surprise. If the rider notices the signs that the horse is about to make some move, he will have time to make a signal of his own, either to encourage or to discourage the horse. Encouraging the horse to do something that he was going to do anyway has the effect of reinforcing the significance of your command, and this is a most important part of the process of building up fluency in the communication between horse and rider.

The position of the foot

From time to time take the opportunity to check the position of your foot in the stirrup. You should not be able to see your toe, but you can lean over from time to time to take a peep. The toe should be pointing forward, not out to the side. If you let your toe turn outward this will bring your knee away from the saddle. Your legs will hang round the horse in an attitude like the legs of a frog. At each jolt, the heels come up against the side of the horse, giving him a signal that you do not intend. If he were to pay attention to this signal, it would mean 'Gallop on', but usually he will have realised that he need not bother to respond. He can ignore this continually repeated signal and treat it as meaningless 'noise' − irritating but not significant. The consequence is that when you really do want to signal to him with your legs he will not be 'listening'.

If your knees are not firmly against the saddle, you will be at a disadvantage if the horse is suddenly startled. His reaction is to drop his weight 4−5 centimetres while he splays his feet out ready to make off in any direction. You will feel the jolt as the saddle first drops and then is suddenly supported again. You will hear the stamp as all four feet come down together in their new positions. The horse's ears are pricked up and his head will make a sudden movement. The horse may either make a dead stop or he may jump to one side. In any case, if your knees are not firmly against the saddle, it will be possible for the saddle to move some way under you before you detect it. This delays your reaction and you may be unbalanced to such an extent that you fall off. With the knee against the saddle you not only get an early warning, but the saddle pushes against your knee and this can itself start you moving in the direction of safety.

To check that your feet are in the correct rest position just over the girth, try the effect of relaxing the pressure against the stirrup. If your foot is too far back, the stirrup will slide forward under your toe as soon as the sole of your foot lifts clear of the stirrup. Similarly, if your foot is too far forward, the stirrup will drop back under the arch of your foot. With your foot in the correct position, the stirrup leather will be vertical and the stirrup will remain in place under the ball of the foot when you lift the front of your foot up and down. Try to do this without lifting the heel, so as not to disturb the position of your knee against the saddle. Repeat on the other side. As well as consolidating your habit of keeping the foot in position over the girth, experiment with other positions, forward for a stop and behind the girth ready for a turn, and get used to the feel of these positions so as to be able to put your foot where you want it when the occasion demands. Return to the rest position: stirrup leather vertical, heel away from the horse, toe pointing forward, heel well down below the base line of the stirrup, knee nestling in the hollow between the knee rolls of the saddle.

When your weight comes onto the stirrup, the leather will have to be vertical. This is why the rest position of the foot should also allow the leather to be vertical. The stirrup is placed under the ball of the foot so that, when the leg moves up and down relative to the saddle during the inevitable jolting of the horse's motion, this leg movement can be taken up by the ankle joint, to keep a steady contact with the stirrup.

The aim is so far as possible to avoid movement of the leg relative to the saddle except when making a deliberate signal to the horse. Nevertheless, because of the movements of the horse, and because of changes in the rider's posture when he shifts his weight, the forces between the leg and the saddle are continually changing. The soft tissues of the rider's leg are squeezed by these changing forces and this inevitably leads to some relative movement of the leg over the saddle. If the stirrup is under the arch of the foot, instead of under the ball, the leg movement comes up against the rigid stop of the stirrup leather, producing a jolt that disturbs the contact between horse and rider. If this happens when going down hill or at the take-off for a jump, when the horse's body rises suddenly, the rider may be thrown out of the saddle. The rider's weight, during active riding, should come on the inside of his knees: not on the stirrups (because he should be able to ride without stirrups) and not on the seat-bones unless the rider deliberately applies his weight there as a signal to the horse.

Training the rider's leg

Once you have some idea of what is needed, you can help yourself to find a comfortable way of achieving the desired posture by an exercise carried out unmounted. Stand on the bottom step of a staircase, facing inward, with your heels overhanging clear of the edge of the step. Steady yourself with a hand and then move up and down using only your ankle joint. Rising onto the toes is a familiar movement. Now try sinking as far as you can, allowing the heel to go down below the level of the step. Throw your weight up and down several times allowing the ankle to relax as much as possible to get the feel of having the heel below the ball of the foot.

The next stage is to have the feet well apart, as they would be on the horse, and set parallel to one another, that is, toes pointing forward. Repeat the 'bouncing' to help free the ankle joint. Then lean forward, bending the knees, and move the arms well forward until the elbows are in front of the knees. The bounces continue until the shoulders come down almost between the knees. Practise balancing in this position, with minimal support from the hands, while bouncing up and down by moving the ankles.

To extend the exercise when mounted, rise in the stirrups, making sure that they are under the ball of the foot, and balance yourself with a hand on the horse's withers or by holding on to the mane. Have the knees as near straight as they will go, then move repeatedly up and down with the ankles as before, emphasising the sinking deep down to get the heel well below the ball of the foot, and keeping the heels out, toes forward. One effect of this exercise is to firm up the muscles of the calf so that they may be used to press on the horse in the various ways needed for signalling in the leg aids. Another effect is to encourage the inward bracing of the knees that provides the basis of a 'good seat'. After some practice it will be possible to hold the position of 'rising in the stirrups', with the knees straight and the seat out of the saddle, even without the stirrups, the weight being taken entirely on the inside of the knees. It is important to remember that in this exercise the reins may not, in any circumstances, be used for balancing.

Riding without stirrups

One of the problems facing the beginner is that he is not used to having the width of the body of the horse between his legs. The unfamiliar attitude of the hip joints becomes uncomfortable after he has been jolted up and down for a few minutes by the movements of the horse. This is particularly so because the horse's movements are also unfamiliar and the beginner needs time to learn how to relax so that his pelvis will smoothly follow the movements of the saddle without jolting the rider's back. A good way to get your hip joints used to the new movements is to spend a few minutes each day riding without stirrups.

You will need your stirrups for mounting and if you just leave them dangling, they will swing about and bang against the horse's side. To put them out of the way, lift them up and cross the leathers over the horse's neck in front of the saddle. This may leave an uncomfortable lump where your thigh passes over the stirrup bar. To avoid this, pull the buckle of the stirrup leather a few centimetres away from the bar and turn the two parts of the leather upward separately so that they lie flat under the skirt of the saddle (*Figure 1.22*).

Ride on at the walk, practising your leg aids, swinging your weight a little from side to side in time with the horse. Remember to keep your toes pointing forward with the heel below the sole of the foot. Try to get the knee as straight as possible. This will emphasise the grip of your knees against the saddle and will give you an increased sense of security. If your leg aids are so vigorous that

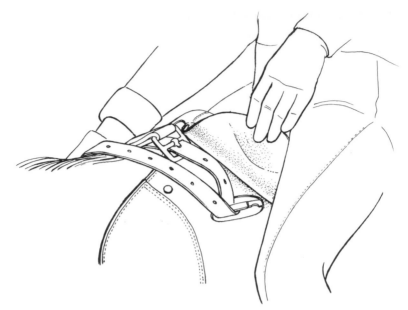

Figure 1.22   *Crossing the stirrups. To avoid an uncomfortable lump under your thigh, pull the buckle of the stirrup leather away from the bar and make sure that both parts of the strap are lying flat under the skirt of the saddle.*

your horse starts to trot, don't panic and grip with your heels because this will only send him on faster. Relax your lower leg, squeeze with your knees, and give a few brief pulls on the rein to tell the horse to slow down.

The leg aids involve movements of the lower leg, out sideways away from the girth and then back again into position over the girth with a slight pressure against the horse's side. The knee stays in place against the saddle. Also try movements of the lower leg forward and back without touching the side of the horse. The aim here is to develop independence of the lower leg so that it can be used to control the horse without disturbing the grip of the knee against the saddle. Move the two legs in opposite directions, as in walking. Also move both legs forward or back at the same time, or move one leg at a time.

Practise also the arm and rein exercises described earlier, changing the rein from one hand to the other in order to free yourself from the feeling of wanting to hold on to the reins for balance. Then combine the arm exercises with the leg exercises until you begin to feel really confident in your balance in the saddle and can move hands or legs quite independently when you need them for signalling to the horse.

Dismounting

When the time comes to dismount, bring your horse to a halt, take both feet out of the stirrups, and sit softly and quietly in the saddle. The horse will then know that you are about to get down. Put both reins in the left hand, with your hand on the withers as for mounting. Put the flat of your right hand firmly on the front of the saddle with the heel of the hand on the pommel (*Figure 1.23*). Bring your right elbow hard in to your side in front of your hip and lean forward, pivoting over your forearm. This will lift your seat out of the saddle. Bend the right knee and, carefully avoiding kicking the horse, swing your right leg backwards up and over the horse. Pause when the two legs come together on the left side of the horse, let yourself slide down gently for a few centimetres, and then drop to the ground. Keep hold of the reins and keep both hands in contact with the horse so as not to fall over backwards. Be prepared to bend your knees as you land on your toes; you are going to drop quite a long way.

It may occasionally happen, after your horse has enjoyed an active excursion with you on his back, that he tries to be too helpful when you are ready to dismount. When he feels your weight coming forward, as part of the dismounting movement, he may think you are overbalancing and about to fall forward over his shoulder. His reaction may be to lift his head to catch you on his neck. He believes this to be helpful, whereas in fact it just hinders your attempt to dismount. The remedy is to bear down steadily on his neck with your left forearm so that he comes to realise that the forward movement of your weight is deliberate and that there is no call for him to rescue you.

Figure 1.23   *Prepare to dismount. Feet out of the stirrups, weight on your hands, right elbow hard against your side, and pivot forward over the right forearm.*

Unsaddling

If the horse is not going to be mounted again immediately, by yourself or by someone else, put the stirrups up into their 'parking' position so that they do not swing about. Slide the stirrup up the inner part of the leather, right up to the bar, and then tuck the free loop of leather through the stirrup. This will hold the stirrup in position. If you have some distance to go to the place where you will take the saddle off, first loosen the girth a couple of holes because, as soon as your weight is out of the saddle, the girth will suddenly feel tighter to the horse. He will appreciate being relieved of this extra tension.

When taking off the tack, take the saddle off first. If you remove the bridle first, the horse may walk away from you with the saddle still in place. His first thought may be to have a good roll, and this won't do your saddle any good! After parking the stirrups, take the reins over his head and loop them over your arm while you are manipulating the saddle. Undo the girth buckles on one side and lift off the saddle, sliding it first backwards a little over the horse's back so as to avoid rubbing the hairs of the coat the wrong way. Lay the girth over the seat of the saddle, horse-side down. The sweat will wipe off easily, whereas any dried mud on the outside of the girth might scratch the saddle. Place the saddle over a gate or over the half-door of the stable until you have finished with the horse. Be careful if you have to lay it on the ground. Keep it well out of the way of the horse's feet. If the front of your saddle is fairly square, you may be able to balance it on the front arch; otherwise you will have to lay it down upright, resting on the back of the panel and on the edges of the saddle-flaps. Keep it away from grit and gravel.

When taking the bridle off, start by putting the rein over the horse's neck, just behind the ears, so that you will be able to retain some control. Have the headcollar or halter ready, looped over one elbow. Undo the buckles of the noseband and throatlash. Then put both hands up to the poll. One hand is to slide the bridle forward over his ears, the other is to discourage him from immediately throwing his head up. Pause with your bridle hand in front of his forehead to allow him to drop the bit. If you don't do this he may throw his head up with the bit still in his mouth. It will rattle against his front teeth and he may plunge about trying to get rid of it. Once his head is up, the bit will not drop out. Even if he does open his mouth, the bit will still be hooked round the lower teeth. An instinctive pull on the bridle doesn't help either. When the horse finally succeeds in getting rid of the bit, it may fly toward you and hit you in the face. You can avoid all this excitement, simply by taking the bridle off gently and pausing to give time for the horse to drop the bit. Once the bit is out of his mouth you can take your hands away from his head. If he starts to move off before you are ready, take hold of both sides of the reins close up to his throat. If you have remembered to put the rein just behind the ears you should have no difficulty in restraining him. Loop the headpiece of the bridle over your elbow in exchange for the headcollar and slip the headcollar into place. You will then have the lead-rope with which to restrain the horse while you lay the bridle aside with the saddle.

Give the horse a rub down, paying particular attention to the damp patches under the saddle and girth. Also rub round the ears and over the face in those places that have been in contact with the bridle. He will appreciate this and may rub his head strongly against you. He intends this in the most friendly manner, but you must be careful not to get your clothes covered in slobber. If you give him a few titbits, remember to keep your hand flat so that he doesn't accidentally close his teeth on your fingers. Don't have sweets in your pocket at this stage. He will smell them and may try to get at them with his teeth. Nibbling at you with his lips is a friendly gesture rather than a vicious attempt at a bite. If he gets too demonstrative, just give him a firm nudge on the side of his face with your knuckles. Don't slap his face or make any sudden movement because this will alarm him and he will become more reluctant to stand close to you. He will also be more difficult to catch. When you are ready to let him free, slip the headcollar off quietly, talk to him, rub his neck and walk away. Do not drive him away from you; leave him standing there. He may stare after you for a bit, then he will probably walk away and have a roll.

Collect up your tack, rinse the bit and go over the leather items with saddle soap, paying particular attention to the panels of the saddle. If these are left to dry they soon become encrusted with hard masses of dried sweat and hair which can eventually cause saddle sores. The sweat wipes off easily if you attend to it promptly.

2 BASIC PRINCIPLES IN MORE DETAIL

When you are guiding a beginner through his first steps in learning to ride, your pupil's reactions to your advice may raise questions in your mind that call for more detail about certain topics. It is a good idea to explain your advice and, of course, it is important to get your explanations right. So much of a rider's later development is affected by the habits that he has acquired when first learning to ride and it is all too easy for a beginner to develop undesirable habits that are very hard to break later.

This chapter is intended to provide the relevant supporting detail. In setting it out, I have found that I need, here and there, to refer to aspects of riding that beginners will not yet have met. They may prefer to postpone the study of this chapter. It should, however, present no problems for the experienced rider who is already familiar with the terms used. If you need any reminders, you will be able to locate detailed definitions through the index.

The saddle and the seat

When we speak of the rider's 'seat', we are referring, not only to his posture in the saddle, but also to his security and elegance when the horse is in motion. All these factors are influenced by the choice of saddle. It is a mistake to use a saddle that does not fit comfortably on the horse's back. A badly fitting saddle not only causes discomfort and possible injury to the horse; it can also be dangerous for the rider, since the horse may come to resent the discomfort and throw the rider off.

Fit the saddle to the rider

Saddles come in many different shapes and sizes. Nevertheless, provided that extremes are avoided, many saddles will fit a variety of horses and riders. So far as the rider is concerned, after deciding on the general type of saddle required, e.g. for jumping, dressage or for general purposes, the important thing to consider is the length of the rider's thigh, from the seat-bones to the knee. The seat-bones are to rest on the lowest part of the dip in the saddle, and the knee should fit into the hollow formed by the knee-rolls of the panel. Children and very short people are best suited by a small saddle, while the very tall require a comparatively large one. Most riders are happily accommodated by the middle range of saddle sizes.

Fit the saddle to the horse

The fit on the horse depends on the shape of the horse's back, as illustrated in *Photos 2.1a-b*. Here a home-made 'outside-profile gauge' has been placed in position to show that the sides of the horse's back form a much flatter angle in the region that will carry the rear portion of the saddle than they do just behind the withers, where the front arch of the saddle is to fit. In *Photos 2.2a-b* an 'inside-profile gauge' is placed against the undersides of the two arches of a saddle to show how the saddlemaker takes account of the shape of the horse's back. In *Photos 2.3a-b* the roles of the two gauges have been reversed. The inside-profile gauge (shown at the bottom) is set to correspond with the shape of the horse's back while the outside-profile gauge (top) represents the shape of the forward arch of the saddle. Fitting the two gauges together makes it clear that, if the saddle is too narrow for the horse, it will fail to engage properly with the ridge of the horse's back. The saddle will then tend to slide round to one side if the rider's weight comes down more heavily on one side than on the other. The rider's weight will also tend to strain the arch of the saddle-tree as

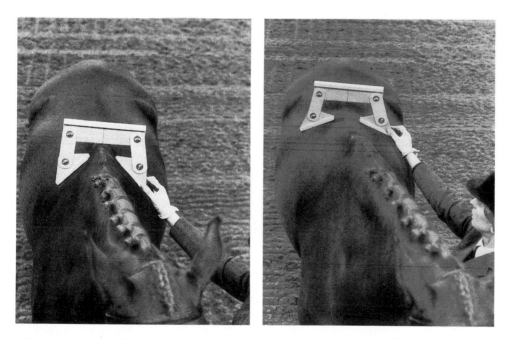

Photo 2.1a-b   *The shape of the horse's back. An 'outside-profile gauge' is laid over the horse's back to indicate the slope of the sides of the body at different positions along the back.* **(a)** *(left) Position for the front arch of the saddle.* **(b)** *(right) Position for the rear arch of the saddle.*

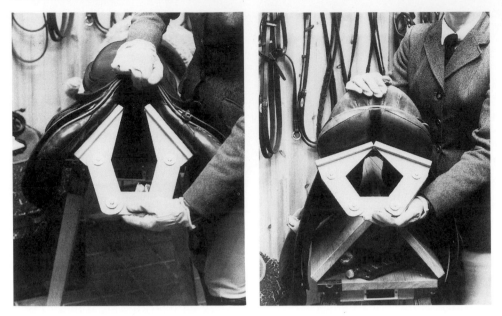

Photo 2.2a-b *The shape of the underside of the saddle. An 'inside-profile gauge' is placed against the saddle to indicate the slopes of the surfaces that will bear against the horse's back. (a) (left) The front arch of the saddle. (b) (right) The rear arch of the saddle.*

well as causing the saddle to pinch the horse's back. At the other extreme, a saddle that is too wide for the horse will fail to keep the rider's weight away from the sensitive bony ridge along the midline of the horse's back. For a very narrow horse with high withers, it is necessary to select a saddle with a cut-away front.

The position taken up on a horse's back by a particular saddle is governed partly by the shape of the saddle in its relation to the shape of the horse's back and partly by the action of the girth, which tends to settle towards the region of minimum circumference of the horse's body. If the girth is tightened when the saddle is not in the optimum position, the later movements of the horse, coupled with the action of the weight of the rider, will tend to move the saddle towards the optimum position and the effect of this is that the girth will go slack.

The position of the rider

There are two features of the design of the saddle that have an important bearing on the rider's position. These are the position of the dip in the saddle and the position of the stirrup bars. The weight of a rider will tend to settle with the rider's seat-bones against the lowest part of the dip in the saddle. It is possible for an inexperienced and tense rider to sit either further forward or

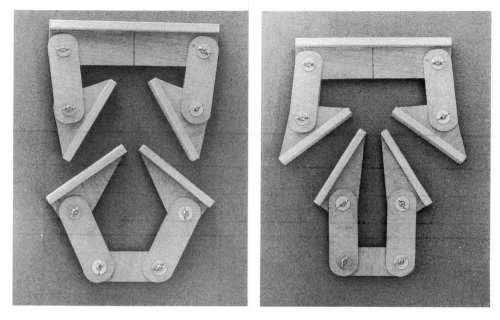

Photo 2.3a-b *The fit of the saddle on the horse's back. The upper profile-gauge is set to indicate the shape of the underside of the front arch of the saddle, while the lower profile-gauge indicates the shape of the horse's back just behind the withers. **(a)** (left) Saddle too narrow for the horse. It fails to engage properly with the ridge of the horse's back and may consequently slip round when the rider attempts to mount. If he succeeds in mounting, there is a risk of splitting the saddle-tree. **(b)** (right) Saddle too wide for the horse. There is a risk that the sensitive ridge along the midline of the horse's back may come into contact with the saddle, causing considerable discomfort to the horse.*

further back than this but it will require muscular effort to retain this position, and it will consequently be tiring as well as insecure.

The effect of the position of the stirrup bars depends on the fact that when part of the rider's weight is taken on the stirrups, as it is during the posting phase at the rising trot or with the rider in the jump-seat position, the stirrup leather must hang vertically to support the weight.

The position of the stirrup bars has a great influence on where the rider's heel will come in relation to the vertical line through the rider's hips, thus contributing to the overall impression given to a competition judge of the elegance of the rider's seat. Some judges regard it as desirable that the rider's ear, shoulder, hip, and heel should all come in the same vertical line. Since the stirrup leather is to be vertical, it is not easy to achieve this vertical alignment of the rider's posture unless the horizontal distance from the stirrup bar to the dip in the saddle is about equal to the distance from the ball of the rider's foot, where it bears against the tread of the stirrup, to the back of the heel of the boot.

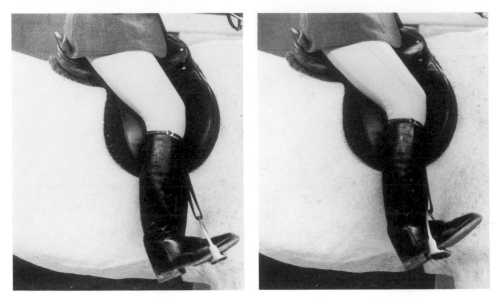

Photo 2.4a-b   *Foot too far forward. (**a**) (left) The stirrup leather is not vertical. If the rider puts weight on the stirrup, this will force the foot backwards. (**b**) (right) The weight has been taken off the stirrup by raising the toe. The stirrup drops back under the rider's instep and when she lowers her toe again, she will be able to feel that the stirrup has moved under the foot.*

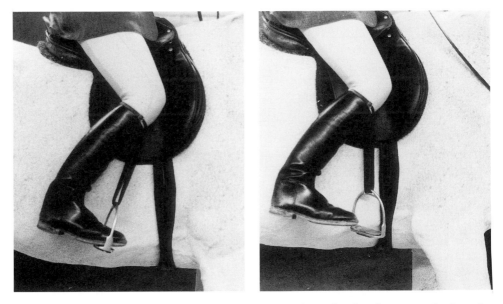

Photo 2.5a-b   *Foot too far back. (**a**) (left) The stirrup leather is not vertical so the foot would swing forward if the rider were to put weight on the stirrup. (**b**) (right) The stirrup has slipped forward when the rider's toe was raised. Lowering the toe again allows the rider to feel the shift of the stirrup.*

You can help the novice rider to become familiar with the feel of the 'correct' position in the dip of the saddle by having him ride round on the lunge without stirrups and with fully relaxed legs. Thereafter he can quickly reassure himself that he is in the right place by wriggling about a little in the saddle.

The rest position of the rider's foot should be with the stirrup leather vertical, for the reasons given earlier. You can help a novice to get used to the feel of having his feet in the right place by demonstrating the effects of exaggerated departures from that position, as illustrated in *Photos 2.4* and *2.5*. If your foot is too far forward (*Photo 2.4a*), then the stirrup will fall back when you raise your toe (*Photo 2.4b*). Similarly, if your foot is too far back (*Photo 2.5a*), the stirrup will slip forward when you raise your toe (*Photo 2.5b*). The procedure for testing the position of the foot, by momentarily lifting the toe to ease the pressure against the stirrup, serves to detect even quite small errors in foot placement.

Length of leathers

In selecting a suitable length for the stirrup leathers, the well-known rule of thumb, that the stirrup-length should correspond with the length of the rider's arm, is of only limited usefulness. This is particularly so in the case of a short rider on a tall horse, where it will often be convenient to let the near-side stirrup down several holes to facilitate mounting. Another point to bear in mind is that reliance on the numbering of the holes in the stirrup leathers is unsatisfactory, since the leathers on the two sides usually stretch unequally in use, because of the extra strain put on the near-side leather during mounting.

If the leathers are too long, you will tend to be tipped forward onto your crotch and will have to reach down with your toe to put weight on the tread of the stirrup, and your knee will tend to be drawn away from its best position in the nest between the knee-rolls (*Photo 2.6a*). There is also a risk that, if you are jolted about and your heel is not below your toe, the stirrup might slip back toward your instep, leaving you unsupported.

If, on the other hand, the leathers are too short (*Photo 2.6b*), your knee will be pushed up out of the nest in the knee-rolls. To avoid having your knee right off the front of the saddle, you may be tempted to sit further back in the saddle, against the cantle. Then the movement of the horse will tend to throw you forward at each bounce as you land on the sloping part of the saddle, behind the dip.

The 'correct' stirrup-length can be arrived at by the following routine. Make sure you are sitting in the bottom of the dip in the saddle. To confirm this, let your legs hang straight down freely, with your feet out of the stirrups and, keeping your heels well away from the horse, swing each leg in turn forward and back a few times, swinging from the hip and, so far as you are able, holding the whole leg out of contact with the horse throughout. You may need to hold on to the pommel while carrying out this settling process. Then, on

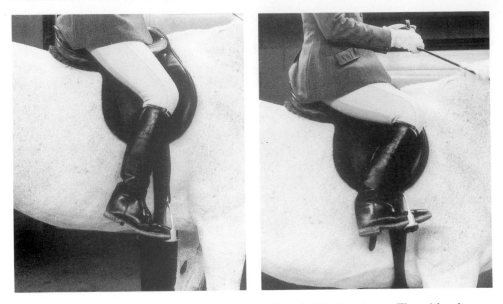

Photo 2.6a-b *Length of stirrup leathers.* ***(a)*** *(left) Too long. The rider has to reach down with her toe, as otherwise her knee will be drawn downward away from the 'nest' provided by the knee-rolls.* ***(b)*** *(right) Too short. The knee is pushed up above the nest in the knee-rolls and the rider may be tempted to sit further back in the saddle to compensate for this.*

each side in turn, locate the 'nest hollow' to be found between the knee-rolls of the panel, and place your knee comfortably in the centre of this nest. Now, with the toe well raised, feel for the stirrup with the inside of your foot. The stirrup will be hanging with the tread more or less parallel with the horse's body, and when you tap the rear upright of the stirrup arch, the stirrup will swing round your foot. Tuck your toe into the stirrup, from the outside. The tread of the stirrup should come to rest against the sole of the foot, under the ball of the foot. If your foot doesn't go easily into the stirrup, the leather is too short. If the tread falls right back against your heel, the leather is too long.

Now check that the two sides are equal. To do this, stand in the stirrups with your legs straight and your heels well away from the horse (*Photo 2.7*). Move your weight up and down a few times by lifting yourself onto your toes and then sinking as far as possible into the stirrups, letting your heels go as far down below your toes as possible. Look down to check that the saddle is centrally placed over the horse's back. If it is not straight, you will be able to slide it round by putting more weight on one side for a moment during the up-and-down surging of your weight. When you are satisfied that the saddle is central, and that both your legs are straight, the feel of your pelvis should tell you whether you are level. Readjust the stirrup leathers as necessary, bring your knees into their nest in the knee-rolls, and lower yourself gently into the saddle.

Photo 2.7 *Testing to see whether the stirrup leathers are equal. The rider stands in the stirrups with knees straight and looks first to see whether the saddle is correctly centred over the horse's withers. It can often get pulled to one side during mounting. If the saddle is not central, its position can be corrected by a sharp push down against the appropriate stirrup. If both of the rider's knees are straight and if her back is upright, any important inequality in the lengths of the stirrup leathers will be revealed by the pelvis feeling pushed over to one side or the other.*

If you neglect the adjustment of the stirrup leathers and ride with unequal contact on the two sides, there is a risk that, at an unexpected jolt, you will come down more heavily on one stirrup than on the other. This will tend to tip you over and will jeopardise your balance.

Stability of the seat

So long as the horse is stationary, you will have no problems of stability because you are in contact with the saddle over an area that is large compared with the vertical distance of your centre of gravity above the saddle. The situation changes when the horse is in active motion: the saddle then tilts, rocks and bobs about in quite complicated ways and pushes against your seat in different directions at different times. If you are not careful, you can be bounced into an awkward position and may even lose your balance altogether. Your first defence is to make sure that you are sitting in the deepest part of the dip in the saddle. The thrust of the saddle against your seat-bones is necessarily at

Photo 2.8a-b   *The rider's position in the saddle.* **(a)** *(above) The drive seat. The rider's seat-bones rest on the lowest part of the dip in the saddle. The knees nestle into the hollows provided by the knee-rolls. The stirrup leather is vertical. The stirrup is under the ball of the foot, with the heel below the toe. The rider sits upright.*

The positions of the centres of gravity of horse and rider have been calculated by

right angles to the surface of contact, and if your weight comes down onto a sloping surface you will inevitably be displaced in the downhill direction. You should also make sure that you remain as supple as possible so that your seat absorbs the most severe part of the jolting.

The function of the contact of your knees with the saddle is to extend the potential area of support. Provided you ensure that you only press vertically down on the saddle with your knees, and do not exert any inclined force, the knees can bear some of your weight. This means that you can move your centre of gravity about without falling over, so long as the movement of your centre of gravity doesn't go too far. If you sit with your body fairly upright over your seat (as in *Photo 2.8a*), and then move your elbows forward in the direction of the horse's mouth without letting your hands come up at all and shortening rein as you go, this will draw your shoulders forward (*Photo 2.8b*) and your seat will come out of the saddle. You are now in the jump-seat position, with your weight taken entirely on the knees and on the inner parts of the lower thighs. There is a small contribution of supporting force from the stirrups, but this

*the method given in Appendix 3. The rider's centre of gravity, as indicated by a dotted cross just below her elbow, lies slightly ahead of the centre of gravity of the horse, as indicated by the vertical dotted line. (**b**) (above) The jump seat. The rider has moved her shoulders forward until her seat has lifted out of the saddle. The positions of the knees and lower legs are unchanged by this manoeuvre.*

Photo 2.9   *The effect of heel position on the contact of the knee with the saddle. Note that the rider's toe points forward. A card has been trapped between the knee and the saddle. If the rider turns her toe out, the card falls, revealing that the knee has come away from the saddle.*

Holding the heel away from the horse has the effect of bringing the knee onto the saddle. A steady contact between the knees and the saddle is essential for the easy maintenance of balance. A tight grip is not necessary except in emergencies.

serves primarily to prevent the knees from sliding down the slope of the saddle-flap. You should not be depending entirely on the stirrups to support your weight.

To maintain the jump-seat position when the horse is in active motion, it is essential that you should keep every part of your body in a state of supple springiness. Complete relaxation is not appropriate, and any undue tenseness is likely to have undesired consequences. The various arm and leg exercises in the text are intended to promote the necessary suppleness. In particular, you should take great care to develop the independence of your hands since, without it, the unavoidable movements of your trunk will be communicated to the reins, thus sending unwanted signals to the horse. On no account should you attempt to hang on to the reins to help keep your balance.

The contact at the knees has another important function. It helps in maintaining lateral stability. The horse's movements tilt the saddle from side to side, and if your trunk is not supple enough, you will be thrown from side to side by the saddle. Your knees can help in controlling such unwanted sideways movements, provided that you always keep them in contact with the saddle. It helps here if you remember to keep your heels away from the horse. If you allow your toes to turn out, the pressure of your knee against the saddle is reduced. In *Photo 2.9*, a card has been trapped between the knee and the saddle. If the rider turns her toe out, the card falls.

Movements of the pelvis

The lateral tilts of the saddle that are produced by the horse's movement can upset the rider unless he trains himself to be able to move his pelvis freely. If you pay attention to the feel of the seat-bones against the saddle you will feel the difference when you put more weight on one seat-bone than on the other. Practise doing this without moving the upper part of your body out of the vertical. In *Photos 2.10a-c* (overleaf), a rider is shown with a marker attached to her waistband to show when one seat-bone has been raised. Another marker hanging from her hat indicates the position of a central vertical line. *Photo 2.10a* shows the normal upright position. In *Photo 2.10b*, the rider has allowed the whole of her body to sway away from the lifted seat-bone, while *Photo 2.10c* shows that she can raise her seat-bone without moving her upper body over. Try this on both sides. You will need this sort of movement to produce the unilateral seat aids used for fine control of the horse. It is this sort of lateral movement of the pelvis relative to the rest of the back that is essential in maintaining balance when the saddle tilts from side to side.

If you habitually keep your knees in contact with the saddle, you will be warned of any tendency to wander from the horse's midline. Such wandering can easily happen if the horse moves to one side or the other while your weight is temporarily out of the saddle after being tossed up by the horse's movement, as often occurs at the canter or over a jump. If you accidentally get out of line while in the air, you will land more heavily on one side or the other and your balance will be seriously upset. With the timely prompting provided by the feel of your knees against the saddle, you can make any necessary preparatory adjustments while still in the air so that you will come down safely, squarely in the middle of the saddle.

Seat aids and weight aids

In addition to the movements of the saddle that are made by the horse, and which affect the rider, it is possible for the rider to move the saddle as a signal to the horse. You can do this laterally, by putting more weight on one seat-bone than on the other, as in the movement described above, or by putting more weight on one knee. Alternatively you can move the saddle in the fore-and-aft

Photo 2.10a-c *Learning about unequal weight on the seat-bones. The rider is sitting on a model horse, so that the saddle remains in the same position through-out. A marker suspended from the rider's waistband indicates the tilting of the pelvis, while a second marker hangs from the rider's hat to indicate the vertical. The line of the pelvic marker is here extended in a dotted line. The vertical through the midline of the saddle is also indicated.* **(a)** *(above) The symmetrical upright*

direction, as in the seat aid that is used in encouraging the horse to move actively forward. The object of this seat aid is to push the saddle forward as a signal to the horse.

One way of learning how to do this is to use a model horse mounted on wheels. The pupil sits in the saddle on the model horse and the instructor makes a small forward and backward movement of the model over the wheels. The pupil can sense the change this produces in the feel of his pelvis. He then tries to reproduce the movement for himself. Success is rewarded by a forward

position with the weight equally distributed between the seat-bones. **(b)** *(above left) The rider has raised her right seat-bone to put more weight on the left. Note that she has, at the same time, allowed her upper body to lean over to the left.* **(c)** *(above right) As in* **(b)** *but this time the rider has kept her upper body vertical while lifting the right seat-bone to put more weight on the left.*

movement of the model horse. The nature of the required movement is a rotation of the pelvis, clockwise as seen from the rider's left, about a horizontal axis through the two hip-joints. This drives the seat-bones forward against the saddle. If you look carefully at *Photos 2.11a-b* (overleaf), comparing the outline of the rider in the two cases, you will see the sort of movement that she has made. A marker hung from the rider's waistband reveals the way the rider has moved her pelvis. Once you have got the idea, you will probably not really need the model horse, which was introduced here primarily to enable a suitable pair of photographs to be taken to illustrate the movement.

Photo 2.11a-b *Practising the seat aid. The rider sits on a wooden horse fitted with large wheels so that it can be moved backwards and forwards very freely. An assistant first moves the 'horse' with a small brisk forward and backward move-ment so that the rider can feel the saddle moving under her. Thereafter the rider attempts to move the horse forward for herself by a rotation of the pelvis to drive the seat-bones forward against the saddle. A marker is suspended from the rider's waistband to draw attention to the nature of the movement. The line of the marker is here extended in a dotted line. This is the movement commonly referred to as 'bracing the back'. **(a)** (left) Preparing to drive the saddle forward. **(b)** (right) After driving the saddle forward by bracing the back. The marker shows that the pelvis has been rotated clockwise as seen from the left.*

The movement to drive the saddle forward with the seat-bones is usually referred to as 'bracing the back'.

In Western-style riding, the weight aids are applied by leaning the whole body to one side or the other. More subtle weight aids are not available because of the relative stiffness of the Western saddle and the fact that the rider sits with legs rather straight.

The leg aids

The effect on the horse of the forward drive of the seat-bones against the saddle in the seat aids depends on what the rider is at the same time doing with his legs.

The lower part of the rider's leg should not be used for balance. It should function primarily for signalling, in conjunction with the rein aids and weight aids. You should be able to move your lower legs about without affecting the contact of your knees with the saddle. I have described, in different places, a number of exercises which will help you to achieve this necessary independence. (You will be able to locate these descriptions through the Index.)

The 'rest position' for the rider's leg is with the stirrup leather vertical. In this position the leg is said to be 'on the girth'. If you consistently hold your lower leg in the rest position most of the time, you can use a change in leg position as an effective signal. You can apply a 'leg aid behind the girth' by drawing your lower leg backwards about one hand's breadth from the rest position. This signal is most useful if it is applied on one side only, so that the horse can detect the asymmetry between your leg positions on the two sides. In giving the positional leg aid you should not allow your knee to wander from its regular position nesting between the knee-rolls of the saddle.

Another type of leg-aid signal is applied by making the lower leg 'active', either on the girth or behind the girth as required. There are two ways of doing this:

- by varying the lateral pressure exerted by the calf against the saddle-flap; and
- by varying the vertical pressure applied by the foot against the tread of the stirrup.

The action of this vertical pressure is a consequence of the fact that the horse's body bulges out to the side so that the stirrup leather does not hang straight down. When you put increased weight on the stirrup, the leather is pressed more firmly into the horse's side. In *Photo 2.12*, a card has been tucked behind the stirrup leather. When the leather is pulled down, as it would be by the rider putting weight on the stirrup, the card is trapped and it cannot be pulled out. Adjusting the downward pressure on the stirrup thus provides a means of applying a very subtle aid, not easily visible to the onlooker.

If the seat aid is combined with an increased pressure of both of the rider's calves against the horse's sides (and/or with an increased downward pressure on the stirrups, which has a corresponding effect on the horse's sides), then the horse responds with an increased eagerness to go forward. Whether he actually accelerates in response to this combination of aids or only shows an increase in 'impulsion' will depend on what rein aids are being applied at the time.

Many aspiring dressage competitors, in their concern to 'ride with a long leg', as is the traditional practice in dressage competitions, get into the habit of allowing their knees to come away from the saddle. The idea here is supposedly to ensure a more intimate contact of the lower leg with the horse. This practice has a number of disadvantages. The constant contact of the rider's lower leg reduces the range of significant variation in the 'feel' of the leg aid to the horse. If the rider tries to move his leg out sideways away from the horse while his

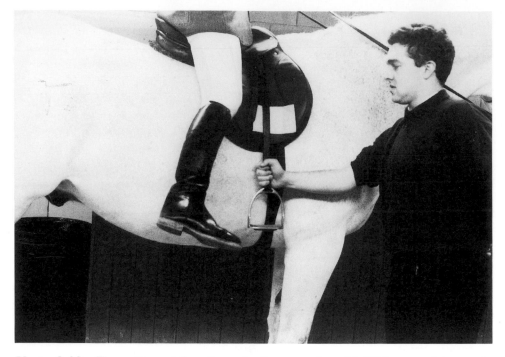

Photo 2.12 *The action of the stirrup leather as a leg aid. With no weight on the stirrup, a card slipped under the stirrup leather can be moved easily. A downward pull on the leather, such as that occurring when the rider applies weight to the stirrup, presses the stirrup leather tightly against the horse's side, thus trapping the card so that it cannot easily be withdrawn.*

Leg aids can accordingly be applied quite effectively by simply altering the downward pressure on the stirrup, without any lateral movement of the rider's leg.

knee is out of contact with the saddle, this will undermine the security of the rider's seat. The horse will then have no way of knowing which leg pressures are intended as signals and which are merely part of the rider's struggle to avoid losing his balance in the saddle. It is preferable to keep your knee lightly on the saddle at all times, allowing complete independence to your lower leg in its signalling function. In lateral work, for example, when you want the horse to yield to your leg on one side, it may help if you move the lower leg on the other side out of contact with the horse's side. You can then bring it back into contact again after the horse has made the single outward step which is all that you should require of him at the first trial.

In building up impulsion at the walk, it may be helpful if, instead of swaying your legs from side to side in the manner that is taught to beginners, you employ a more sophisticated action that emphasises the vertical movement of your foot rather than the lateral movement of your calf. For this leg-aid system it is essential that your weight should be taken mainly on the seat, lower thighs, and knees, with only a small contribution of support by the stirrups. You can

Photo 2.13   *Contact point for the leg aids. A card has been trapped between the rider's calf and the side of the horse to show where the pressure of the leg acts on the horse. There is no virtue in attempting to make contact with the horse by using a lower part of the leg or the heel.*

then press down on the stirrup with the ball of your foot on one side to apply a signal through the tension in the stirrup leather. The action of pressing down with the ball of the foot tenses the muscles of the calf and the horse can feel this as well as the increased pressure of the stirrup leather against his side. While you are pressing down with your foot it will be natural for you to put a little more weight on that knee. You can reinforce the effectiveness of this manoeuvre by a unilateral seat aid, using the seat-bone of the same side to push the saddle forward. This gives you the following full combination: unilateral seat aid, unilateral weight aid on the knee, and unilateral pressure on the stirrup. To encourage the walk, you then use this combination on each side in turn, in time with the swaying of the horse's trunk.

The level at which the leg-aid pressure is effective is shown in *Photo 2.13*, in which a card has been inserted under the rider's calf. You should not attempt to bring your heel into contact with the horse. Resorting to 'kicking on' is a sign of desperation in a rider who has not learned how to give intelligible signals to his horse. The effect is to punish the horse, unjustly, for the rider's incompetence.

The effect of the direct leg aid, applied over the girth either by a lateral movement of the leg or by an adjustment of the weight on the stirrup, is to make the horse tend to reach forward more vigorously with the hindleg of that side. Such leg aids are used in alternation to encourage the walk, the rider's right leg being applied while the horse is swaying to the left, and the left leg during the sway to the right. Leg aids over the girth are used together on the two sides to encourage forward movement, as in the transition to the trot, and in developing impulsion.

The action of the leg aid behind the girth depends on what the horse is doing at the time, and on what other aids are also being used at that moment. Thus:

- If the horse is going freely forward, the application of the left leg behind the girth will produce a turn to the right. You can produce this effect by the leg alone, without the reinforcement of any rein aid. It is particularly valuable to practise the combination of the leg aid behind the girth on one side with the unilateral weight aid on the other side, without using the rein. Remember that the weight aid is to be applied on the side to which you want the horse to turn.
- On the other hand, if the horse is well collected and the rein aids are symmetrical, the application of the left leg behind the girth will produce 'leg-yielding', the horse moving on a diagonal path toward the right, without change of bend.
- The same combination, symmetrical reins coupled with left leg aid behind the girth, when used with yielding hands and supported by symmetrical seat aids and a direct leg aid on the right, produces a strike-off into canter on the right lead.
- If the horse is asked to turn his head to the right during the leg-yielding manoeuvre, the combined effect is to produce a half-pass to the right.
- In shoulder-in to the right, where the horse moves diagonally forward toward the left in response to the rider's right leg applied over the girth, the left leg is held behind the girth, but inactive and kept in readiness. It is made active only when the horse shows a tendency to wander out to the left with his hindquarters.
- If the left leg is applied behind the girth when the horse is at the halt, he will start to turn on the forehand to the left.
- The application of the left leg behind the girth during a rein-back causes the horse to step out to the right with his hindquarters.

If, instead of squeezing with your calves on both sides (or pressing down on the stirrups) while giving the seat aid to drive the saddle forward, you emphasise the downward pressure of your knees against the saddle, the result is a downward transition in gait, leading to a full halt. This combination can be effective even on a loose rein, that is to say, even without the confirmation of the firmly resisting rein aid that normally accompanies the seat aid when asking for a brisk halt.

On a side-saddle (*Photo 2.14*), the rider's right leg is not available for the application of leg aids, but a stiff cane carried by the rider serves to give corresponding indications. If the horse tends to veer to the right under the

Photo 2.14 *Side-saddle, for comparison with Photo 2.8, same rider, same horse. Note that, because the rider's right leg lies over the horse's withers, her weight comes a little further back than when riding astride. The rider's centre of gravity, shown by the dotted cross, is almost exactly over that of the horse, as indicated by the vertical dotted line.*

influence of the unsymmetrical leg aids, this can be corrected by a judicious use of the right indirect rein behind the withers.

The feel of the bit

The bit is used as a channel of communication between the rider and his horse. It is accordingly of interest to consider what the bit feels like to the horse.

The snaffle bit

When the horse first finds the bit in his mouth he cannot be expected to know what to do with it. To guide him he has only his own sensations: smell, taste and touch. Both the smell and the taste may have been disguised either deliberately by the person presenting the bit as part of the technique for persuading the horse to take the bit into his mouth, or from the bit having been at some time previously in the mouth of another horse. The taste and smell of the metal itself will be something quite unusual. The metal will feel cold, and the horse will soon discover that it is hard.

In exploring the feel of the bit, he will try to move it about with his tongue. This reveals that the bit does not fall out when he opens his mouth. He also finds it awkward to bring the bit into range of his teeth. The attachment of the bit rings to the cheekpieces of the bridle has the effect that the corners of the mouth are forced well back if he tries to crush the bit with his grinding teeth, and he cannot push the bit down into contact with his incisors. In any case he soon discovers that the metal is so hard as to discourage attempts to grind it. The bit is clearly not edible, but equally clearly he can't get rid of it in the way that he would normally reject other non-edible objects such as stones.

The horse cannot ignore the bit in the way a human comes to forget about well-fitting dentures or the clothes on his back. The sense of touch is very dependent on movement, as we can demonstrate easily for ourselves. If you rest your hands quietly in your lap with the fingers of one hand loosely clasped in those of the other without moving, you soon lose awareness of the contact between the hands. But move one finger by just a fraction and you are instantly aware of it. The bit is not fixed in the horse's mouth like a well-fitting denture in a person's mouth but is free to move, and the horse's tongue is in continual motion. The presence of the bit thus makes itself felt continually. The horse can regard it either as a nuisance or as something interesting.

Feeling the presence of the reins

When the rider takes up the reins, the feel of the bit in the horse's mouth will change dramatically. It is no longer an inert object responding passively to the movements of the horse's tongue. It starts to press against the horse's tongue and it is no longer easily pushed about. The feeling of something pulling on the mouth will be to some extent familiar, resembling a type of experience encountered when grazing, browsing leaves from a tree, or pulling hay from a manger or haynet. The horse's natural reaction is to hold on and swing his head to free the food morsel from whatever it is that is restraining it. If the rider is an unsuspecting child who hangs on to the rein with unyielding arms, when the pony pulls, the child may be pulled right out of the saddle.

The bridle supports the bit in that part of the horse's mouth where there is a gap, on each side, in the row of teeth, the jaw in this region being known as a 'bar'. In many books on riding, it is stated that the bit normally acts on the bars of the horse's mouth. However, in the forward part of the horse's mouth, the two sides of the lower jaw lie very close beside one another for some distance, to form a bony floor to the mouth. The arrangement is not like that in man, where the tongue can lie comfortably within the arc of the lower jaw. There is no room in the horse's mouth for the tongue to lie between the bars, so the bit will normally rest against the tongue rather than on the bars. If you are using a jointed bit, a strong pull on the reins can, of course, bring the bit into hard contact with the bars, as well as painfully squeezing the tongue, and it is not uncommon for a vet to see signs of quite severe bruising of the bars where the bit has pressed against them. But if you can avoid pulling too hard, and will concentrate on maintaining a very light tension in the rein, the horse will be able to carry the bit on his tongue all the time, the bit making only occasional light contact with the bars. The tongue is very much more sensitive than the bars, so this practice of using only a very light tension in the reins has much to recommend it.

By judicious manipulation of the rein tension, the skilled rider establishes communication with the horse. You first have to teach the horse that there is no profit in swinging his head in an attempt to pull the bit free. To achieve this you maintain a small steady tension in the rein and allow your hands to move freely forward when the horse pulls. The horse then never gets the satisfaction of pulling the rein free. The pressure of the bit on the tongue remains much the same whatever the horse tries to do.

Another strategy for discouraging the horse from attempting to snatch the rein free is to take a very firm grip on the rein and to push the knuckles of both hands strongly into the horse's crest so that the rein cannot be pulled forward. The horse will then discover that, when he pulls on the bit, he is pulling against himself.

The alerting signal

The next stage is for you to make the bit interesting, by making small changes in the rein tension, rather like a gentle tickling. The usual technique here is to grip the rein between thumb and forefinger while the other fingers are loosely curled round the part of the rein that runs to the horse's mouth. You close and loosen the two middle fingers to impart a fluctuating tension of a few tens of grams around the steady tension of about 1 kg or a little less. This tickling action of the rein makes the bit interesting to the horse and acts as an alerting signal. The horse may react by pulling on the bit. You discourage this by yielding or blocking as before. As soon as the horse relaxes his pull, you yield also, allowing the tension to fall to a somewhat lower level, but never allowing the rein to go completely slack.

A device to facilitate the learning of this tickling movement is illustrated in *Photo 2.15*. Here a 'rein' strap pulls on a length of soft rubber, the other end of which is anchored. A small bell is fitted at the junction. The alerting signal is produced with the two middle fingers, which close and relax together in rapid alternation, while the thumb and forefinger retain a steady grip on the rein (see *Figure 1.15*). A successful tickling action is rewarded by a tinkling of the bell.

The finger action that rings the bell is really a very strong signal to the horse, rather like that of someone who, at a very noisy party, climbs on a chair and calls out 'Can I have your attention, please!'. When you have established a reasonable working relationship with your horse, a much more gentle signal, equivalent to a whispered 'Psst!', will be sufficient.

This quiet signal is produced by the same finger movements as those needed

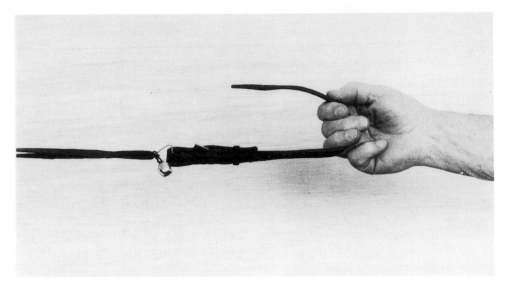

Photo 2.15   *Device for teaching the technique for 'tickling' the bit with the rein. The 'rein' strap pulls on a length of soft rubber, the other end of which is anchored. A small bell is fitted at the junction. The alerting signal is produced with the ring and middle fingers, which close and relax together in rapid alternation, while the thumb and forefinger retain a steady grip on the rein. A successful tickling action is rewarded by a tinkling of the bell.*

to ring the bell, but the movements are very much slower, taking two or three seconds for each phase of increasing or decreasing rein tension. The resulting subtle action on the horse's mouth is remarkably compelling.

The 'softening' response

The object is to persuade the horse to 'soften his mouth', that is to say, to pay attention to the bit, moving it about in his mouth and exploring what it feels like. You can detect that the horse is responding in this way because you can feel the horse 'giving' with his lower jaw. You may hear the bit jangling, and, when the horse turns his head, you will be able to see that the horse is salivating. This salivation is a reflex response to the friction of the tongue against the inside of the mouth as the horse moves the bit about with his tongue.

To achieve this softening of the mouth, you use the slowly fluctuating tension in the rein in a variety of ways. You may tickle with one hand at a time, giving an unsymmetrical effect on the bit, or you may tickle with both hands at the same time. You may also move your hands a little from side to side, or up and down a little way, to provide variation.

You will, of course, have to let your hand move with the forward and

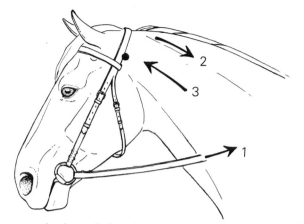

Figure 2.1 *Forces on the horse's head associated with tension in the snaffle rein. The skull pivots on the joint with the bones of the neck (filled circle). (1) Pressure on the horse's mouth, tending to rotate the head anti-clockwise. (2) Tension in the muscles of the neck, tending to rotate the head clockwise. (3) Reaction thrust of the bones of the neck.*

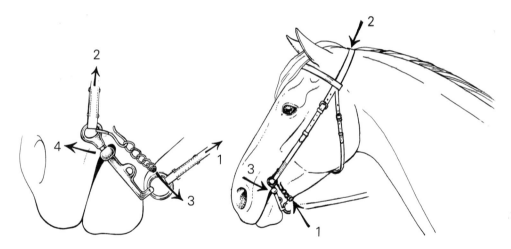

Figure 2.2 *Forces associated with the curb bit. **(a)** Forces on the curb bit. (1) Tension in the rein. (2) Tension in the cheekpiece of the bridle. (3) Tension in the curb chain. (4) Pressure of the horse's mouth against the bit. This may be several times as great as the tension in the curb rein (over five times in this case) because of the leverage. The lever factor is not the same as the ratio between the lengths of the shanks of the bit. Because the line of action of the tension in the curb chain is not at right angles to the shank of the bit, the offset distance for this force is considerably less than the length of the upper shank of the bit. The effective lever factor is correspondingly increased. **(b)** Actions of the curb bit on the horse's head. (1) Pressure of the curb chain against the underside of the jaw. (2) Pressure of the bridle against the poll. (3) Pressure of the bit against the mouth.*

backward movements of the horse's head to keep up the small but steady background tension on which to superimpose this signal. If the rein is allowed to go slack, it will inevitably come taut again with a snap a moment later, and the horse will soon learn that the resulting fluctuation in rein tension doesn't really mean anything, although it feels just like a shouted command to stop. Very soon the horse will decide to ignore most of your rein signals, recognising that he has a beginner on his back, so that he can do as he likes.

When the horse has become accustomed to having the bit in his mouth and has learned about the sorts of pressure to be expected from the bit when he has a skilled rider on his back, he gets into the habit of feeling for this pressure. If the rein tension then falls off, the horse moves his mouth forward to restore the pressure on the bit, and if the bit pressure rises, the horse moves his mouth nearer to his chest to ease the pressure. You reward this yielding behaviour with lavish caresses and encouraging sounds until the horse joins in the game of maintaining a steady pressure on the bit. Signals now pass both ways along the rein. You can see from the lifting of the head and pricking of the ears that the horse is taking an interest, and the horse can feel the way the bit pressure changes actively rather than passively in response to his head movements. This procedure, for persuading the horse to 'enter into dialogue with the rider' through the bit, is called 'putting the horse on the bit'.

With the snaffle bit, the pressure of the bit on the horse's mouth corresponds directly to the tension in the rein. This tension exerted against the head is supported by a compressive thrust in the neck, just as the tension in a bowstring is supported by the compression of the bow. Since these two forces on the horse's head do not act in the same line, their combination tends to rotate the head to bring the mouth nearer to the horse's chest (*Figure 2.1*). This tendency to rotate is checked by those neck muscles that are also used in pulling hay from a haynet. For this reason you have to exert a good deal of tact to persuade the horse to accept the rein tension and not to attempt to pull the rein free.

The curb bit

With a curb bit, the relation between rein tension and the pressure of the bit on the mouth is somewhat different from that with the snaffle bit. A large part of the force with which the curb bit presses backwards on the mouth is supported by the forward pressure of the curb chain under the jaw, as a consequence of the lever action of the shanks of the cheekpieces (see *Photo 2.16* and *Figure 2.2a*). The effect of this is that, when the horse tries to move his mouth forward with a particular amount of effort by the neck muscles, he feels a greater pressure on his mouth from the curb bit than he does when pulling against a snaffle bit. You can take advantage of this to use the curb bit to encourage the horse to bend his neck at the poll. You have to exercise considerable tact to achieve this result. Trying to bring his head in by a bullying application of force is more likely to produce antagonism than co-operation.

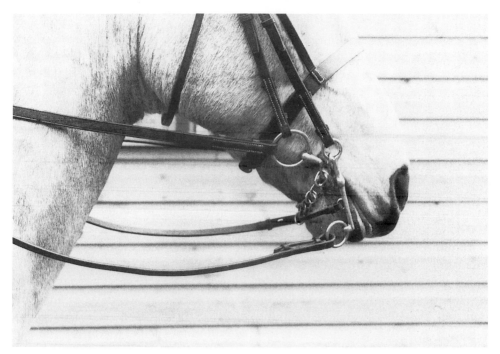

Photo 2.16a-b   *The double bridle. **(a)** (above) Curb rein inactive; no tension in the curb chain. **(b)** (below) Curb rein active: the cheekpieces of the curb bit rotate to tighten the curb chain and bring extra pressure to bear on the bit in the mouth.*

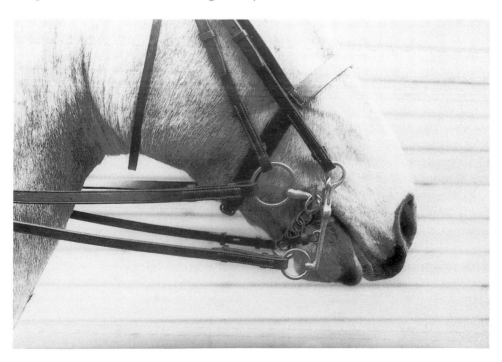

Double bridle

The combination of snaffle bit and curb bit in the double bridle provides the rider with a sophisticated signalling system, using the two bits to produce different effects. You use the curb bit to encourage the horse to maintain his head posture with the line of his face just in front of the vertical. In this posture, the snaffle bit works across the line of the jaw, rather than up toward the angle of the mouth. It is in this direction that the different rein aids are most readily distinguished by the horse. The combination of curb and snaffle, used thus with appropriate subtlety, gives the rider a very delicate control over the behaviour of the horse. It is just such a delicate control that is essential for the elegant execution of the dressage movements called for in the advanced stages of competition. When a snaffle bit is used in combination with a curb bit, the snaffle is usually referred to as a 'bridoon bit'.

To get yourself and your horse used to the curb bit, you may find the Pelham bit useful. This is a curb bit with the usual chain and long-shanked cheekpiece, but it differs from the normal curb bit in that it has two sets of rings for the reins. One set is at the lower end of the shank of the cheekpiece as in a normal curb bit. The other is attached at the level of the mouthpiece itself. Two sets of reins are used. The upper one acts just like a normal snaffle; the lower one acts like a curb rein. With this arrangement, you can get used to handling the two sets of reins, and the horse can get used to the feel of the curb chain and to the unusual pressure of the bit against his mouth, without at the same time having to get used to having two bits in his mouth.

Some people use a Pelham bit with a 'rounding' on each side. Each of these is a short strap attached at its ends to the two rein rings of the bit. A single rein has a sliding attachment to the loop in the rounding on each side. The Kimblewick is an all-metal version of the same device. The idea is that the rider has only one rein to worry about. If the horse takes a strong pull, the rein slides down the rounding and exerts more effect on the curb bit. Such devices are often fitted on children's ponies, with the hope of giving the children better control. The whole idea is based on a misconception of the role of the curb bit, which is here used to punish the horse for pulling, instead of only as a means of very subtle fine control. The horse may react by just pulling even harder, in the attempt to relieve himself of the painful object in his mouth.

In Western-style riding a curb bit is used without a bridoon. The rider usually holds both reins in the same hand with hardly any tension at all in the rein. Steering is achieved primarily by neck-reining.

The response to rein signals

The horse can feel whether the bit is being made 'active', as by the rider's alerting signal, or is simply passive although still pressing steadily against the tongue. He can feel any asymmetry such as one side being active while the other is passive, or if the pressure is greater on one side than on the other; and he can feel any change in the direction in which the rein is pulling on the bit. His response to these asymmetries is to move his head until the bit feels symmetrical again. Thus, if you have both hands in the 'regular', direct rein, position but make your right hand active while the left is quiet, the reins remaining equal, the horse will turn his head to the right. If, however, your right hand yields as well as being active, the horse will turn to the left.

These head movements affect the thrusts developed by the legs against the ground in one of a set of automatic reactions known to physiologists as the 'neck reflexes'. When the head is moved to one side, the limbs on that side develop stronger thrusts, with a corresponding reduction in thrust on the opposite side. This is a useful reaction because the movement of the head shifts the centre of gravity of the body as a whole, putting more weight on the limbs on the side to which the head has been turned. The neck-reflex reaction provides the extra thrust needed to support the increased load. The neck-reflex reactions are seen in their pure form only when the head movement is in the horizontal plane. Head movements in other directions involve tilting the skull and this brings into play another set of automatic reactions originating in the balancing organs of the inner ear.

When a horse is walking briskly forward, he nods his head, throwing it up strongly at each stride. Because of the weight of the head, this repeated action facilitates the lifting in turn of the individual hindlegs. Another consequence is that, commonly, the distance between the horse's mouth and his chest fluctuates continually. If you do not move your hands appropriately, the nodding head movement will affect the feel of the bit in the horse's mouth. If the bit pressure rises when the horse's mouth is moving forward, this discourages the act of progression and slows the walk, shortening the stride. Conversely, if you move your hands in rhythm with the nodding of the head in such a way that the rein tension rises slightly when the mouth is moving back and decreases when the mouth is moving forward, this encourages the swinging of the horse's head and leads to a more vigorous walk with longer strides.

Swinging movements of the horse's head also occur at the canter and gallop. Here again you can adjust the stride length by judiciously timed variations in rein tension. One often sees racing jockeys engaged in this manoeuvre when urging their mounts toward the finishing line. At the trot, the nodding actions are less noticeable since they are masked by the bouncing motion of the trunk as a whole.

Comparatively small movements of the rider's hands affect the feel of the bit in the horse's mouth and can act as effective signals to the horse, provided that there are no interfering factors. It must often be very hard for the horse to make sense of what is happening to the bit when the reins are in the hands of an unskilled rider. All sorts of inadvertent, and often contradictory, signals are transmitted to the bit. It is accordingly no surprise that the hand movements of an unskilled rider often produce unexpected and even undesirable effects on the horse.

3 GETTING GOING

If you decided to postpone Chapter 2 during your first read-through, this is where you should resume.

If, on the other hand, you have read straight through, do not be surprised now to come across, here and there, phrases that sound familiar. Remember that it is sometimes instructive to look again at a particular idea from a different point of view, or in a different context. For example, in one place you will find an action described in a context where we are looking at various ways in which that particular action can be used. In another place you find the same action described among others that are to be used in combination to produce a particular effect.

Impulsion

When you get your leg aids working properly at the walk (closing your legs alternately against each side of the horse in turn when the shoulder of that side is coming back toward you) and if you can avoid jerking the rein, you will usually find that the horse gradually increases the vigour of his walk. He may walk faster, or step out more, or lift his feet higher at each step. At the same time the nodding of his head becomes more and more pronounced. You can accentuate the nodding by rhythmically varying the pressure of your fingers on the rein.

Apart from the grip of thumb and forefinger, which should be just enough to prevent the rein from sliding through your hand, the fingers are only lightly curled against the rein. The pull on the rein is just enough to carry the weight of your hand hanging against it and the flexibility of your relaxed arm and shoulder allows the hand to be moved freely backward and forward by the movements of the horse's head. Unless you deliberately intend it, there should be no fluctuation in the tension in the rein. You should feel the rein by pressing lightly with your fingers and you should be on the look-out for moments when the rein goes slack and then snaps taut again. If this happens, you will feel the slight jerk. The horse easily notices the very slightest jerk and responds by slowing down, unless he has decided that the jerks are happening all the time and that they can therefore be ignored.

You encourage the nodding by pulling a little when he gives and by giving a little when he pulls, at each nod of the head. The change that is produced in the horse's readiness to go forward by the combination of your repeated leg aids together with the action of your hands, is called 'impulsion'. This is a very important idea. It is not the same as 'acceleration' or 'speed', and it is not quite the same as 'eagerness' or 'spirit'. It is a contained eagerness to go forward. The horse holds back, waiting for the rider's authorisation, so that he is ready to surge forward promptly on command.

To build up impulsion you first practise changing the speed over the ground by adjusting the steady tension in the rein. You need to start by increasing the pressure on the bit surreptitiously, taking up the rein a little at a time and keeping the speed going by the action of your legs. If the horse slows up, at once ease the rein and increase the vigour of your leg aids. The action of the leg aids can be reinforced by adding the seat aid, bracing the back, and using the rotation of the pelvis to drive the saddle forward (see pp 36 and 76). After a few strides with increased rein pressure, relax the rein a little and watch for the horse moving his head forward to follow your hand and lengthening his stride. Then take up the rein again cautiously, to meet the increased pressure that the horse is now putting on the bit. Keep the leg aids going while the horse shortens his stride. After a few strides with this increased rein tension, relax the rein again and allow the horse to go ahead with longer strides.

Extended walk

You now have two sorts of variation in the feel of the rein to keep going at the same time. There is the regular coming and going with the nodding of the horse's head and there is the slower and more sustained variation to produce shortening and lengthening of the horse's stride. Persist with your practice of the changes in speed until you can obtain three clearly differentiated speeds at the walk. In the 'extended walk' the horse steps out briskly, each stride being noticeably longer than those taken at the relaxed 'medium' walk which is his more natural pace.

Collection

The 'collected walk' is more difficult to achieve. Usually, when you increase the pressure on the rein, the horse will slow up and he may stop altogether. What you have to aim for, by tactful adjustments in the intensity of your aids with leg and rein, is a shortening of the stride with at the same time an increase in the vigour of the action of the horse's legs. The horse lifts his feet well up at each stride and arches his neck without pulling too heavily on the rein. He is responding to the leg aids by increasing the vigour of all his movements. At the same time he is holding back in readiness for whatever you tell him to do next. He should not be fighting against your restraint, but holding himself in without leaning on the rein. As soon as you move your hand forward, he responds by surging forward. If you move one hand forward he advances more on that side and goes into a turn. You should practise the turns asked for by giving with the outside hand, as well as those produced by pulling with the inside hand and those produced by leg aids alone.

Also try to recognise the general feel of the horse's movements. When properly collected, the horse feels more 'bouncy' under you. Distinguish this controlled bounciness from the excited 'tittuping' that horses sometimes perform when they are very keen to get on with something but cannot quite make up their minds exactly what is required of them. A horse that is accustomed to go forward freely and to lead other horses when out hacking, will start tittuping if he is held back and sees the other horses in the ride going past him or away from him. He may be fighting the bit that is holding him back if the rider gives in to the temptation to pull back at him, or, if the rider has a light enough hand, he may just throw his head up and down without pulling. He makes lots of little steps with his hindlegs and plunges up and down on the forelegs as though about to take off at a gallop. Indeed, he will gallop on as soon as the rider indicates that this is permitted. He may prance about all over the place, even going backwards, and seems obsessed with the idea of violent activity and pays no attention to what he is doing. To calm him you may have to turn him away from the other horses, caress his neck and talk soothingly to him. If there is room to walk on, this will usually settle him. Because of the problems associated with tittuping, you have to be very tactful with a lively horse when asking for collection. Be content with just a little collection to start with.

Transition from walk to trot

After practising the changes of speed at the walk you will begin to be able to feel changes in the horse's impulsion. By working with your legs and at the same time restraining his forward acceleration, by increasing the weight of your hands on the reins, you will feel the horse being 'wound up' like a spring compressed between the forward drive of your legs and the backward restraint of your hands. When the horse is wound up, he will surge forward as soon as you move your hands forward to relieve the tension in the rein. To get the change of gait from the walk to a trot, all that is now needed is the appropriate signal from your legs.

The leg aids for the walk are the alternating pressures, one at a time, of the calf muscles of your leg on each side. To tell the horse to trot, you squeeze simultaneously with both legs, each leg applying the same sort of pressure as you have been using at the walk. These leg aids are applied over the girth. There is no need to kick backwards.

Just as you used a combination of signals to give the command to walk on — leg, rein and saddle — so you need a similar combination for the command to trot. Before asking the horse to walk on, you have learned to warn him that you are ready by giving the 'alerting' command, tickling the bit with the rein. He then goes forward when you relax the rein at the moment of giving the aids with leg and saddle. To make the transition from walk to trot you first prepare by building up impulsion at the walk, using active leg aids accompanied by a restraining hand. You will then have some tension in the rein which can be relaxed as part of the command to trot.

It may be helpful for the beginner if other horses are ridden alongside and all start the trot together. The beginner's horse will then trot by imitation and this helps the novice rider to learn the timing of his moves. The instructor first calls 'Prepare to trot'. Each rider then collects his horse and starts building up impulsion so that the horse can feel the relaxation in the rein as the rider's hand moves forward. At the command 'and ... ter-rot!', all riders apply their leg aids simultaneously and give with their hands. All the horses then start to trot at the same time.

Halt and rein-back

The preparation for each change of gait involves an effort by the rider to get the horse alert and ready for the next command. The rider makes his wishes known to the horse by 'winding him up' between the forward drive asked for by the leg aids and the restraint indicated by the reins. The combination of leg and rein should be used for the halt as well as for an increase in forward speed. Do not expect a clean halt in response to rein action alone. Remember that the effective part of your signal with the rein is the change in tension. Use brief pulls and make a distinct release of tension as you give between the pulls. A steady pull just encourages the horse to lean his weight against your hand. He may lunge his head forward to escape the steady pressure on the bit and try to pull you forward out of the saddle.

You build up impulsion by squeezing with the legs while restraining with your hand. Then, if you give with the hand while squeezing with the legs, the horse will move ahead. If, instead of giving, you increase the pressure on the bit, the horse will slow down. If he is already at the halt, he will walk backwards. Thus the preparation for the rein-back is the same as the preparation for the walk-on. The only difference is in the rein pressure. A decreased pressure means 'walk on', and an increased pressure means 'walk backwards', provided you start from a suitable state of alert collection.

Do not attempt to produce the rein-back simply by a strong pull on the rein alone. If you happen to raise your hands while you are pulling strongly, the horse may respond by rearing. If you are not ready for this, it can be very frightening.

Your reaction to rearing must be to grip firmly with the knees and to throw your weight well forward (*Figure 3.1*), arms round the horse's neck if need be. Relax the rein. If you need something to hold on to, grasp the mane rather than the rein. If you happen to tip backward and try to save yourself by hanging on to the rein, the effect may be just to overbalance the horse. He may then fall

Figure 3.1   *Rearing. When a trained horse rears on command, the rider grips with his knees and bends forward at the hips so that his body remains upright in spite of the backward tilt of the saddle. The drill for rearing is very similar to that for riding up hill (see Figure 4.2).*

backwards on top of you. Pulling his head to one side may help because he can twist in the air to land on his forefeet. In any case, if the horse goes well up, get your feet out of the stirrups, so that, if you do start to slide, you can land on your feet.

If you feel that your horse is about to rear, quickly urge him to go forward with active leg aids and relaxed rein as he cannot both go forward and rear at the same time. Then return to what you were trying to do before, but this time be a little more tactful.

When you first try the rein-back, the horse may not understand what it is you want him to do. To explain this to him, ride him toward a high wall that he cannot see over. Come to a halt square on to the wall and very close to it. Pause for a moment, then give strong leg aids and brief pulls on the rein, keeping your hands low, and reinforcing the leg aids with the seat aid if necessary. The leg aids and seat aid in combination tell the horse to get moving, but the wall prevents him from going forward. He may then realise that the pulls on the rein, which are in any case increasing rather than decreasing at the time when he is feeling the leg aids, must this time mean 'Walk back'.

Watch out for attempts to turn out to one side and indicate briskly with the rein that this is not what you want. If he takes one step back, reward him warmly by your voice and by your hand on his neck. Be content at first with even a single step back and go on to do something else. Leave the follow-up till later. This gives the lesson a chance to sink in. Too much insistence all at once can have the undesirable effect of building up resistance.

Notice that, in calling for the half-halt, the full halt, and the rein-back, the actions of the seat aids and leg aids are, in each case, those appropriate to urging the horse to move forward. The speed over the ground is governed by the rein aids, the distinctions between the responses being achieved by judicious adjustment of the intensity with which the rein aids are applied, as well as by adjustment of the timing.

Movements of the rider at trot

When you have achieved the rein-back you will have begun to get the feel of having your horse wound up between leg and hand. Thereafter, you should have no trouble in making the transition from walk to trot, so long as you can avoid giving the horse accidental jerks on the bit, by the rein alternately going slack and snapping taut.

As soon as the horse starts to trot, the rider is faced with a whole set of new sensations. In place of the rolling and horizontal surging of the saddle, forwards as well as sideways, the saddle suddenly starts to hop up and down. The reins, which were previously moving forward and backward through 15−20 centimetres at each stride, suddenly go slack. However, although the horse has stopped nodding his head, the rider himself is now bouncing about. This presents a new set of problems in the task of avoiding jerks on the reins. The horse's head is comparatively steady, but now the rider's hands tend to be thrown about by the bouncing of his body.

The first reaction of the beginner is to stiffen his back and grip with the legs. Both of these movements only serve to make matters worse. With a stiff back, the upward movement of the saddle has to lift the whole of the rider's weight all at once. This means a hard impact and severe jarring. If the rider can relax his back, then the shoulders can keep on going downward for a bit after the seat has struck the saddle. The first impact then has to lift only the lower half of the body. The descent of the shoulders and upper part of the body is cushioned by the springiness of the back. The shoulders thus land, and are thrown up, later than the lower part of the body. The effect of the springiness of the back is to distribute the forces on the body so that they act over a longer period of time. This means that the peak force at impact is much reduced and there is consequently a great deal less jarring.

The effect of gripping with the legs is twofold. It will usually bring the knee away from the saddle and at the same time it presses the rider's lower legs against the horse's side. Because the rider is bouncing up and down, his legs tend to thump against the horse. This will feel to the horse like a command to go faster, which may not be what the rider intends.

Instead of trying to wrap his legs round the horse's belly, the rider should think about keeping his heels away from the horse while pointing his toes forward. This will have the effect of pushing his knees against the saddle, which is where they will be of most use. With the knees against the saddle on each side, the rider's weight remains centred over the saddle even though everything is bouncing up and down. When the knee grip is slack, the occasional small sideways movements of the horse will have the effect that the rider does not always hit the saddle square in the middle at each bounce. If the impact is even a little to one side it will tend to tip the rider over to the other side. The next bounce will then be even further from the midline and after a very few bounces the rider is rattling about all over the place and feeling increasingly uncomfortable. He becomes more and more insecure with each stride.

With your knees firmly against the saddle you can take some of your weight on the knees. You can push your knees down as your seat comes out of the saddle. In this way your knee and lower leg stay in position on the saddle and do not move relative to the horse in spite of the up-and-down movements of your trunk. You can also use your thigh muscles to check the descent of your trunk, taking more weight on the knee each time the body comes down toward the saddle. This provides further cushioning of the impact.

Posting (rising trot)

If, on alternate strides, you push down harder onto your knees, you can then, for these strides, absorb the whole of the impact when your body is coming down toward the saddle. Doing this reduces the main up-and-down movement of your body to half as often as before. That is, you are thrown up and down in the saddle once for every two bounces of the horse, instead of at every stride. This mode of progression, called the 'rising trot', involves much less jolting than the 'sitting trot' in which the rider's seat comes down into the saddle at each bounce of the horse. The procedure of taking the weight intermittently on the knees is called 'posting'. At successive bounces the main part of the rider's weight comes alternately on his knees and on his seat. He should be taking some weight on his knees all the time.

Some beginners get the idea that they are meant to stand upright in the stirrups while posting at the rising trot. They actively throw the pelvis forward into a standing posture for one stride, letting their seat down into the saddle with a thump for the next stride, then again throw themselves forward, and again thump back, and so on. Often the stirrups will swing backwards and forwards as the weight on them comes and goes, and the rider's calves get nipped uncomfortably between the stirrup leather and the saddle.

There is no need for all this excess activity. Just keep yourself supple and let the horse do the throwing. Cushion yourself against the saddle by relaxing your back and putting weight on your knees. Let your knees follow the up-and-down movement of the horse and use your thigh muscles to catch you on the descent, using a bit more push against the knees at alternate strides so that your seat just grazes the saddle at the rising stride and just gently sinks into the saddle at the sitting stride. In this way you not only get a more comfortable ride, you will leave your lower leg free to be moved independently when you need it for giving the leg-aid signals to your horse.

The beginner should be given the chance to get used to the motion of the trot with the horse on the lunge and with the reins attached to the cavesson or headcollar instead of to the bit. To get the trot started he emphasises his walk aids, builds up pressure in the reins and then gives the combined aids for 'trot'. Then, as soon as the horse starts to trot, the rider should relax his body as much as he can. Let the reins go slack, relax the back and shoulders and let the lower leg dangle. Think only about keeping the heels out and toes forward with a relaxed lower leg. Get used to the feel of the knees pressing snugly into the saddle. You can let your hands rest on your knees to encourage relaxation in the arms, and just jog round and round for two or three minutes each way, with rests at the walk in between. If you feel very insecure, hook two fingers of one hand under the arch of the saddle in front of the pommel to help you to keep your weight over the midline.

The next stage is to let go of the reins and hold your hands out to the side in a straight line from the shoulders, palms upward, as in the exercise already practised at the walk. The idea here is to develop the balance of the trunk without the rider being tempted to hold on with his hands. It is essential to achieve independence of the hands before you start to take up the rein. You can now start to move the shoulders forward, trotting all the time with a supple back. This brings more weight onto the knees. Bring your hands forward also, aiming to get your elbows in front of your knees and relying as little as possible on contact with your hands for balance.

While you are leaning forward, pay attention to the position of your feet. Don't let the feet come back. The lower leg should be hanging freely below the knee with the stirrup leather vertical and the stirrup on the ball of the foot. After a little practice you will find that most of your weight comes on your knees and that your seat is just grazing the saddle at each bump. Now sit up a little and use your legs to take more weight on alternate strides, letting your seat down gently into the saddle in between. You are now doing the rising trot. Practise this while circling on the lunge in both directions.

Notice that at each bounce your lower leg swings inward against the horse's side. The leg aid for encouraging the trot is simply to emphasise these natural intermittent leg contacts. Squeeze a little at each bounce, using the calf of your leg which will be tensed automatically by the increase in the pressure of the stirrup against the ball of your foot as your weight comes down. If the horse accelerates more than you want, push your heel out to the side so that your calves no longer touch the horse and your knee-grip is intensified. If, at the same time, you drop back into the sitting trot, the horse should slow down, even without a pull on the rein.

When you have become accustomed to riding with a supple back at the trot you can begin to take up the rein. At first have the rein attached to the headcollar so as not to jerk the bit accidentally. Practise changing the rein from one hand to the other without either jerking the rein or losing contact with the horse's head. Then put the reins back in their proper place on the bit and watch for the horse's reactions to your accidental and deliberate changes in the tension in the rein. Convince yourself that the horse will stop when you want, and you are then ready to ride at the trot without the lunge rein.

Movements of the horse at trot

The reason for the marked difference in the rider's sensations when the horse starts to trot lies in the very nature of the trotting action itself. At the walk the horse always has some feet on the ground, and the movements of the four legs are equally spaced out in time. At the trot, the timing is altered so that the two feet of each diagonal pair of legs are moved simultaneously and strike the ground at almost the same instant. The horse's body is then for a moment supported on this diagonal pair of legs before being again thrown up into the air to produce a period of so-called 'suspension'. All four feet are then off the ground at the same time until the horse lands on the feet of the other diagonal pair.

When the body is in 'suspension' after being tossed upward, it is actually falling freely under gravity, just as when you toss a ball in the air it first rises and then falls. It takes some effort to throw the heavy body of the horse into the air, and there is a good deal of momentum to be absorbed on landing. This means that the horse's legs have to push very hard against the ground. They have to exert all their effort within a very short space of time and it is this sudden sharp push that produces the jolting motion of the horse's body. We are not much aware of the jolting of our own bodies when we run to cover the ground quickly, but it becomes much more obvious if we run on the spot, particularly if we make the action brisk enough to clear a skipping-rope. The horse usually lifts his feet well clear of the ground at the trot, so the up-and-down motion is very like that of a person skipping.

Just as the legs of the trotting horse have to catch the falling weight of the horse's body and throw it upward again at each stride, so they must also catch and throw the weight of the rider. If the rider allows himself to be thrown clear at each stride, he will still be coming down after the horse's body has already started to rise at the next stride. This is why the impact of the rider's seat with the saddle can be so severe if he tenses his back. For the rider's comfort it is essential to use the thigh muscles and to press down with the knees to cushion the impact.

The sequence of the horse's leg movements at the trot is indicated in *Figure*

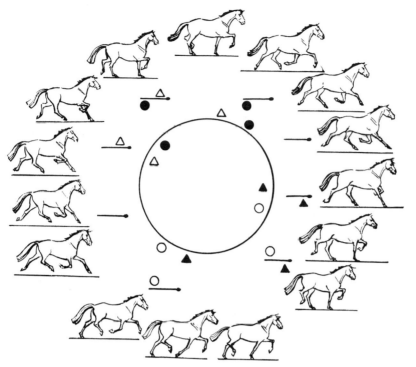

Figure 3.2 *Cycle of leg movements and support patterns at the trot. (Symbols as in Figure 1.6; clockface as in Figure 1.19; side views from Muybridge (1893).) The body is tossed from one diagonal pair of legs to the other.*

3.2. When we compare this diagram with that for the walk (*Figure 1.20*) we see that the hindlegs are lifted relatively earlier and that the placings of the forelegs are much delayed. At the moment of transition from the walk to the trot, the horse has to take an extra-long stride with one hindleg in order to catch up with the diagonal foreleg. He can then use this diagonal pair of legs in a simultaneous push to throw the body up for the first stride at the trot. When in the air, he delays the moment of placing the foreleg of the same side and brings the opposite hindleg forward to make an almost synchronised landing on the other diagonal pair.

This analysis explains the working of the leg aids. It has already been mentioned that the effect of the rider's leg aid on a given side is to increase the vigour of the movements of the horse's legs on that side. For the transition from walk to trot, both hindlegs need to make an extra reach forward. We ask for this by giving leg aids simultaneously on the two sides.

Because of the substantial forces involved in the thrusts of the legs to catch and throw the body at each stride, the muscles of the horse's trunk also have to work hard to stiffen the body. The upthrusts of a diagonal pair of legs have a strong twisting action on the trunk, the direction of the twist being reversed for the alternating diagonals. The horse does not swing his head about much when he is trotting, but he has to catch and throw the weight of the head at each stride just like the weight of any other part of the body. The neck muscles thus must also be stiffened to provide intermittent strong lifting action on the head even though we don't see the head move much. Without some controlled intermittent muscular action in the neck, the head would tend to be jolted wildly up and down at each stride just as the rider is.

There is a very small nodding action of the head as the weight is taken at each stride by the neck muscles. This means that the reins move backwards and forwards a little, though not nearly so much as at the walk. It is the stiffening of the neck that brings the nose in a little at the start of the trot. That is why the rider has to be ready to take up the rein. He can help to speed up the trot by encouraging the swing of the head by alternately pulling slightly when the nose is coming back and giving when it is going forward. He must remember that his own shoulders are probably moving about much more than the horse's mouth. It is therefore essential to develop great suppleness in the arms to avoid accidental jerks on the bit.

Exercises at trot

Once the rider has become used to riding at the trot, there are several exercises that he can practise to develop his confidence and to increase both his enjoyment of riding and his security in the saddle. These exercises will also help him to develop feel for those changes in the horse under him which are indications of what the horse is going to do next. The horse usually has to shift his weight before making any new move. If the rider is alert to this he will feel the changes in the horse's muscles that bring about the shift of weight, and thus will be better able to anticipate the horse's movement. He can then either encourage or discourage this movement by the application of the appropriate aids. In this way he keeps up a continual conversation with the horse. The rider 'listens' to the horse's movements and the horse 'listens' for the rider's intentions as communicated through the rein, through the feel of the rider's legs against the horse's side and of the shifts of weight in the saddle, through the rider's tone of voice, and even through the rider's unspoken intention. This latter may perhaps be communicated by movements of which the rider is unaware, but we should not disregard the possibility of direct telepathy.

The objectives of these exercises can be summarised as: to develop suppleness in the rider's body and shoulders; to improve his balance; to confirm the grip of his knees against the saddle; to consolidate the correct habitual position for the rider's foot; to ensure that the rider can move his hands and lower legs independently of the movements of his body; and to develop the responsiveness of the horse to each of the various commands indicated to him by the rider's hands and legs and by the shift of the rider's weight.

In the early stages it will be appropriate, in the leg aids, to make a fairly definite, even exaggerated, movement. Then, as horse and rider come to understand one another better, the aids can be reduced to nudges that are almost imperceptible to an onlooker. One should remember that the aids given both by the leg and by the reins are to act only as signals. They do not operate like the controls of a car where the driver pushes harder against the appropriate pedal to produce more acceleration or more braking action. The signals to the horse are intensified by brisk repetition, not by submerging the signal in a strong pull or by kicking harder. At all times the rider's hands have to be supple enough to allow the horse to move his head freely whenever the need arises, either during the rhythmic movements of normal locomotion or in the sudden movements the horse needs to make in order to regain his balance after a stumble. The rider must learn not to hang on to the reins to preserve his own balance because this will inevitably mean inappropriate jerking of the bit in the horse's mouth.

Arm and rein exercises at trot

One may start by carrying out at the trot the exercises already performed at the walk. The rein is passed from one hand to the other, and the rider sometimes has the reins separated in the two hands and sometimes rides with both reins in the same hand. The arm not engaged with the rein is held out horizontally sideways straight out from the shoulder, palm up. All the time the rider is to maintain a steady light contact with the bit, making just sufficient difference between the pressures on the two reins to steer as may be necessary.

One variation on this exercise is to make more extensive movements with the disengaged arm. Instead of just holding it out sideways straight out from the shoulder, raise the arm straight upward and then sweep it right round backward and downward to make a complete circle, like a windmill, before taking the rein again into the two hands. Repeat with the other arm.

Handling the short riding whip

You may from time to time have occasion to carry a whip and this is a good time to get used to managing it. The whip is normally carried with the butt end upward and with the tip pointing backward along the thigh toward the hip. The wrist strap fitted to many whips is not used during normal riding. It is provided merely to save dropping the whip when all the fingers are needed for some special task such as putting on gloves or the like. To change the whip from one hand to the other, first take both reins into the hand that is already holding the whip (*Figure 3.3*). Draw the whip through the slightly relaxed fingers of the rein hand. Rearrange the whip in the free hand. Then take the rein back into the two hands. This leads to the following practice routine:

(1)   Start with the reins in the two hands, whip in the left hand. Separate the hands.

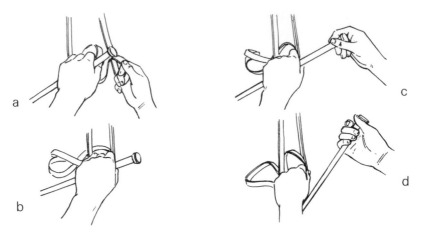

Figure 3.3   *Changing the whip from one hand to the other. Take both reins into the hand that is carrying the whip. Draw the whip through into the other hand. Rearrange the fingers round the whip. Take back the rein into this hand.*

(2)   Take both reins, together with the whip, into the left hand, hold the right hand straight out sideways from the shoulder.

(3)   Both reins still in the left hand, take the whip in the right hand and hold it out from the shoulder.

(4)   Take the reins into the two hands, whip in the right hand. Separate the hands.

(5)   Put both reins, and the whip, in the right hand, left arm out.

(6)   Reins in right hand, whip in left hand held out from the shoulder.

(7)   As (1), and repeat the whole sequence.

The exercise is carried out both at sitting trot and at rising trot. All the time the rider should be just feeling the reins to keep up a steady light pressure of the bit in the horse's mouth, and he should steer in a figure-of-eight to confirm that the rein aids are working properly.

When you want to use the whip, remember to take both reins into the other hand. It is a mistake to attempt to use the whip while you still have your whip-hand on the rein. The object of using the whip is to reinforce a leg aid that the horse has ignored. The leg aid is a signal to increase forward impulsion, but if the hand wielding the whip is also holding the rein, there will inevitably be a jerk on the horse's mouth, meaning 'Stop!', happening at the same time as the horse receives the blow from the whip. It is unfair to give the horse commands calling for both 'stop' and 'go' at the same time. He will just become confused and upset.

Before using the whip, reverse it in your hand so that the butt comes against the heel of your hand. You will need to practise this manoeuvre. It is easiest if you let your hand drop to your side while the point of the whip swings forward.

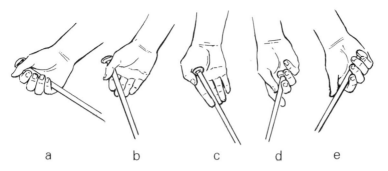

a   b   c   d   e

Figure 3.4 *Reversing the whip. As the hand swings downward the whip is swung forward and the fingers pass the butt of the whip across the palm of the hand.*

You can then relax your fingers and work your thumb over the end of the butt (*Figure 3.4*). For the return to the carrying position you just reverse the sequence. Start with your hand down by your side holding the whip which you then rotate as you bring your hand up toward the rein.

The place to aim for with the whip is the side of the horse's belly just behind your heel. This makes quite clear to the horse your intention to make him 'listen' to the leg aid. You have to be very prompt, applying the whip within a couple of seconds of the leg aid, otherwise the horse will not understand what you are about. Remember that the horse lives, as it were, from one stride to the next. There is no reason for him to remember what he was doing two or three strides earlier. He will, however, remember vividly any situation in which he was particularly uncomfortable. If you are too late with your whip he will associate the chastisement with having you on his back instead of with the command to which he failed to respond. A good rule is to use the whip sparingly but to be quite definite in your intention when you do use it. Give quite a sharp blow so that the horse will feel it. There is no point in just patting him with the whip as he will not then feel any urgency to pay special attention to it.

Sometimes you may need to assert yourself when you don't happen to be carrying a whip. You can then use the spare loop in the reins to hit the horse on the front of the shoulder. With the reins in the two hands, and with the hands close together, place the slack rein from the left hand over that in the right so that the spare loop lies between right thumb and forefinger (*Figure 3.5*). Move both hands forward, close together, to avoid jerking the bit, and swing the loop of rein over the top from one side to the other by twisting the right hand at the wrist, letting the loop come down smartly on the side of the horse's neck at the top of the shoulder. Be very careful not to jerk the bit.

The arm and rein exercises, with and without the whip, serve to develop the rider's skill in maintaining a light contact with the horse's mouth without jerks even while the rider's body is being thrown up and down by the horse's

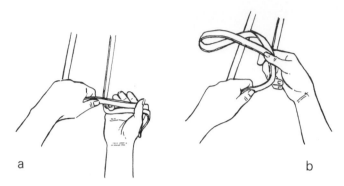

a   b

Figure 3.5   *Using the spare rein as a whip, without jerking the bit.*

movements. Once past this hurdle the rider can practise the stop from the trot and when this also can be achieved with confidence, then he is ready to include some gentle trotting when out hacking with more experienced riders.

Balancing exercises

The next aim is to consolidate the security of your seat in the saddle. For this it helps to spend a little time each day trotting round on the lunge. Tie a knot in the reins and let them lie on the horse's neck so that you can do the balancing exercises without touching them.

By this time you should no longer feel the urgent need to hang on to something with your hands. Keep the trot going by rhythmic squeezing with your calves and knees and hold both hands out sideways to their full extent, palms upward and level with your shoulders ('aeroplane'). Then, keeping the elbows well up, swing the hands in toward your chest and out again, either both together or one at a time. Also turn your head from side to side, looking first at one fully extended hand, then at the other. Do the exercise both at the sitting trot and at the rising trot. The aim is to develop an upright carriage, with a supple back.

To help loosen up your shoulders, try arm-circling. The arms are held straight and are swung round from the shoulder in full circles, forward, upward, backward and downward ('windmill'); first one arm at a time, then the two arms alternately, and after that the two arms rising and falling at the same time. Repeat with forward circling.

Now, with both arms out (as in 'aeroplane'), circle with your head, bending the neck well forward, sideways, and backwards. Make clockwise and anti-clockwise circles. Also turn your head from side to side, going as far round as you can in each direction.

Stretch one arm above your head as far as it will go while the other arm is stretched down by your side as far as it will go. Hold the position for a moment, then change over and repeat on the other side ('arm stretching').

Stretch one arm up and have the other down by your side, lean forward, and bring your raised hand down to touch first the stirrup on the same side then, after going right up overhead again, come down to touch the stirrup on the opposite side. Repeat with the other hand.

With both arms out to the side, lean forward till your seat begins to come out of the saddle. Then lean backward as far as you can, gripping with the knees and keeping the heels away from the horse all the time. Then come forward again.

After a few sessions trotting round on the lunge and doing these balancing exercises you will be surprised how relaxed and confident you become. Movements which felt very precarious when first attempted gradually come to feel quite easy and natural. As your confidence grows, you will be able to do all these exercises without stirrups. Here you should pay attention to what is happening to your feet. The lower leg should hang straight down, toes pointing forward and heels out. When you need to give a leg aid to keep the trot going, tense your calf muscles by lifting the sole of your foot until it is above the heel. If the horse goes ahead too fast, push your heels out to the side so that your calves no longer touch the horse's side. This will emphasise the pressure of your knee against the saddle. The knee should never move from its nest in the side of the saddle.

Leg exercises

While continuing in sitting trot on the lunge, without stirrups, bring your arms up to the 'aeroplane' position and practise the independence of your lower legs. Without moving the knee, push one heel away from the horse and swing the foot forward and backward without at any time touching the horse. Repeat with the other leg. Make circling movements with each foot in turn, clockwise and anticlockwise, always without touching the horse.

Now halt, take your stirrups again, and hold your hands just above the pommel in the rest position for holding the reins. With the horse standing at the halt, lean forward with your weight on your knees until your seat comes out of the saddle. Straighten up without sitting back, and balance in this position with your seat out of the saddle. Sit down again in the saddle and repeat two or three times.

Then give the leg aids to start the trot and practise the following sequence:
- Four strides sitting trot.
- Four strides standing in the stirrups, that is to say, balancing on your knees as just described.
- Four strides rising trot.
- Sit, two, three, four, stand, two, three, four.
- Sit, stand, sit, stand, sit, stand, sit, stand.
- Sit two, three, four, stand, two, three, four.
- Sit, stand, sit, stand, sit, stand, sit, stand.

After practising this sequence a few times without holding the rein, take the reins in your hands and repeat the exercise paying particular attention to the rein to make sure that the contact with the bit remains the same all the time without ever jerking or letting the rein go slack.

The aim in all these exercises is to learn to 'sit deep' into the saddle and to let yourself 'feel tall'. All the joints in your body should become supple and well sprung, with no stiffnesses anywhere. Each part of the body should appear to be carried without effort so that it feels light, almost as though floating, yet ready at any moment to react promptly to any sudden call for action either for balance or to control the horse.

More about steering

After practising the exercises described above, the rider should feel more comfortable in the saddle and he should be better able to control the rein. It is now time to give more thought to the delicate and extensive topic of steering. This is a much more subtle business than steering a car or a boat. Setting aside telepathy and word of command, we have three ways to communicate our desires to the horse: through the reins; with our legs; and by shifting our weight in the saddle. We use various combinations of these kinds of 'aid' to produce changes in speed and in gait as well as changes in direction. Moreover, there are many ways in which the horse may change direction. He can shift the body over the feet in almost any direction either with or without at the same time changing the direction in which he is facing. He can also bend the body, the neck, and the head, to one side or the other, the bends in each case not necessarily being in the same direction. From time to time we may wish to ask the horse to make particular kinds of 'change of direction' and for this we need to establish a workable code with which to make our intention clear. The tests used in competitive dressage are, in effect, tests of fluency in interpreting the code. Specific problems are posed to determine how effectively the rider can communicate with his mount.

At first it will be sufficient to use the basic aids for turning described in the previous chapter for turns at the walk. These are: weight on the inside knee; inside leg straight down; outside leg back a little, just behind the girth; and just enough difference between the two reins to bring into view the outside corner of the horse's eye on the side to which the turn is to be made. Practise making the turns by giving with the outside hand as well as by pulling with the inside hand. If you have sufficient impulsion from your leg aids, the horse should move his head forward to maintain the even pressure on the bit. He will thus feel the same asymmetry of the bit in his mouth when you give with one hand as he does when you pull with the other. Also practise making turns as much as possible with the legs and weight-shift alone, using the minimum of rein action.

A circle to the right is referred to as 'on the right rein'. When you steer out of a circle to the right and into a circle to the left, this is called 'changing the rein'. A figure-of-eight involves a change of rein at each crossover. Another useful practice figure is the 'serpentine'. This is a sequence of half-circles in alternate directions. Choose an imaginary line on the ground and change the rein every time you cross this line, making half-circles alternately on the left and right reins.

Diagonals

When circling at the rising trot, pay attention to the movements of the horse's shoulders. You will see the point of the shoulder coming back toward you on each side alternately. The shoulder moves back when the corresponding foreleg is on the ground. At this time the opposite hindleg is also on the ground and the horse is supported on a diagonal pair of legs. The two diagonals are named according to which foreleg is involved. On a circle to the right, the expression 'outside diagonal' means the left diagonal, that is to say, the left foreleg and the right hindleg, and so on. You will be posting on one diagonal and sitting down on the other. Work out which diagonal is on the ground when your seat is in the saddle.

To change from one diagonal to the other you break the strict alternation of sitting and posting by sitting down for two bumps in succession, thus: sit, stand, sit, stand, sit, sit, stand, sit, stand, sit, stand, and so on. Get into the habit of always sitting on the outside diagonal. Then, every time you change the rein at the rising trot, you also change the diagonal. In the figure-of-eight you change the diagonal every time you pass the crossover point. In the serpentine you change every time you cross the line down the centre of the pattern.

Practising the turns

A variation of simple circling is to make the circle gradually smaller and smaller so that you ride in a spiral. As you near the centre, change the rein and ride a gradually expanding spiral. Notice that, as the circles get smaller, the horse begins to curve his spine. He bends round your inside leg. Avoid pulling his head round because this will encourage him to bend his neck instead of his trunk. The effect of excessive bending of the neck will be to lose impulsion. (Remember, to stop a runaway the rider pulls the horse's head to one side.)

If your horse seems reluctant to turn in response to a slight pull on the inside rein or to a small relaxation of the outer rein, resist the temptation to pull harder with the inside rein. Instead, hold the inside rein firm and tickle the bit with the outside rein by working on the rein with a rapid curling and uncurling of the fingers as described earlier for 'alerting'. This draws the horse's attention to the bit. He lines up his mouth with the bit to give an equal feel on the two sides. This produces the required bend of the head into the turn.

The sharpness of the turn is indicated to the horse by the frequency and briskness of the repeated squeezes with the outside leg behind the girth and by the way you distort the saddle with your knees. You bring more of your weight on to the inside knee. The inside leg is held straight down and its calf presses on the side of the horse at the girth. When you move your outside leg back slightly to give the leg aid for turning, you also press the knee of that leg into the side of the saddle. The combined action of the two legs tends to twist the saddle round on the horse's back in the direction of the turn, and this encourages him to bend his spine.

Drill patterns in the dressage arena

You may find that when practising turns it helps to have a track to follow. You can then judge whether or not you are making the turns as precisely as you would like. A number of useful imaginary tracks can be set up in a standard dressage arena of 40 m by 20 m. (A longer arena, 60 m by 20 m, is used in some advanced dressage tests. These are the dimensions of the Winter Riding School in Vienna, home of the famous Spanish Riding School.) It is a good idea to fix in your mind some convenient landmarks in your practice area which will mark out a suitably sized rectangle with the proportions of a double square

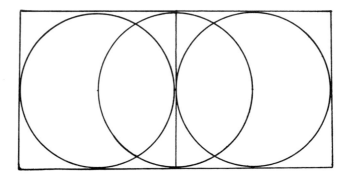

Figure 3.6   *A practice arena in the form of a double square, each of about 20 m along the side. This gives three positions for a 20 m circle.*

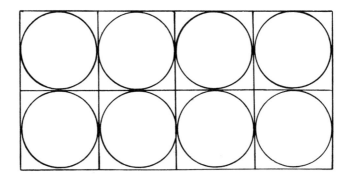

Figure 3.7   *Positions, within the practice arena, of eight 10 m circles.*

(*Figure 3.6*). This gives three positions for a 'large circle' of about 20 m diameter, one at each end and one overlapping in the middle. You can pass from one end-circle to the other by changing the rein as you ride through the centre of the arena, or you can go from one circle to another by keeping straight for the appropriate distance along one of the long sides.

If you now imagine each of the two large squares to be cut in half in each

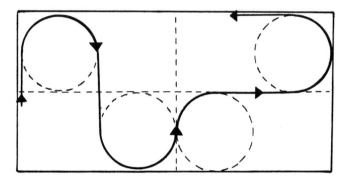

Figure 3.8   *Examples of tracks made up of straight lines joining segments of 10 m circles.*

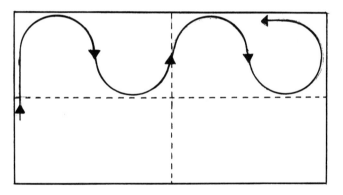

Figure 3.9   *Serpentine down the long side.*

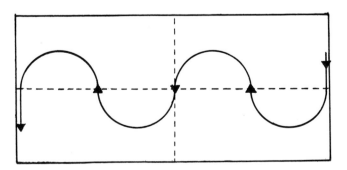

Figure 3.10   *Serpentine along the centre-line.*

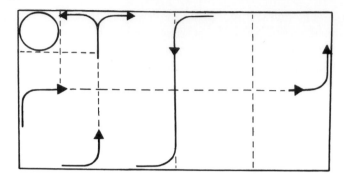

Figure 3.11   *Corners formed from segments of 5 m circles.*

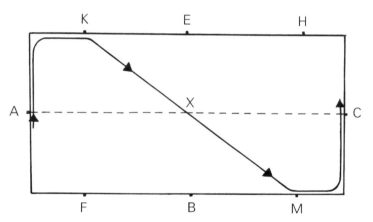

Figure 3.12   *Diagonal change of hand from one quarter-marker to another in the dressage arena.*

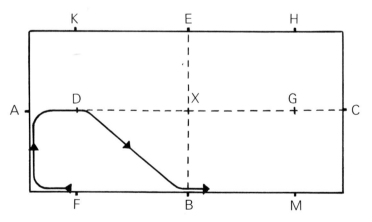

Figure 3.13   *Change of hand on a diagonal moving away from the centre-line.*

direction, this will produce eight squares in each of which you can ride a 10 m circle (*Figure 3.7*). Again you can pass from one circle to another with a change of rein where the circles touch, or you can join up parts of different

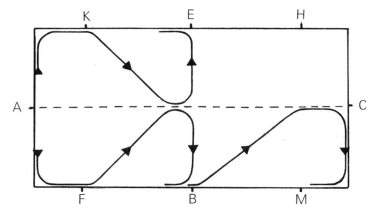

Figure 3.14 *Examples of reversed change of hand, on diagonals toward the centre-line.*

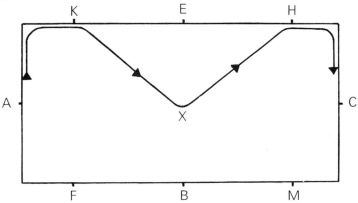

Figure 3.15 *Counter change of hand. Two changes are required, one on the diagonal from K to X, the other on the diagonal from X to rejoin the long side at H.*

circles with straight tracks along the edges of the squares (*Figure 3.8*). The pattern formed by a succession of half-circles (*Figure 3.9*) is the serpentine already referred to earlier. You can also ride a serpentine along the centre-line (*Figure 3.10*).

The 10 m circle is about as sharp a turn as the horse can negotiate safely when travelling fast. At the walk or slow trot he can manage a 5 m circle. Four of these fit into each of our eight 10 m squares (*Figure 3.11*). When you are riding a corner at a moderate pace your track should follow a quarter of one of these 5 m circles. In a regular dressage arena the 'quarter-markers' are placed at 6 m from the corners to correspond with the subdivisions of the 60 m arena, which has markers 12 m apart along the long sides. The dressage rules of the British Horse Society prescribe that, when riding corners, the horse should describe one quarter of a circle of approximately 6 m diameter at collected and working paces, or a quarter of a circle of approximately 10 m diameter at medium and extended paces. (The expression 'working pace' implies that the horse is responding to the rider's demand for impulsion and is not just strolling along without paying much attention to the rider. In a 'medium pace' the horse is being encouraged to go forward fairly freely but he is not yet showing the full extension of which he is capable.)

Using regular corners you can build up patterns including straight-line segments in various directions. You can ride along the centre-line or across the arena along a line parallel to the short sides leaving the long side at any point. When you reach the outside track, or at any of the intersections of the rectangular grid in *Figure 3.11*, you can turn either way.

Another variation is to include diagonal lines as in *Figure 3.12*. In riding a diagonal, do not aim for the corner, but remember to allow room to make a correct arc of a 5 m circle both on rejoining the long side of the arena, and again on arriving at the corners. The track in *Figure 3.12* shows the rider as on the right rein from A to K and on the left rein from M to C. This pattern is called a 'diagonal change of hand'. If you are proceeding at the rising trot, remember to 'change the diagonal' by sitting twice as you cross the centre-line, in order to be posting on the correct leg for the next turn. Notice that the word 'diagonal' is used in two senses here:

(1) The diagonal track across the arena.
(2) The diagonal pair of legs used by the horse in successive strides at the trot.

A diagonal change of hand can be executed in one half of the arena either from the centre-line (*Figure 3.13*), or, in a 'reversed change of hand' (*Figure 3.14*), starting from the long side near to a corner and regaining the same long side by turning in on the opposite rein from the middle of the arena.

If you ride from one diagonal track to another, changing in the middle of the arena, you will rejoin the long side on the same rein as you started. This manoeuvre (*Figure 3.15*) is called 'a counter change of hand'. In fact, two changes of hand are needed, one in each of the diagonal parts of the track.

Although the dressage arena is not itself very large, the repertoire of different patterns of track described above makes it possible to continue riding in a restricted space, such as an indoor riding school, for extended periods of time, and day after day, without at any stage becoming bored. You string the patterns together in whatever sequence you choose and at the same time introduce other variables, such as changes of gait and changes of speed. At all times concentrate on keeping strictly to the chosen pattern without allowing the horse to wander from the straight lines or to cut the corners. Circles are to be performed precisely, as though drawn with a pair of compasses. Do not accept irregular patterns like the outline of an ink blot. In this way you teach yourself to watch for any indication that the horse is preparing to deviate from the pattern you have chosen.

Of course, the horse has no idea what pattern of track you have selected to ride. As he moves along, you inevitably shift about to some extent in the saddle. In consequence, each stride will feel different to the horse and he will be liable at any time to do something unexpected with his next stride. You have to be alert to feel what is happening so that you can signal back to him if what he apparently proposes is not precisely what you want. It is here that it helps to have a set pattern in mind. If you let the horse wander about just anyhow and allow him to carry you where he happens to go, the likelihood is that you will both soon become very bored as you would with a human companion if neither of you made any attempt at conversation. It is the communication that provides much of the interest.

The secret is to have a definite plan in mind so that you have some standard against which to compare the behaviour of the horse. You can then watch to see whether the horse keeps his head pointing in the direction you have chosen. He will turn his head if he is distracted. This means that he is not concentrating on what you are doing with the bit, and you will need to do something to remind him to pay attention. Alternatively he may step off the track. If he does this with a foreleg, this indicates an uncertainty of aiming. If he deviates with a hindleg, his haunches will cease to follow the forequarters, indicating that he is escaping from the control of your legs, or perhaps that one of your legs is accidentally giving a spurious signal.

Concentric circles

It is, at first, easier to spot the moments when the horse is inattentive if you are not at the same time continually changing course. You can ride for some time on the same large circle, concentrating on maintaining a steady rhythm with the horse's neck bent toward the inside of the circle just enough to bring the corner of his eye into view. From time to time alter the steady pressure on the rein to produce either more collection or a more extended pace. When the horse has settled to a steady rhythm, move in onto a new circle about 2 m inside the original one. The slightly tighter curve causes the horse to make each movement a little more precisely. His action will then become more springy and he should respond more positively when you ask for more collection or more extension.

Continue on the second circle until the horse has settled to the new rhythm. Then move in another 2 m onto a yet smaller circle and repeat the process of polishing up the horse's precision. Then see if you can maintain the same lively action when you move out again onto one of the larger circles, or while riding a straight segment of track.

┌4┐ RIDING IN COMPANY

Group lessons

When you are first starting to ride, you will probably be on your own with your instructor for the first few lessons. These will, one hopes, have been conducted in a restricted and securely fenced area where your instructor could come quickly to your rescue at the first sign of your getting into difficulties. Later, when you are better able to control your horse on your own, you will probably be expected to join others in a group lesson. You will be asked to ride in line, one behind the other, and this will provide you with new problems to face because of the presence of the other horses.

When riding in a group in a riding school like this you may hear the instructor calling 'Close up!' or 'Keep your distance!'. The idea is that you should, at all times, keep a constant distance between your horse and the one in front. Usually one and a half lengths will be about right. Never let your horse get closer to the horse in front than about one length. If you get too far behind, this will interfere with the pattern of the lesson, and the instructor will be shouting at you.

Since it often happens that the different horses being ridden together in a lesson are of different sizes and temperaments, the task of keeping one's distance when riding in line ahead (in single file) calls for continual attention to the speed over the ground. Sometimes you will need to urge your horse onward to avoid getting left behind. At other times you will need to slow down so as not to get too close. The ability to control the speed over the ground is a valuable, indeed an essential, equestrian skill, but all too often the instructor does not explain this, and you may get the impression that he is asking you to do something simply for his own convenience. Riding in line ahead while keeping a precisely controlled distance between the horses is an exercise of fundamental importance. The resulting skill can be extremely useful in all sorts of different situations.

You will be told that the reason for keeping your distance is to avoid having your horse kicked by the one in front. In this context, you may recall seeing horses galloping about in the open in a closely packed group, sometimes actually touching one another and you may be tempted to ask what the fuss is all about.

The explanation is that the horses that you have seen galloping in company are all members of the same well-established group. It is in the nature of horses to form such groups. In the wild, a stallion will herd his 'harem' together so that all the individuals in the harem get used to one another and form a group. Similar close-knit groups also form spontaneously among domesticated horses, but it is not always clear why some of the horses in a field belong to a particular group while others do not, even though they all spend long periods together in the same field.

When horses are at liberty, they drive away unwelcome strangers by adopting a special threat posture. If an 'outsider' approaches too close to an established group, he will be repelled by threats. One form of threat is that used by the stallion in discouraging members of his harem from straying. He intercepts the straggler, presenting his broadside with head lowered and ears laid back (*Figure 4.1*). If the straggler doesn't turn back to rejoin the harem, the stallion will lunge toward her with bared teeth. A similar threat is used by the 'boss horse' of any group at the approach of a stranger, lungeing toward the intruder with lowered head and ears laid back. Usually the threatened horse will lift his head and turn away. If he doesn't move away fast enough, the threatener will bare his teeth and charge, aiming to take a bite out of the flank of the offender.

The defence against such a charge is for the fleeing horse to throw up his heels and kick out at the head of his pursuer. It is this defensive reaction of the pursued horse that is the potential cause of trouble in the riding school. If you come up too close behind another horse, there is always a risk that the horse in front may feel threatened and kick out. You need to keep well clear because it is surprising how far a horse can reach and he can do a lot of damage. He can kick out quite effectively even when travelling at a considerable speed. You

Figure 4.1   *Threat posture adopted by a stallion when herding a group of mares and when defending his harem from an intruder. The head is lowered with ears laid back, signalling that his next move will be to attack, lungeing toward the offender with bared teeth.*

Photo 4.1 *Turning out of line ahead. The rider of the second horse, to avoid getting too close to the horse in front, turns out of the line and circles to join the rear of the ride.*

need to keep at least a length between your horse's nose and the tail of the horse in front. If you have occasion to overtake, you need to be at least half a length clear to the side.

When a horse is contemplating making a defensive threat, he usually starts by preparing himself with a small sideways movement of his hindquarters. This is a sign to be on the look-out for. It is a positive danger signal warning you to keep clear.

If your horse is over-eager and continually tends to close the gap, bringing you too close to the horse in front, it may be sensible to turn away from the line of the other horses and to circle to join up with the rear of the ride (*Photo 4.1*).

A useful variation from just riding round in line ahead is for all the riders to turn simuitaneously away from the long side of the arena (*Photo 4.2*) to form a line abreast. Each rider has then to watch his neighbours and adjust his speed to maintain the straight-line formation. The riders then all arrive together at the other side of the arena and turn simultaneously to re-form the well-spaced line ahead.

Riding in pairs, or three abreast, on a track involving turns (*Photo 4.3*) provides the opportunity to practise keeping abreast while at the same time preserving the spacing of the line ahead.

A more advanced manoeuvre is the 'wheel' (*Photo 4.4*). Here a group of riders perform a turn while riding in line abreast. The rider on the inside of the

Photo 4.2a-b *Line ahead to line abreast. **(a)** (above) All the riders prepare to turn across the school at the same time, as may be seen from the positions of the horses' heads. **(b)** (below) After making the turn, the riders need to watch their neighbours and control their own speed over the ground to maintain the straightness of the line abreast. At this attempt the riders have not been entirely successful.*

Photo 4.3a-b *Riding in pairs, adjusting the speed on the turns. **(a)** (above) Turning to cross the school. The horse on the inside of the turn has to take short steps, while the horse on the outside has to take longer steps so that the pair will keep abreast of one another. Each pair has to keep the proper spacing behind the pair in front. **(b)** (below) Arriving at the long side, the pairs turn onto the track.*

Photo 4.4a-b   *The 'wheel' at line abreast. Each rider has to adjust his speed during the turns to keep accurately in line abreast, slowing on the inside of the turn and speeding up on the outside. **(a)** (above) Preparing to wheel across the school. **(b)** (below) Arriving at the long side.*

turn has to collect his horse to hold back, while at the same time those further out have to extend in order to press on to cover the ground more quickly, as otherwise they will be left behind and will fail to maintain the line-abreast formation.

An entertaining manoeuvre for a large group of riders is the 'in-and-out spiral'. Here the leader rides a decreasing spiral, starting from as large a circle as the arena will allow. The others follow in strict line ahead, being careful not to allow their horses to 'cut the corner'. When the leader judges that he is already making as sharp a turn as is comfortable, he turns outward to change the rein and rides an increasing spiral in the opposite direction. In doing this he has to thread his way between the oncoming lines of the riders who are still riding on the inwardly decreasing spiral. Until all the riders involved have become extremely expert, it is advisable that this manoeuvre be performed only at the walk. When performed by well-trained riders at the collected canter, with a half-pirouette at the change of rein in the centre, this manoeuvre forms a very effective display, bordering on the 'haute école', and demonstrating skills of steering as well as of control of the speed over the ground.

Hacking

Learning to control your horse's speed over the ground is a natural progression from learning to start moving forward and learning to stop. These are all essential skills. So long as there is no uncertainty about the effectiveness of the command to stop, it will be quite beneficial for a novice rider to go for a quiet hack in company with two or three more experienced riders. It is noticeable that horses like to keep together in a group; so where the experienced riders go, the beginner can accompany them without too many problems. Nevertheless, it is important, when a group includes less experienced riders, to ensure that one of the more experienced riders takes upon himself the responsibility of keeping an eye on the less experienced.

The beginner should keep practising his steering and his control of the speed over the ground. He should be particularly careful to avoid being taken too near the hindquarters of another horse. He should always maintain a clearance of at least one horse's length. If he gets too close, the horse in front will feel threatened and may kick out. Don't rely too much on assurances that 'My horse doesn't kick'. Just keep your distance and be safe.

Particular care is required if, during your hack, you have occasion to ride through a field containing loose horses. The 'boss' of the local group may come thundering up to investigate. If he feels that you are encroaching on his territory, he may charge in an attempt to drive you off. He can approach at full speed, stop suddenly at very close range, spin round, and let fly with his heels. An attack of this kind can be very unnerving. Accordingly you need to be especially vigilant. Keep well away from the loose horses and ride steadily by, taking care to avoid giving the impression of an invading force.

It is well not to venture onto roads where there is likely to be a lot of traffic unless everyone in the party is experienced enough to be in full control of his horse. Riders should at all times respect the needs of other road users. They should keep well in to the side, keep a look-out for other traffic, and give clear signals when necessary. If there are a number of riders in the party, they should split up into groups with not more than four riders in each group. Leave gaps between the groups so that overtaking vehicles can pass the groups one at a time and can draw in between the groups if oncoming traffic makes this advisable.

One consequence of the preference of horses for keeping in a group is that they will tend to join up with faster moving companions, so as not to get left behind. The experienced riders in a group should keep this in mind since a novice rider can be unsettled if his mount unexpectedly accelerates to keep pace with another horse that is overtaking.

If there is a beginner in the party, who is not yet secure at the trot, the others should not trot either, because when one horse trots, all the others are likely to imitate him. It is also important not to let the beginner become separated from the others. If, for some reason, he gets stuck and falls behind, go back and join him, because his horse may become agitated as soon as the others move away, and could become more and more difficult for the beginner to control. This principle is especially important if there are gates to be negotiated. If a friend has dismounted to open and shut the gate, do not ride off until your friend is safely back in the saddle. If you are alone and your horse is getting worked up because you have been left at the gate, turn your horse away from the others and point his nose over the closed gate while you mount up. Talk to him and pat his neck to quiet him. Run your hands up and down his neck just beside the crest.

If during the ride you happen to stop for a chat to a pedestrian, you may have difficulty in keeping your horse quiet. He will not understand why you want him to continue standing still while you remain sitting on his back. He will keep trying to walk on and he may become excited if you repeatedly restrain him. It will be better to allow him to walk around in small circles while you continue your conversation. This gives him something to think about so that he doesn't get quite so impatient. Alternatively you can dismount, but even then he may wonder what all the delay is about and may start pawing at the ground. This is a polite way of telling you to get a move on. Remember not to ask your horse to stand about too long in a cold wind when his coat is wet with sweat from earlier exertions.

Shying

In the wild, the horse depends on his vigilance for survival, so you will find that, as you ride along, your horse's attention is continually being distracted, to one side or the other, often by things you yourself do not bother about, such as a piece of paper blown by the wind. He may stop suddenly, or he may swing suddenly to one side. In an extreme case he may stop very suddenly with a quick stamp of all four feet and throw his head first down and then violently upward, following through with an upward and sideways rearing lurch of the forequarters as he jumps to the side. It may thereafter be very hard to persuade him to go back to the spot.

If your horse shies like this, be very careful not to dig your heels in and pull on the reins. This will only excite him further. Put your heels firmly away from the horse, forward if possible, to bring your knees hard into the saddle. Reach forward with your hands and shoulders to get your hands onto the side of his neck where the contact will have a soothing effect. Try to relax, and speak reassuringly to the horse, patting him on the neck and rubbing your hand up and down beside the mane. Wait quietly for a moment or two before trying to move on again.

It is a great help to have another quiet horse to walk alongside, and slightly in front, to help you get your own horse past a point where he has shied. Here you are using the principle of 'giving a lead'. Because horses like to keep together, they will often tackle obstacles, when they are in a group led by a confident leader, that they would repeatedly shy away from and refuse if presented with the same situation when on their own.

Giving a lead

The strategy of giving a lead may be employed to deal with many other awkward situations. For example, the beginner will often find that he has difficulty in persuading his horse to leave a group of other horses. The root of the problem here may be either that the rider is not sufficiently unambiguous in his commands, or that the horse has not learned that leaving the others is one of the things he is expected to do. The beginner is likely to feel rather frustrated when his horse will not move off when asked. There is a strong temptation to kick the horse on and, as the rider's exasperation grows and his movements become more and more vigorous, he tends not to notice that at the same time as kicking backwards at the horse, he is also throwing his shoulders and arms about and accidentally jerking the reins.

In response, the horse starts throwing up his head and generally 'playing up', sometimes even walking backwards. It is important that the rider should restrain himself. If he allows himself to get excited when his horse is misbehaving, the result will be a 'shouting match', and a shouting match based on a misunderstanding doesn't usually solve anything. The rider should make an effort to keep calm and to proceed quietly, and step by step, through the routine described earlier for walking forward.

First of all, calm the horse by rubbing your hand up and down his neck alongside the crest and talking soothingly to him. Then ask for his attention by tickling the bit with the rein. Finally, drive on with seat and legs while at the same time easing the rein. If this does not work you may need to ask one of the other riders to give you a lead.

The idea of giving a lead in this context is that the horse's natural desire to keep with others can be directed to the lead horse as well as to the stationary group. If the lead horse is moving, it exerts a particularly strong attraction. Accordingly, if your horse refuses to leave a group of stationary horses, have another rider come alongside you, preferably between you and the others, and give your 'walk on' commands just as he passes you. The two of you then ride round one behind the other on a fairly large circle, coming back close to the group of stationary horses each time round. As you pass the group, emphasise your walk aids with legs, rein and seat, and pay particular attention to the steering. After a few trials you can try going round the circle on your own without the lead horse. In this way you allow your horse to become accustomed to walking past other horses without stopping.

Heading for home

The liking for the company of other horses produces another effect that can be troublesome for the beginner when he starts to go out hacking. Horses seem to know their way about the countryside quite well and they know which gateways or turnings will take them back to the stable. If they have made up their mind that the rider is somewhat ineffective in asserting his will, they will try to go home when they feel like it, without waiting for the rider's indication. They will sometimes show great reluctance to be ridden away from the stable, or past a turning toward home that they have taken on a previous excursion. Firm leg aids are needed in situations such as this.

Do not expect to be able to exert your will by exaggerating your commands through the rein. You must, of course, be quite firm in your intention, so that any effect of telepathy will work in your favour, but do not try to pull the horse round by his head. I described earlier how to stop a runaway by steering strongly into ever-decreasing circles. This is the only situation in which there is any point in pulling the horse's head round toward your knee. The effect of this is to slow him down and eventually to stop him. When you remember this you will see that to pull the horse's head round when he is standing still, in an effort to get him to move away from the direction he has chosen, is not going to have much chance of success. You are asking him to move on in response to a command to stop. It is better to turn the horse's head only slightly, just enough to bring his eye into view on the side to which he is·to turn. Then get him to walk on, straight ahead at first if need be, even if this is not the way you want to go eventually. Then get him to make the turn at the walk, using strong leg aids, behind the girth on the outside of the turn and on the girth with the inside leg. Turns on the spot may be useful here (described in the next chapter), but until you have mastered these, it is better to get the horse moving first, and then to make the turn at the walk.

If the horse persists in making for home, bring him firmly to a halt, speak to him, set his head ready for a turn, and walk on, as described above, making the desired turn firmly with your legs once he is in motion and using as light a hand on the rein as possible. Any jerking or pulling on the rein at this point just undermines the effectiveness of your leg command to walk on. If you still have difficulty, ask one of your companions to ride his horse across in front of you and try to get your horse to follow on. As a last resort, dismount, lead your horse a few yards in the direction you wish to go, and then get up again. Watch out for any suspicion of an intent to turn for home and give firm leg aids to make clear to the horse what you want him to do.

Refusing to go forward (jibbing)

It can be very frustrating if your horse refuses to go forward in spite of your active seat aids and leg aids. If you find yourself in such a conflict with your horse, watch out in case he starts to walk backwards. This reaction is a particularly dangerous habit. When the horse is fighting against the bit he does not look where he is going and he may walk backwards into trouble. For example, he may back into oncoming traffic or over an edge into a ditch. On no account should a beginner be put up on a horse that has this vice, because the beginner's reaction to the undesired and unexpected movement is often to tighten up on the rein as though this will put on the brakes. What happens is precisely the opposite. The pull on the rein is an encouragement to back and the horse just goes backwards faster than ever.

To cure a horse of this habit you need an experienced rider who knows how to manage the spurs and who can deal with any sudden reaction of the horse. As soon as the horse starts to back, the rider should apply firm pressure with the spurs well behind the girth on both sides. Be careful not to have a tight rein but be on the alert for any sudden move the horse may make. If necessary the action of the spur can be reinforced by a sharp blow with the whip, applied just behind the boot, but not always on the same side. Remember here that, to be effective, any punishment like this must be extremely prompt. If you delay even a couple of seconds, the horse will not associate the punishment with what he has been doing. It will just reinforce his notion that he is in a situation from which he must exert himself violently to escape.

Pulling

A horse will go forward much more eagerly once you have reached the home-ward leg of your hack. Here is your chance to practise the stops. It is better to stop many times, and to ride with a light rein in between, rather than to allow your horse to pull against you all the way home. The tug-of-war is an irritating bad habit. Some horses will open their mouths and throw their heads about to evade the bit while pulling very strongly, almost hard enough sometimes to pull you right out of the saddle. Do not put up with this. Even more important, do not encourage the horse by pulling against him. Give when he pulls and quickly take up the slack again as soon as you can. Try to keep a constant gentle pressure in spite of all his head shaking. If he starts to go faster, make a definite stop with a few brief pulls on the reins, returning at once to the gentle contact as soon as you get any response.

It is important not to get too tensed up. Keep your heels well away from the horse, because if you cling on, this will only make him want to go faster. Run your hand up and down his neck beside the mane. Speak to him calmly. Although you are practising stops, do not let your companions get too far away ahead.

Up hill and down hill

It is very good practice, both for horse and for rider, to take any opportunity that presents itself, when out hacking, to walk up and down hills, banks and other rough places. But be careful to avoid slippery places. Even a quite moderately inclined metalled road can be quite treacherous. A surface that is admirable for the wheels of a car can be quite dangerous for horses. Their iron horseshoes make no indentations in a hard road so that there is nothing to grip with, and the horses slide all over the place. On a hill they can easily fall and hurt both themselves and their riders.

When going up a steep hill, sit well forward in the saddle, gripping with your knees and reaching along the horse's neck with your hands (*Figure 4.2*). Let the reins be fairly slack to allow the horse to make the plunging movements with his head that he needs. If you have to hold on with your hands, use the neck strap if there is one, or hang on to the mane. Do not try to save yourself from slipping back by pulling on the rein. Aim to get your weight well forward, over your knees if you can. If you start to slide in the saddle, get your feet out of the stirrups quickly and hang on to the pommel of the saddle so that, if you do slide right off, you will land on your feet. Horses seem to enjoy going up hill. On a moderate slope they will canter if given half a chance. Very steep slopes are taken in a series of bounds and it is essential to lean well forward with your seat out of the saddle and with your weight on your knees to avoid being thrown about violently by the saddle each time the horse surges upward.

You also need to keep your weight on your knees when going down hill.

When you realise you are about to go down a steep place, pause and check the girth. You don't want the saddle to go sliding along the horse's neck. Then put your feet well forward, knees almost straight, heels out and toes in, and check that the stirrups are under the ball of the foot (*Figure 4.3*). The cushioning action of the ankle joint provides an important contribution to your security. Lean your shoulders a little forward, if anything, rather than back, to make sure you are not pressing on the saddle with your seat-bones. It is permissible for your seat to brush the saddle momentarily from time to time, but if you are

Figure 4.2   *Going up hill. Lean well forward with your weight out of the saddle, arms round the horse's neck if need be. Have a slack rein and grip with your knees. If you start to slip, hold on to the mane, to the neck strap, or to the saddle. Do not try to save yourself by holding on to the rein.*

sitting back with your weight on the saddle, the sudden movements as the horse lifts up each of his hindlegs in turn will throw you forward quite sharply. If you overbalance forward you will have nothing to hold on to. So keep your weight out of the saddle, grip firmly with your knees and balance yourself with knee and ankle. Let the rein go reasonably slack, so as not to restrict the movements of the horse's head. Just give a touch on the rein occasionally on one side or the other to keep the horse aimed in the desired direction.

You will feel that the movements of the saddle are very much more pronounced than they are on level ground. This is because the horse prevents himself from pitching forward by strong thrusts of the forelegs. The horse doesn't have a collarbone to connect his shoulderblade to the skeleton of the trunk and in consequence the increased forces that the forelegs have to bear when the horse is going down hill produce large movements of the shoulderblades under the saddle. You will feel yourself being thrown from side to side as well as plunging downward in a series of lunges.

The horse will hold his head a long way down and, because the hill is sloping away in front, you will feel a very long way from the ground. Don't let this worry you. Horses are quite used to going down steep hills and they don't mind going down quite fast. The essential thing is to aim straight down if the slope is at all steep or slippery. Then if the horse starts to slide, he will just sit down on his hindquarters and slither along until he gets a grip or reaches the

Figure 4.3   *Going down hill. Weight on your knees, feet slightly forward rather than back, heels away from the horse. Let the horse have his head free.*

bottom. So long as he is going straight down he can keep his forelegs out in front of him and he can easily remain upright. On no account attempt to go down a steep slope at an angle because, if the horse should happen to lose his footing, you will both go rolling down together, with serious risk of injury to both horse and rider.

The extensive movements of the saddle, as the horse negotiates the uphill and downhill slopes, compel the rider to bend his back. To retain his balance he has to keep his shoulders vertically above his seat while his pelvis is being rocked from side to side and while his weight is being pushed alternately forward and backward. This is a very good exercise and it helps considerably in developing the rider's suppleness. It is also very good for the horse, strengthening his muscles.

Another advantage of practising riding up and down steep places is that it brings home to the rider the importance of the shock-absorbing action of the ankle. He will get the benefit of this only if he rides with the stirrup under the ball of the foot. This should become a matter of habit.

Faster work

Most riders will wish to enjoy the canter as soon as they have become reasonably confident at the trot. However, although many horses will break into a canter quite freely when you urge them forward at the trot, others present problems, particularly to a beginner. Your horse may canter readily enough alongside other horses when these are asked to canter, but will obstinately refuse to canter on his own when not given a lead. The reason for this is that successful control of the canter calls for the aids to be different on the two sides of the horse. You will find that all your problems with the canter usually disappear after you have become familiar with the actions of the individual aids, both separately and in combination. For this reason I have postponed my explanations of how to control canters and jumps to Chapter 8, and concentrate first on the actions of the aids.

There are advantages in studying the variations in lateral work to be described in the next few chapters, and in learning to develop the collected and extended gaits, even if you have no intention of ever submitting yourself to the scrutiny of a judge in a competition. Occasions for the use of these manoeuvres arise from time to time, even during casual hacking. You will find that lateral work and the turns on the spot, for instance, together with the rein-back, will be useful to you in negotiating gates. Collection and extension are useful in adjusting the pace of your horse to suit that of a companion, and you should not really venture onto a public road until you can keep your mount in to the side of the road, by leg-yielding, to allow room for other traffic.

DEVELOPING PRECISION

The rein aids

After you have worked for some time with fairly simple controls and when you are beginning to 'get a feel for' the way the horse prepares his various movements, you can start to experiment with more sophisticated manipulation of the reins. An essential preliminary is to achieve sufficient relaxation of the arm so that the position of your hand is governed entirely by the feel of the rein against your fingers and not at all by the movements of your shoulder caused by your being bounced up and down by the horse. When the horse's head moves towards or away from the saddle, your hand should go with this movement without any change in rein tension. In particular, the rein should never be allowed to sag loosely. If it does, the rein will snap taut again and produce an unintended jab to the horse's mouth.

Rein-tension training machine

I have devised a machine to assist riders to develop their ability to maintain a constant tension in the reins in spite of the movements of the horse's head (*Photos 5.1a-b*).

> The principles of operation of this device are illustrated in *Figure 5.1*. The two reins that the pupil is to handle are each attached to a length of flexible braided nylon cord. These two cords pass, each over a separate pulley, to a triangular yoke-piece, the apex of which is attached, by another length of cord, to a motor-driven crank (*Figure 5.1b*). The motor turns the crank at about 60 rpm, imposing on the yoke-piece a vertical excursion of about 18 cm up and down every second. This simulates the forward and backward movement of the horse's mouth. The function of the yoke-piece is to permit variation in the relative tensions in the individual reins, over the range from 0% to 100%. If the yoke-piece tilts down on the right, the left rein will carry a larger proportion of the tension, and so on.
>
> The pulleys form part of the tension-indicating mechanism (*Figure 5.1a*). Each is fitted on the end of a horizontal pivoted arm about 10 cm long. Vertical support for the pulley is provided by a horizontal lever with two supports, one of which incorporates a spring. The free end of this lever carries a pointer

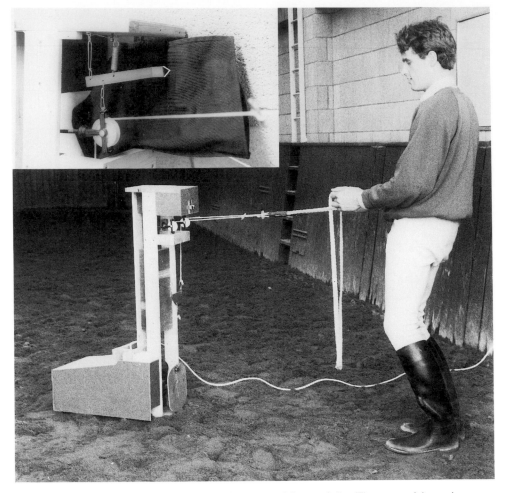

Photo 5.1a-b *Rein-tension training machine.* **(a)** *The machine in use.* **(b)** *(Inset) Detail of the tension-indicating device, to show the simplicity of its construction. The cover has been removed and the second indicator is screened off to avoid confusion.*

which moves along a fixed scale.

There are four equal forces on the pulley, two horizontal and two vertical. The action of the pulley ensures that the downward pull exerted on the cord by the movements of the crank is transmitted to the horizontal pull in the cord running to the pupil's hand. The horizontal pull in the cord is met by the resistance of the frame supporting the pivoted arm of the pulley, while the vertical force in the cord is transmitted to the indicating lever. Excursions of the pointer thus indicate what is happening in the rein while the pupil's hands are being pulled forward and back.

The motorised crank is not essential. The necessary movement may alterna-

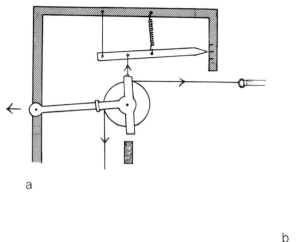
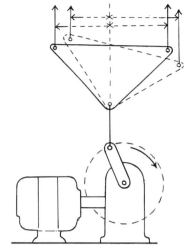

a

b

Figure 5.1 *Rein-tension training machine: principles of operation. (a) Tension-indicating mechanism, side view (one side only is shown). A pulley is tethered to the frame by a pivoted arm and supported by a spring. A cord running over the pulley connects the pupil's rein to the pulling device. Overload protection is provided by a fixed block that prevents the pulley from being pulled down too far. (b) Pulling device, front view. A motor-driven crank rotates at about once per second. The crank is coupled to the two reins by a triangular yoke-piece that allows the two reins to bear different tensions. If the yoke-piece tips downward on the right, the left rein will carry a larger proportion of the applied tension.*

tively be imposed on the yoke-piece by an instructor who pulls a cord which passes round a fixed pulley to preserve the verticality of the downward pull on the yoke-piece.

The virtue of this device is that it imposes a movement on the pupil's hands while at the same time indicating to him what is happening to the tension in the rein. It thus gives the pupil the opportunity to appreciate how important it is for him to keep his arms supple. It takes only a little practice for novice riders to gain a clear impression of what is required of them by the instruction to keep a constant small tension in the rein in spite of the relative movement occurring between the horse's mouth and the rider's shoulders. Some quite experienced riders have found that a trial with the machine is extremely salutary. Many had not been aware of just how strong a pull they were habitually applying to the reins.

The thirteen positions of the hand

Up to this point we have been considering practice routines in which the hand is held always in or near a single standard position, just clear of the withers and just in front of the pommel of the saddle. When seen from the side the hand is so placed that the forearm and rein appear to form a single straight line from the bit to the rider's elbow. The upper arms hang straight down from the shoulders with the elbows just brushing against the waist, above the hips. The thumbs are uppermost and about 12−15 centimetres apart. The wrists turn in very slightly in continual supple motion to provide the 'springiness' which is needed to absorb the effects of sudden movements either of the horse's head or of the rider's shoulders.

We now examine some useful deviations from the standard position. In the first place, the hand may be raised by bending the elbow (*Figure 5.2*). In the right conditions this may help the horse to put more weight on his hindquarters and thus may make it easier for the rider to persuade an over-eager horse to drop back from the trot into the walk. If the hands are habitually held high this will encourage the horse to 'poke his nose' in a 'star-gazing' posture which has several disadvantages. This makes it more difficult for the rider to control his horse, and it may interfere with the horse's ability to see where he is going to put his feet. An injudicious pull on the reins with the hands held high may provoke rearing.

There are some situations in which it is useful to hold the hands low down beside the horse's neck, even as far down as the point of the shoulder. This encourages the horse to bring his nose in toward his chest. The effect is very like that aimed at with draw reins. The lowered hand has a great advantage over the draw reins in that it permits a more supple action on the bit, as well as being always available and quickly dispensed with at a moment's notice.

As well as raising and lowering the hand, we may move it to one side or the other. These changes in the lateral position of the hands alter the angle at which the rein meets the bit. Five possibilities are shown in *Figure 5.3*.

The 'regular' position, which we have been using up to now, is No. 2, the 'direct rein'. If the hand is moved to the side, away from the horse's neck, we have the 'opening rein', No. 1. This leads the horse into a turn. Alternatively, we may apply an 'indirect rein' by moving the hand toward the centre-line of the neck with the line of the rein either behind the withers, No. 3, or in front of the withers, No. 4. Each of these four directions can be adopted either with the hand at the regular height or with the hand raised.

With the hand below the withers we can apply both the direct rein and the opening rein. An effect similar to that of the indirect rein may be obtained by pressing the lowered hand firmly into the side of the horse's neck.

The more extreme deviation across the horse's neck, No. 5 in *Figure 5.3*, is used with the raised hand in the action of 'neck reining' by Western-style riders, where both reins are usually held in the one hand.

The rein is also taken across the middle of the horse's neck in one of the manoeuvres for stopping a runaway (*Photo 5.2*). One hand, say the left, is moved well down the rein, toward the horse's mouth. Then, gripping the rein firmly, the hand is brought across the neck until the fist can be pressed strongly

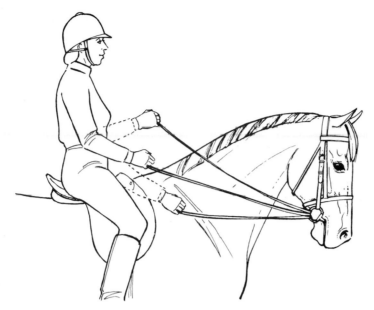

Figure 5.2 *Vertical positions of the hand. Two alternatives to the regular position are shown, one raised, the other lowered.*

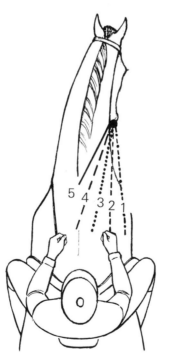

Figure 5.3 *Five horizontal directions for the rein. From right to left: **(1)** opening rein; **(2)** direct rein; **(3)** indirect rein behind the withers; **(4)** indirect rein in front of the withers; **(5)** neck rein.*

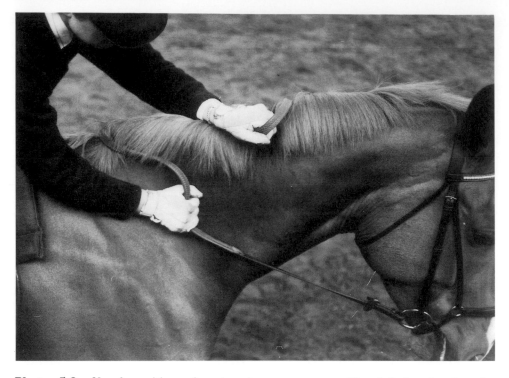

Photo 5.2 *Hand positions for stopping a runaway. The left hand grips the shortened rein and leans across the horse's neck to provide an unyielding anchorage for the rein as well as some support for the rider's weight. The right hand is lowered and applies a fluctuating strong tension to the rein, aiming to pull the horse's nose round to the rider's knee. A steady pull is much less effective. The rider's feet are held well forward, heels away from the horse, in an attitude like that of an athlete landing after a long-jump.*

into the right side of the neck beside the crest. Meanwhile the other hand, held well down at the level of the horse's shoulder, pulls in the 'opening rein' direction, repeatedly increasing and decreasing the pressure on the bit to insist on a turn toward that side. The 'blocking' of the left rein, by thrusting the fist into the right side of the neck, ensures that the bit does not get pulled right through the horse's mouth.

Thus, each of the five rein directions shown (*Figure 5.3*) may be used with the hand at either of two heights, and there are, in addition, three rein directions available with the hand below the withers. In all, there are thirteen distinct positions of the hand.

The horse seems able to distinguish the different effects of the rein on the bit and produces appropriately different responses without special training. This is in contrast with the responses to the leg aids, which, apart from the simple response of lifting the hindleg, will have to be carefully taught.

The indirect rein

We may convince ourselves of the naturalness of the responses to different rein actions by the following exercise. Have the horse going on steadily at a moderate pace, either at the walk or at the trot, with enough impulsion for the horse to be leaning slightly on the bit. Keep up an unchanging pressure on the rein with each hand and do not make any deliberate shift of weight. Keep the leg aids symmetrical. Hold one hand, say the left, steady in the 'direct rein' position and apply 'opening rein' with the other (right) hand, still without any change in the tension on the rein. The horse will turn to the right. After a few strides, return the right hand to the direct rein position. The horse goes straight ahead. Now carry the right hand across to the left, still without altering the tension in the rein. The horse veers to the left. Also try the opening and indirect reins with the left hand, keeping the right hand always in the direct rein position. The horse will veer left and right as before.

The next stage is to look for differences in the responses to the indirect rein, when the line of the rein passes in front of or behind the withers. If we apply the right indirect rein in front of the withers the horse moves his head and shoulders to the left and makes a turn. If the indirect rein is applied behind the withers it affects the haunches as well as the forequarters. The whole body of the horse moves to the left in a diagonal direction, with the forelegs and hindlegs following different tracks. If your horse does not appear to understand the difference between these two rein signals, it may be that he is not yet adequately collected. You will need to give him more practice in developing impulsion.

The subtle language of the rein (*See also* Chapter 6)

There are a great many different things you can do with the rein and any particular action you make can have a different meaning to the horse according to the precise moment at which the signal is given and according to what the horse's head happens to be doing at the time. For example, the horse's head may be turned to the left, or to the right, or it may be pointing straight ahead. The mouth may be moving toward the saddle or away from it. This gives six possibilities, without considering the details of the timing in relation to the stride.

Your hand may be keeping a steady tension, or it may pull with increased tension, or give with reduced tension, or it may be imposing a fluctuating tension, as in 'tickling the bit' by rapidly repeated curling and uncurling of the fingers − four possibilities for rein action in each position of the hand. Each hand can thus give fifty-two different indications − four ways of manipulating the tension in each of thirteen positions. If we suppose the two hands to be independent, and take account of the six different conditions of the horse's head, we arrive at 16,224 different ways of signalling with the rein!

will then encourage him to bring his hocks forward under him until he is supported on a shorter base. His back becomes more rounded and his action is altogether more bouncy, like that of a stallion in his aggressive display.

Up to now we have been concentrating on allowing the hand to move with the horse's mouth, keeping a steady tension and never allowing the reins to flap or to be jerked taut. As the horse's mouth moves in toward the saddle and away again, we have followed in with the hand and let out again as the tension in the rein begins to rise. If we exaggerate the movement of the hand, this encourages the horse to swing his head and he steps out in a more extended stride (*Photo 5.4*). To produce a more collected action, we alter the timing of our changes in the pressure of the fingers on the rein. When the horse's mouth is coming back toward the saddle, instead of following it in all the way, we relax the pressure slightly, being careful never to let the rein go completely slack. Then, as the horse's mouth moves forward, we first check a little, allowing the tension to build up, then tickle the bit, and finally give again as soon as the horse responds and yields to the increased pressure on the rein. We are now working against the natural swing of the horse's head instead of encouraging it.

After a time, the horse comes to hold his mouth always at the same distance from the saddle. He continues to nod his head and neck up and down, but the rider's hand no longer moves backwards and forwards with each stride. We can now start gradually shortening the rein, stealing a little at each stride at the moment when the tension is slackening off. If the horse begins to lean heavily on the bit, let go suddenly and then immediately take up the tension again. This prevents him from getting into the habit of letting you carry the weight of his head. Meanwhile keep up the forward drive with legs and seat.

Do not insist on prolonged periods of extreme collection but do allow the horse from time to time to go forward freely in extended trot. By alternating in this way you can gradually build up the contrast between the different forms of the trot. Ideally the extended trot should have very much the same rhythm as the collected trot, but the horse should cover a great deal more ground at each stride. To help to emphasise the difference between the collected and extended trots, you can post when riding the extended trot and sit down again for the collected trot. Another variation is to introduce what is called the 'jump seat'.

Jump seat and drive seat

When a horse takes off for a jump his body makes a sudden surge upward and forward. If you happen to be sitting down hard in the saddle at this precise moment, you will be catapulted into the air and there is no knowing where you will land. It is much safer to have a more springy contact with the horse at the moment of take-off. Then, instead of a sudden jolt, you receive a less severe, but more prolonged, push which is much easier to cope with. It is appropriate to practise the safe posture so as to be ready for the jump when it comes.

Figure 5.4 *The jump seat: weight on the knees; seat out of the saddle; stirrup on the ball of the foot; ankle springy; heel down. (See also Photo 2.8b)*

An extreme form of the 'jump seat' (*Figure 5.4*) is that adopted by professional racing jockeys who usually ride with the seat well out of the saddle. The rider carries his shoulders well forward to bring all his weight out of the saddle. The stirrup is kept on the ball of the foot with the stirrup leather vertical, as usual, but only a little of the weight is actually on the stirrups. Most of the weight is taken on the knees. This makes it easier to balance. Because the knee is several centimetres in front of the stirrup leather, a tendency to pitch forward or backward over the knees can be corrected by adjusting the push of the feet against the stirrups. It may be convenient to move the hands down the reins to bring them nearer to the horse's mouth. You can then use the pressure of your knuckles against the horse's neck as an additional aid to balance. But you should try, so far as possible, to manage without this so that you do not interfere with the independence of your hand which is so necessary for controlling the horse. A useful practice routine is to alternate collected trot in the jump seat position with extended trot in the normal sitting trot position.

If the pelvis is being used energetically at the sitting trot, this becomes the 'drive seat' position. The rider's shoulders, neck and upper back are kept supple, to provide springy support, while the lower back is intermittently braced to rotate the pelvis and to drive the seat-bones forward against the saddle at each stride. The knees and thighs press firmly against the saddle, so that the driving action of the seat-bones is distributed over the whole of the saddle and urges it forward. Meanwhile the lower leg below the knee maintains its independence ready to give whatever directional leg aids may be required.

The horse should accelerate briskly when you relax the rein and sit down into the drive seat after a period of collected trot in the jump seat position. You will need this kind of surging acceleration later for the approach to a jump. Just before the actual moment of take-off, however, you fold forward into the jump seat to cushion yourself against the sudden rise of the saddle.

In the jump seat position, the rider can no longer drive the saddle forward with his seat. He can, however, develop an additional strong leg aid as follows. The support provided by the knees and ankles is a very springy one and the rider's lower leg accordingly slides up and down over the horse's side with each stride. The rider's weight is pressed down into the saddle at the moment when the horse is landing and thrusting off again. This winds up the spring of the muscles supporting the rider so that, as soon as the horse's thrust is over, the rider's legs tend to lift him upward away from the saddle. If the rider squeezes with his legs at this point, he can apply a sort of 'lifting' pressure against the horse's side as well as the earlier squeeze associated with the moment of landing. This lifting leg aid encourages the horse to spring higher at each step and the increased vigour of his action is reflected in increased impulsion.

Bringing his nose in

It may be that your attempts to build up impulsion have succeeded in making your horse alert and responsive, but he is still holding his head up in an attitude like that of *Figure 5.5a*, whereas what you are aiming at is a posture more like that of *Figure 5.5b*. Notice here that the line of the rein indicates a very light tension, showing that the horse is holding his head in for himself. His head is not being pulled in by the rein. The action of the rein is much more effective here, where the pull is across the line of the mouth, than it would be in an attitude such as that in *Figure 5.5a*, where the bit would be pulled up into the corner of the mouth.

To achieve the arched neck and upright head-carriage you need first to explain to the horse what you want him to do. Paradoxically, the first step is to persuade him to stretch forward and downward. This is where the lowered hand becomes important. Ride a succession of turns either at the walk or at a slow trot. Come forward into the jump seat position and get your hands as far down the horse's shoulder as you can (*Photo 5.5*). Tickle the bit, first on one side then on the other and make the turns by giving with the outside hand. Keep up the impulsion with your legs. When you feel the horse reaching for the bit, reward him with your voice and by caressing his neck with the inside of your forearm.

Figure 5.5 *Attitudes of the horse's head. **(a)** Alert but unrestrained. **(b)** Nose in and neck arched, paying close attention to the bit and ready to respond to the rider's slightest indication.*

From time to time encourage him to relax further by running your hand up and down his neck close beside the crest. You will need to be patient. After a time he will begin to lower his head into the turns, stretching his neck forward. Continue tickling the bit and gradually start stealing a little rein whenever he gives you a chance. Keep your hands very low.

The draw reins

If you find you get tired quickly in this position you can try using the draw reins. These are long reins that pass through the rings on the ends of the bit and run downward to an anchorage on the girth under the mid-line of the belly (*Photo 5.6a-b*). The line of action of the force exerted by the draw rein upon the bit bisects the angle between the parts of the rein above and below the bit. This means that you can hold your hands at the normal level, just above the withers, and still pull the bit down toward the horse's shoulder, as you were previously doing with the lowered hand.

The disadvantage of the draw rein is that, because of the extra purchase of the pulley-action where the rein passes through the bit-ring, it is possible to

Photo 5.5   *Reaching for the bit. The rider sits forward, in jump-seat position with hands low, and tickles the bit in a sequence of turns to alternate sides, until the horse responds by lowering his head and reaching his nose forward to play his part in maintaining a small steady tension in the rein.*

pull the horse's head down by sheer force. This encourages him to pull back with the muscles that lift his head, whereas what you want him to do is to relax these same muscles and hold his head freely in the nose-in position.

You will probably need the draw reins for only a few minutes because, once your horse has grasped the idea of what you want him to do, you can go back to the regular rein. This allows a much more delicate control of the bit.

If you find that your horse is slow to learn to keep his nose in and continually fights against the rein, try working with draw reins and ordinary reins in different hands, using for each hand the modified single-handed grip (*Figure 6.19*). You can then alternate between the two reins, using the draw rein when he pokes his nose out, and changing to the ordinary rein when he starts to get a little overbent and when he puts his nose too far down in response to the draw rein. It is important to keep up the impulsion by driving with the seat. This will encourage him to keep his head up and when he eventually learns to keep his nose in it will be with an arched neck.

Some people anchor the ends of the draw reins to the girth straps instead of to the middle of the girth between the forelegs. This gives the extra purchase of the pulley-action round the rings of the bit, but the line of the pull on the bit is not lowered very much below that of the hand in the regular position. One thus

Photo 5.6a-b *Draw reins in position, held in the left hand and controlled separately from the ordinary rein which is held in the right hand.* **(a)** *(above) Draw rein inactive.* **(b)** *(below) Draw rein active. The line of action of the resultant force exerted on the bit is indicated by the dotted line. Compare with Photo 5.5.*

achieves the disadvantages of the draw rein without the advantages. The object of bringing his nose in is to persuade him to arch his neck as part of the process of collection. There is no point in pulling his nose right in to his chest if he doesn't arch his neck.

Corners

When riding turns in the jump seat position you will notice that your weight comes naturally on to the inside knee at the beginning of the turn. This, in itself, is an effective instruction to the horse to make the turn. Do not over-emphasise the shift of weight, however, because this may encourage the horse to 'fall in' on the turns, cutting the corner by stepping sideways with his forelegs. One aspect of the precision that one tries to achieve is that, unless one is deliberately asking the horse to go on two tracks, the hindquarters should follow directly behind the forequarters through all turns and corners. If your horse tends to step across the corners with his forelegs, correct him by using indirect rein instead of opening rein on the inside of the turn, asking for the turn by yielding with the outside rein. Also apply your inside leg over the girth or a little in front of it. An effective way to do this when in the jump seat is to work with the ankle of the inside foot to apply repeated brief pressures down onto the stirrup. This tenses the calf muscle against the side of the horse in a rapid sequence of nudges.

It is good practice to ask your horse to go well into each of the corners when you are riding a pattern involving right-angle turns. Do not make the mistake of allowing the horse to bend too much at the neck. You need little more than just enough to bring the corner of his eye into view. He can quite easily turn his head beyond a right angle, but if you allow him to do this he may become 'rubber-necked'. He will then tend to respond to the rein by turning his head alone, continuing to go straight on, instead of moving into a turn when you want him to.

Bending

If all is going well, you may feel that the horse is actually bending his spine as well as his neck. He cannot, however, bend the main part of his spine very much in a sideways direction, and most of the apparent bend will be in the relative positions of the shoulders and haunches. The outer shoulder reaches forward while the inner shoulder is held back. This gives a very slight deflection of the withers as the start of a smooth curve running along the whole length of the neck up to the poll. The haunch on the inner side also reaches forward more than the outer haunch, producing a slight sideways bend of the lumbar part of the back.

This stage in the education of horse and rider is one that demands and repays prolonged practice. You should work on the development of impulsion by bracing the back, and you should keep encouraging your horse to hold his nose in without leaning heavily on the rein. Pay attention to the smoothness of the bend when riding on a circle and check that the hindquarters are correctly tracking exactly behind the forequarters. The concentric circles are an appropriate pattern to use because no change of direction is required and you can concentrate on maintaining a steady rhythm while varying the speed over the ground, periodically collecting up for a time and then encouraging full extension for a number of strides.

Stiff on one side

You should, of course, practise turns both to the right and to the left. You will probably find that there is a distinct difference between the two sides both in the smoothness with which the horse takes up the bend in his spine and in the steadiness with which he goes forward. He appears to be stiffer on one side than on the other. Make up your mind which is the stiff side and start your bending practice for the day with circles to the easy side. When the horse is warmed up, start to work on the stiff side, beginning with a number of fairly large circles and gradually reducing the diameter. After spending some minutes on this, move on to figures-of-eight. Here you should pay attention to the symmetry of the track making sure that the alternating circles to right and to left are of precisely the same size, as well as both being perfectly round.

Ask a friend to watch you carefully to see whether the asymmetry in the horse can be attributed to an asymmetry in the rider. It is very easy to get into the habit of riding with a little more weight on one side than the other without being aware of it. If you happen to have developed such a habit, you will at first feel lopsided when you move into a position that your friend says is straight. However, it will be worth while to persist. You will be rewarded by finding that your horse becomes more symmetrical in his behaviour as you cure yourself of the habit.

One way to make yourself more aware of your own asymmetry is to ride for a little with your weight deliberately more on one side than the other, and then change over to the other side. Then, after you have been riding for a time without thinking about the possibility of asymmetry, just try out the feel of momentarily putting more weight first on one side and then on the other. Ask yourself whether the two sides feel the same. If your usual position is asymmetrical, you will probably feel that the deliberate shifts of weight to the two sides do not call for the same amount of effort.

Signs of restlessness

While you are riding round and round trying to get your horse settled, watch what he is doing with his head and ears. This will tell you whether he is being distracted by things going on round about. You may also be able to tell whether he is uncertain about what you are trying to tell him by your movements of the bit. He may throw his head about and pluck at the rein.

Another common sign of restlessness, tail swishing, is not so easily seen from the saddle, though it is immediately obvious to an onlooker. In the wild, tail swishing from side to side is a sign to other horses to be on their guard. It is not a full alarm signal. It just indicates a state of unease; the horse does not feel it is safe to relax but he is not quite sure what the problem is.

When your horse has relaxed and is content to carry you steadily round the circle his actions will indicate this. His tail swishing stops, he no longer throws his head about, he works the bit gently in his mouth to maintain a light tension, and he extends his neck and lowers his head slightly without actually changing the distance between his mouth and the saddle. This neck movement is characteristic but rather subtle. You will recognise it once you have seen it.

The halt and half-halt

As well as practising the turns, to encourage the horse to bend his spine, you should also practise the halt. To produce a really smart halt you need to brace your back to drive the horse into a restraining hand. The aids are similar to those needed to increase collection but with a firmer tension in the rein. The effect is to bring the horse's hindlegs forward under his weight. If you ask for a sudden halt with the rein alone, he will tend to throw out his forelegs and will stop with his weight on the forequarters. He will probably bring his head down at the same time so that you are in danger of sliding forward over his neck.

The horse will need first to be warned of your intention to halt. You indicate this by a brief pull on the rein. You then apply a firmer resistance to those movements of the rein produced by the horse so that he knows not to go forward, and at the same time you drive the saddle forward with a braced back. The horse is, so to speak, driven up into the bit. It may be necessary to reinforce your rein signal by adding a few brief pulls to the steady tension in the rein. The process of coming to a halt is a gradual one, the horse making shorter and shorter steps. The hindfeet start to catch up with the forefeet. The horse 'sits back' into the halt instead of pitching forward.

The full halt takes two or three strides, so you can ease the rein again before the horse actually comes to a standstill. This manoeuvre is called a 'half-halt'. The horse is brought 'to attention', with increased collection. It is appropriate to ask for a half-halt as a preliminary to any manoeuvre, such as a change of gait, which you want the horse to execute with some precision. When you release the rein after a half-halt the horse should surge forward with increasing extension.

Transition from trot to walk

In a dressage competition you may be required to make certain changes of gait at specified points in the arena. This calls for a certain delicacy in balancing the actions of the seat and hands which can be achieved only with practice. Decide upon some fixed landmark in your practice area and try to make the transition from trot to walk at the precise moment at which your body passes the marker. Warn the horse of your intention when you are still a few strides away from the transition point. Ask for a half-halt. Keep up a gradually increasing rein pressure and then give an extra brief pull on the rein just as you are coming up to the mark. As soon as the horse drops to the walk, ease the rein and relax your seat. Thereafter gradually build up the pattern of alternating leg aids appropriate to the walk. If your horse is particularly lively and is reluctant to drop back into the walk, it may help if you lift your hands briefly just as you are coming up to the moment when you want him to change.

The aids for the transition from trot to walk are just like those for the halt, except that you ease the rein before the horse comes to a standstill. The smoothness of the transition depends on accurate timing. If you relax your tension too soon, he will continue in trot and you achieve only a half-halt. If you are too late in relaxing, he will stop completely and you will have to restart him again at the walk. To get the timing right, you have to be aware of what he is doing.

At the walk, the horse does not throw himself clear of the ground at each step in the way he does at the trot. To make the transition, he must first make a soft landing on one diagonal. You can feel his trunk muscles getting ready for this since the preparation for a soft landing is not the same as the preparation for the jolt that is involved, at each stride of the trot, in catching the weight on a single diagonal pair of legs and throwing it up again for the next stride.

Another difference between trot and walk is that each leg steps individually at the walk instead of being paired with its diagonal. Just after the soft landing on one diagonal, the opposite forefoot is brought to the ground early to give three-point support. Meanwhile the placing of the hindfoot of that diagonal is delayed. Then, just before this hindfoot touches down, the forefoot on the same side is lifted in the start of the walking pattern. As well as relaxing his trunk muscles to make the soft landing for the walk, the horse also relaxes his neck muscles, so that his head sinks further at the moment of the soft landing. The upward return movement of the head, while the trunk is supported on three legs, helps the horse to reach forward with the hindleg, which is still in the air at this point. If you are alert to all the small components of the horse's movement, there are several signs that you can look for as indications that the horse is about to make the change from trot to walk. In this way you teach yourself to adjust the timing of the change in your aids until the transition is achieved smoothly at the precise moment you intend.

Turn on the forehand

An exercise that helps to develop the rider's awareness of the horse's movements is the turn on the forehand. This manoeuvre is also a good introduction to

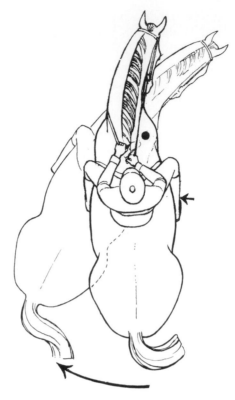

Figure 5.6   *Turn on the forehand, to the right in this case. The horse pivots on the right forefoot, replacing it on the same spot after each step.* (See text.)

lateral work, in which the horse is trained to respond to leg aids which are different on the two sides. We have, up to this point, been dealing mainly with aids that the horse appears to understand naturally. Where the leg aids have been different on the two sides they have been accompanied by shifts of the rider's weight in the saddle. The shift of weight is understood naturally, and the leg aids have been used merely as reinforcement. We are now ready to try out the effects of leg aids given in new combinations with weight shift, rein aid, and position of the horse's head.

The turn on the forehand is carried out from the halt, with the horse in a good state of alertness (*Figure 5.6*). He is to be asked to move his haunches sideways to pivot on a single forefoot. This pivoting foot does not remain rooted to the ground, but each time it is lifted it is put down again on the same spot. We start by tickling the bit and bracing the back to bring the horse to a state of readiness. We then warn the horse of what is coming. If the turn is to be made to the right, we ask the horse to shift his nose round slightly toward the right by being a little firmer with the right rein and giving a little with the left. We now want him to step to the left with his hindlegs. Bring the weight forward a little in the saddle, to help free the hindquarters, and work actively

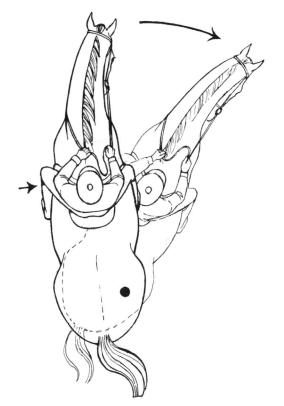

Figure 5.7 *Turn on the haunches, to the right. The horse pivots on the right hindfoot, which is replaced on the same spot after each step.* (See text.)

with the right leg, giving a series of little pats with the calf against the girth or a little behind it.

The natural response to the leg aid is for the horse to lift his hindleg on that side. We restrain him from stepping forward by pressing more firmly with the rein just at this point. Do not press too hard or he will step backward. The right rein should be in the position for the indirect rein behind the withers, while the left hand gives indirect rein in front of the withers. Both reins are opposing forward movement of the horse. Their lateral effects on the forequarters cancel out, leaving the influence on the hindquarters of the right indirect rein behind the withers. The effect of this is to ask the horse to move his haunches to the left. His nose is already turned to the right and a leftward movement of the haunches would tend to straighten his spine. We encourage him to step to the left by putting a little more weight on the right knee and by tapping harder with the right leg. He may cross one hindleg in front of the other or he may just bring his right foot closer to the left. In any case he will then step out to the left with his left hindfoot, make a small forward step with the left forefoot and will lift and replace the right forefoot.

When you feel the haunches starting to move across to the left, you should apply the left leg aid, to encourage him to lift his left hindleg, and then apply steady pressure with your left leg to tell the horse to pause after making this one step in the desired direction. Relax, and reward him with your voice and by caressing his neck before asking for another step. Do not attempt too much at one time. The situation for the horse is a little unusual and he has a lot to assimilate.

Concentrate on feeling what the horse is doing. Make each step separately so that you can anticipate each stage in the movement of the horse, being ready to hold him in if he starts to move forward or to urge him on if he starts to back. Practise the turns in both directions, then take two steps round one way followed by two steps in the opposite direction. Finally, after one step, say to the left, step back again to the right.

This exercise is a first stage in teaching the horse to move away from your leg. This is not a natural reaction. Some horses will move toward your leg, particularly if you are wearing a spur. When at liberty, they will look for a tree or a post to rub themselves against to dislodge anything that is irritating the skin, so it is natural to push against the irritation of the spur. In making the turn on the forehand two signals tell the horse not to push back against your leg. In the first place we start with the head turned to one side so that he would need to bend even further to push against the leg aid. Secondly, we apply the indirect rein behind the withers. Even if he does not understand this at first, the intention becomes clear when it is applied on the side to which the head is already turned.

After several repetitions he comes to associate the leg aid with the response he is making naturally to the indirect rein behind the withers. Thereafter he will give the same response to the leg even if the rein aid is reduced. We consolidate this by asking for the turn on the forehand with less and less preliminary turning of the head, until eventually he will make the turn even when the head is first turned the opposite way. That is to say, he learns to move his haunches to the left, in response to the rider's right leg, even when his head is already turned to the left. This movement is the basis of all lateral work.

Do not overpractise the simple turn on the forehand because your horse may get into the undesirable habit of swinging his haunches whenever you ask him to bend his neck. When you set his head to the right, for example, he may move his haunches to the left, spinning round to follow his head, and keeping his body straight instead of developing a bend. In contrast, the turn on the forehand in which the haunches are moved to the same side as the head is a most valuable suppling exercise even though it is not at first easy to perform.

Haunches-in

A variation on the advanced form of the turn on the forehand is to call for a similar lateral displacement of the haunches while riding a circle. The commands for steering into the circle include a leg aid given behind the girth by the rider's outside leg. In the normal course the rider's leg would return to the regular position over the girth as soon as the horse has settled onto the circular path. To ask the horse to displace his haunches toward the inside of the circle in the manoeuvre known as 'haunches-in', the rider moves his outside leg back and applies a series of nudging leg aids just behind the girth. The knee of the rider's inside leg presses firmly into the saddle with the lower leg straight down. Meanwhile the rider gives indirect rein behind the withers with the outside rein and uses the inside rein in the direct rein position to maintain the inward bend of the horse's neck. The horse should step across into the circle with his hindlegs and thereafter the horse's feet should make two separate tracks, the hoofprints of the hindfeet falling on a slightly smaller circle than those of the forefeet. It is important to maintain plenty of impulsion to ensure that the rein aids have their proper effect.

Leg-yielding

Once the horse has learned to move away from the rider's leg in the context of the turn on the forehand and when turning a circle with haunches-in, the rider can start to use the leg aid on its own. We have already seen that if the horse is going straight ahead with symmetrical aids from leg, seat and reins, the effect of moving one hand toward the neck to give the indirect rein behind the withers is to cause the horse to incline sideways, moving both fore- and hindquarters to the side away from the rein, while continuing to aim his head and body in the same forward direction.

Some horses respond to the indirect rein behind the withers more readily than others. Those that do not at first move readily to the side can be encouraged to do so by giving active unilateral leg aids on the same side as the rein aid, provided that they have first been taught not to push back against the rider's leg. After practising this for some time on a straight track, give the unilateral leg aid without the rein aid. Your horse should now move diagonally to the side in response to the leg aid alone. This response is called 'leg-yielding'. It is convenient to practise this when hacking along quiet roads, asking the horse to move out to the middle of the road and then back to the side while all the time facing directly forward. The diagonal movement may be asked for either by the rein alone, using the indirect rein behind the withers, or by the leg aid alone, both hands being maintained in the direct rein position.

Steering the rein-back

When your horse has learned to respond to the leg aid applied on one side only, the other leg being inactive, and when you have made yourself familiar with the different responses you can produce with the rein, you will be in a position to improve the precision of all the manoeuvres already in your repertoire.

During the rein-back, for example, you will be alert for signs that the horse is going to deviate from the straight path. When he moves his haunches to one side, you can correct, both with the appropriate leg aid and by applying indirect rein behind the withers.

Rein-back balance

You should also be able to regulate the speed with which the horse steps back. Try to persuade him to pause after each step. The pattern of leg movements during the rein-back is not the same as that for forward walking. The horse tends to step back with a diagonal pair of legs rather than with one leg at a time. With a little practice you will be able to make him pause after a single step and then, instead of stepping back further, make him go forward again for a single step. The step back and the step forward are both performed with the same diagonal pair of legs, the other diagonal remaining on the ground. The horse balances backward and forward over the stationary diagonal. Repeat on the other diagonal.

A variation on this is to go straight into a rein-back from the forward walk, without pausing in between. This manoeuvre is achieved by judiciously balancing the effect of your restraining hand against the forward impulsion of your seat and legs. You may have found your horse doing this accidentally when you were really asking for a halt, but did not relax your pull on the rein at quite the right moment.

Turn on the haunches

For a straight rein-back your hands should be in the 'direct rein' position. If you move your hands to one side, the horse will step sideways with the forelegs and you can use your seat to hold him from stepping back with the hindlegs. He then executes a turn on the haunches, the forelegs moving round in a circle while the horse pivots on one of the hindlegs, which is replaced on the same spot each time it is lifted (*Figure 5.7*).

To make the turn on the haunches to the right, start by bracing your back to make sure the horse is fully alert. Then give opening rein with the right hand and at the same time give indirect rein in front of the withers with the left hand in the raised position. Keep up the impulsion with your seat and press the left knee sideways into the saddle. It may help to sit back a little to relieve the weight on the forequarters. The horse should step out to the side with his forelegs. Be content at first with a single step. Apply the right leg aid to tell the horse to halt, then relax and reward the horse.

Practise turns on the haunches in both directions, making the turn in a series of separate steps with pauses in between. It is easier to develop precision if you proceed slowly like this. Do not be in too much of a hurry.

The 'chain'

You build up precision in your control of the horse by insisting on a proper distinction between the turn on the forehand and the turn on the haunches. In each case the horse should pivot on a single leg, which is put down again on the same spot each time it is lifted. Do not be content with a sloppy turn in

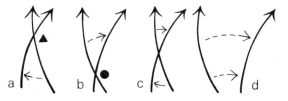

Figure 5.8 *Distinctions between kinds of turn. (a) Turn on the forehand, pivoting on a foreleg. (b) Turn on the haunches, pivoting on a hindleg. (c) Spin, or sloppy turn, with forelegs and hindlegs moving sideways in opposite directions. (d) Pirouette; forelegs and hindlegs both move sideways, but in the same direction. When the spin (c) is performed deliberately it is referred to as 'a turn on the centre'.*

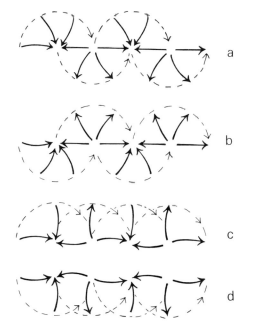

Figure 5.9 *Examples of the 'chain', a sequence of half-turns alternately on the forehand and on the haunches. (a) Turn to the right on the forehand, followed by turn to the left on the haunches, with change of bend. (b) Turn to the left on the forehand, followed by turn to the right on the haunches, with change of bend. (c) Turn to the right on the forehand, followed by turn also to the right on the haunches, the bend being to the right throughout. (d) As (c) but to the left. Great care is needed to preserve precision in cases (c) and (d) and to avoid the turns degenerating into spins.*

which the feet just tramp all over the place (*Figure 5.8*).

An elegant exercise which helps horse and rider to understand one another is the 'chain'. This is a sequence of half-turns carried out alternately on the forehand and on the haunches (*Figure 5.9*). As the horse pivots first on a foreleg and then on a hindleg, the succession of half-turns results in a progression. The hindlegs walk round a foreleg and then the forelegs walk round a hindleg. It is this succession of small semi-circles that gives the manoeuvre its name. The successive turns may be made in various ways. If you turn in alternate directions, you make either all the turns on the forehand to the right and all the turns on the haunches to the left or all the forehand turns to the left and all the turns on the haunches to the right, changing the bend for each half-turn. Alternatively, all the turns may be made in the same direction either to the right or to the left, pivoting alternately on the forehand and on the haunches, and keeping the same bend throughout.

The full pass

The discipline of carrying out the pivoting turns one step at a time leads directly into the 'full pass' (moving sideways without forward progression). Suppose that you make one step to the right with the forelegs, using the aids for a turn on the haunches, pause, and then make one step to the right with the hindlegs, using the aids for the turn on the forehand. The result is that the horse has stepped out to the right with all four legs.

The next stage is to alternate smoothly between the two sets of aids in order to reduce the duration of the pause. Then, instead of pivoting at each stride, he moves steadily to the side on two tracks in a direction at right angles to the long axis of his body. If the steps are large enough he should cross his legs, the left legs stepping over in front of the right legs. This exercise makes considerable demands on the horse and one should not ask for more than a few steps. The full pass should be practised to the left as well as to the right.

Gates

The rein-back balance, the pivoting turns on the forehand and on the haunches, and the full pass, all contribute to the mobility needed for opening and closing gates without dismounting. One can bring one's horse close up to the gate, and position the shoulders near the fastening. In leaning over to manipulate the fastening, be careful not to move your breastbone too far away from the horse's withers or you will lose your balance. If the horse moves, do not hold on to the gate, but let go and quickly move back into position on the saddle. Reposition the horse and start again.

After releasing the fastening ask your horse to move in an arc to follow the movement of the gate, backing if it opens toward you or edging forward if it opens away. Pass through the opening, pivoting round the end of the gate, if possible keeping a hand on it to prevent it swinging. Then move back with the gate to close it. Get your horse to stand close to the gatepost and to stand still while you do up the fastening. Pivot, turn away, and ride on. If your horse gets excited when he is close to the gate, do not persist, but dismount to deal with the gate and try again on another day. You can get into serious difficulties if your horse charges through the narrow gap left by inadequately opening a gate that opens toward you. If anything catches on the end of the gate as you go through, the horse will be trapped against the gatepost and all his efforts to get through will just pull the gatepost harder and harder into his side. He could injure himself, and you, very badly. However, once warned, you are less likely to allow yourself to drift into such a situation.

6 MORE ABOUT FINE CONTROL

In this chapter we consider in more detail how to set about persuading your horse to do just what you want, precisely on cue. I use the expression 'persuading' advisedly, since the task of controlling a horse is very different from that of controlling a mechanical vehicle, where steering-wheel, accelerator and brake each have separate functions. The reaction of the horse to any particular one of the rider's aids at a particular time depends on a number of factors. We need to take account of what the horse is already doing at the time the aid is applied, and also what other aids are being used in combination with it.

The horse is in full control of his own movements, so what he does depends on what he himself decides to do. If he is in co-operative mood, he may, but only if he feels like it, take account of the rider's movements that come to his attention. In the present context we are concerned primarily with signals that we apply to the horse with the intention of influencing his behaviour, and which are conveyed to him through his sense of touch. We need to build up the effectiveness of our signals by systematic practice with clear and unambiguous movements so that the horse will come to understand what is required of him.

The rider's hands can act in several different ways so that there are a large number of signals that can be communicated to the horse through the reins. What each signal means to the horse depends on what the horse happens to be doing at the time. Only a very few of these signals are really useful. The others are either meaningless or, worse still, downright confusing to the horse. You should, therefore, do your best to make sure that your signals are unambiguous and you should as far as possible avoid over-large or uncontrolled hand movements or unintentional changes in rein tension.

A common source of difficulty arises from the requirement in competitive dressage that the rider's aids should be inconspicuous to the onlooker. With this in mind, your instructor may keep telling you to hold your hands as still as possible. The problem is that, until you have established fluent communication with your horse using well-marked aids, he will not know what to do about your less distinct movements and you may get yourself into a muddle.

Before looking at the effects of aids in combination, we need to remind ourselves of the actions of the individual rein aids when each is applied on its own, without the reinforcement of the seat aids and leg aids.

Rein aids alone

Photo 6.1a illustrates the 'regular' position of the hands. Both hands are inactive in the direct-rein position and the horse is facing straight ahead. In this position your thumbs should be uppermost with the hands slightly rotated so that you can just see the tips of your fingers. Your wrists should be slightly bent inwards. Keep your wrists and arms supple and springy so that your hands can be carried freely forward and backward as required by the movements of the horse's head. It is essential that the position of your hands should be independent of the movements of your trunk. In this way you can keep a steady small tension in the rein without jerking it or allowing it to go slack.

In addition to this 'coming and going' with the nodding of the horse's head, you need to keep adjusting the length of the rein between your hands and the horse's mouth if your hands are not to be taken too far away from the 'ideal' position, just in front of the pommel. When the horse changes the posture of his head, you must either work your fingers up the rein, as in *Figure 1.14*, or allow the rein to slide a little through your fingers, as the situation demands, in order to be able to maintain the same steady tension at all times.

The responses to individual rein aids do not have to be specifically taught. Even an untrained horse, once in the right mood, will respond in the way described here, provided the aid is clear. This is where the problem usually lies. You need to take great care to distinguish between messages that are intended to produce different responses.

In studying the actions of the individual aids on their own, it is necessary to have the horse 'on the bit'. This means that you must first take steps to build up impulsion by working with your seat aids to drive the saddle forward while, at the same time, using your hands to keep the horse from actually accelerating forward. The effect of this is to make the horse more attentive to what you are doing. He becomes 'wound up' and eager to surge forward as soon as you indicate, by slightly reducing the rein tension, that this is permitted.

Effect of activity of hand

Each hand can be *active*, in the sense of giving the quiet alerting signal described in Chapter 2, or it can be *inactive*. In addition, your hand may (1) '*yield*', moving forward or backward to keep the same steady small tension in the rein in spite of the movements of the horse's head, or (2) '*restrain*', by increasing the rein tension, or (3) '*block*' the rein, by being held in much the same place relative to the saddle in spite of the horse's head movements. The effect of blocking the rein is that a forward movement of the horse's head is met with increasing resistance and a movement of the horse's mouth toward his chest is rewarded with a reduction in rein tension.

Consider the effects produced by your right hand alone, with your left hand inactive, and with the horse 'on the bit' and going forward steadily.

Photo 6.1a-d *Rein aids. Effect of hand position alone with the horse moving freely forward with his head pointing straight ahead. The hands are inactive in each case.* **(a)** *(above left) Both hands in the direct-rein position. The horse goes straight ahead. This is the 'regular' position for the hands. (In this photograph, the rider's wrists are somewhat bent back, in an attitude that tends to introduce undesirable stiffness into the control of the rein. It is preferable to hold the wrists straight or slightly bent inward.)* **(b)** *(above right) Right hand in opening-rein*

If the horse is responsive, he will tend to explore the 'feel' of the bit on the right side when your right hand is active, by extending his neck on that side. If your right hand 'yields', this allows the horse to bend his head to the left and, if you keep on with the aid, he will turn to the left.

If you make your right hand active, but not yielding, even perhaps momentarily increasing the rein tension and then keeping your hand in a fixed position, the horse will feel the inequality in pressure on the two sides of the bit and respond by turning his head to the right to equalise the pressure. If you keep on with the aid, he will turn to the right.

If you make both hands active and unyielding, the horse will tend to slow up unless you actively discourage this by increasing the intensity of your seat aids so as to develop increased impulsion. If you do not keep up the increased rein tension, the result will be a half-halt. A more insistent application of increased tension brings the horse to a full halt. Even further persistence with this rein aid produces a rein-back.

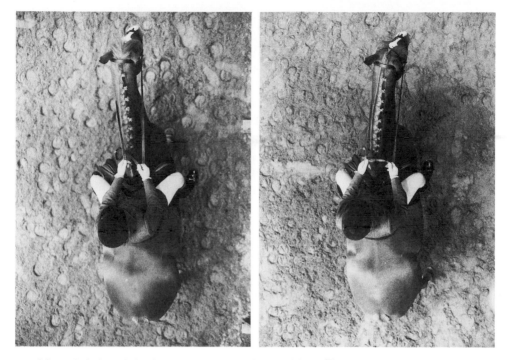

position, left hand in 'regular' direct-rein position. The horse turns to the right.
(c) *(above left) Right hand in direct-rein position, left hand in position for 'indirect rein in front of the withers'. The horse turns to the right.* ***(d)*** *(above right) Normal turn to the right. Both hands are moved a little to the right from their 'regular' position. Note that a much smaller movement is effective when both hands are used at the same time.*

If the horse pulls back strongly when you make your hands active and restrain with a positive increase in rein tension, you will have to allow the rein tension to drop suddenly to zero for a moment, to discourage the incipient tug-of-war. Immediately after the momentary slackening of tension, take up the previous rein tension again. When the horse responds by bringing his nose in, don't allow your hands to follow. The horse is then rewarded by a reduction in rein tension.

Effect of hand position

We now consider the way the horse responds to a change in the angle at which the rein pulls on the bit, as a separate effect from the response to changes in the rein tension. These responses have already been referred to briefly in the previous chapter. You need to have the horse going freely forward either at the walk or at the trot, again keeping up the impulsion by symmetrical seat aids and leg aids. Adjust the reins to have the horse's head pointing straight ahead with your hands symmetrical, just in front of the pommel and each about 6−7 centimetres from the midline. This is the 'regular' or direct-rein position already referred to (*Photo 6.1a*). Each of the reins will be roughly parallel to the horse's spine.

Now move your right hand out to the right a further 6 centimetres or so, into the opening-rein position (*Photo 6.1b*), keeping your left hand where it was and being careful not to vary the tension in the rein or the degree of activity of either hand. The horse will turn to the right, and will keep turning so long as your right hand stays in the opening-rein position. When you return your right hand to the direct-rein position, the horse will straighten out and carry on straight ahead.

The next hand position to try is the indirect rein in front of the withers. Starting with both hands in the direct-rein position and the horse going freely forward, move your left hand inward almost to the midline, leaving your right hand in the direct-rein position and without changing the tension in the rein on either side (*Photo 6.1c*). The horse again turns to the right and continues turning until your left hand returns to the direct-rein position. Try these two single-rein effects on the other side also.

Rein aids in combination

After convincing yourself that the horse will respond to a change in the position of one hand alone, try moving both hands at the same time a little to the right (*Photo 6.1d*). The horse will turn to the right. Notice that a much smaller movement is effective when you move both hands at the same time. This is, in fact, the normal rein aid for a turn to the right. It is usually supported by a unilateral leg aid with the left leg behind the girth, but it is instructive to observe that the horse will respond to the rein aid alone, and that he can detect even quite small changes in the position of the rider's hands.

Indirect reins

The actions of the indirect reins with active hands are quite complicated, since the position of the horse's head has to be taken into account. You can set the horse's head to one side or the other by judicious manipulation of the rein tension, slightly increasing the tension for a moment on one side while briefly easing the tension on the other side, or by making one hand momentarily more active or more resisting than the other. Once the head has moved, you can resume the symmetrical handling of the reins. There need be no change in the position of your hands as compared with the one you adopted with the horse's head facing straight ahead.

If the horse holds his head to one side at the walk, the effect of the changed weight-bearing activity of the two forelegs is to permit a freer forward swing of the foreleg on the opposite side. The horse reaches further forward with this leg and this causes him to veer in the direction toward which he has turned his head. As we have seen, you can produce this indirect steering action of the reins in several different ways: by making one hand more active than the other, by applying more tension with one hand than with the other, or merely by moving one hand laterally away from the direct-rein position.

Because the horse's neck is relatively long and supple, it can be bent in different directions in different places. Thus he can turn his head to the right while the part of his neck further back is turned a little way to the left. This is what happens when you move your right hand into the position for indirect rein behind the withers. The horse responds by stepping to the left both with his forefeet and with his hindfeet, in diagonally-forward progression on two tracks.

The indirect reins are usually applied in combination with leg aids, as we have already seen in the previous chapter in relation to the turns from the halt and the full pass. We now need to look in more detail at the different ways in which the horse can move laterally on two tracks.

Lateral work on two tracks

Exercises involving the 'lateral movements' were originally conceived as suppling exercises for the horse and, indeed, they are excellent for this purpose. It takes some skill on the part of the rider for the manoeuvres to be performed neatly and precisely on cue, and it is for this reason that these movements are included in the schedules for the more advanced dressage tests. An unfortunate consequence of this has been that many riders have come to think of the lateral movements as being primarily display manoeuvres appropriate only to the higher standards of competitive dressage. Many instructors will even discourage their pupils from attempting the movements until they have 'qualified' in competition at more elementary levels. This attitude deprives the non-competitive rider, and his horse, of the benefits to be gained from the exercises and of the satisfaction of being able to perform them successfully.

In these movements the horse moves diagonally forward and to one side with the axis of his trunk at an angle to the direction of travel. Forelegs and hindlegs follow two separate tracks as in leg-yielding. For competition purposes, the regulation angle at which the horse's body is inclined to the direction of progression corresponds to the diagonal between the quarter-markers in the 40 m dressage arena, for example from F to H or from D to E in *Figure 6.1*. The horse may be asked to proceed along a track parallel to the long sides of the arena while facing along a diagonal, or he may proceed along a diagonal while his body remains parallel to the long side of the arena. The head may be either to the right or to the left of the trunk. The horse's trunk may be held straight as in leg-yielding, or alternatively it may be bent either toward or away from the direction of progression. In proceeding from F to H in *Figure 6.1* with the head to the left of the track, the axis of the horse's body should be parallel to a line

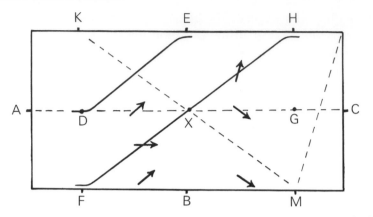

Figure 6.1 *Lateral work on two tracks. Relationships between the inclination of the axis of the horse's body to the direction of progression and to the sides and diagonals of the dressage arena. (See text.) On the diagonal from X to H, with the nose to the left of the track, the horse's body should be parallel to the dashed line from M to the corner between H and C, rather than parallel to the short side of the arena.*

from the quarter-marker at M to the corner of the arena between C and H, not parallel to the short side of the arena.

When riding on circles we ask the horse to bend as well as turn. In leg-yielding we ask for an inclined track without bending. The first stage in developing the other lateral movements is to teach the horse to perform the bend without change of direction.

The signal that tells the horse that he is to bend his spine sideways is made up of a combination of all the various things that the trained rider normally does when asking his horse to make a turn.

'Position' in the saddle

After you have learned to make both the turn on the forehand from the halt and the turn on the haunches from the halt, you will find that you naturally tend to take up an unsymmetrical position in the saddle whenever you want your horse to make a turn, even when he is going forward. Thus, for a turn to the right, you take up 'position right' as in *Figure 6.2*, and for a turn to the left you take up 'position left'. When you put more weight on one side of the saddle than on the other, the steering effect on the horse is similar to that on a skate-board, surf-board or ski. In each case the turn is towards the side of the increased downward pressure.

The expressions 'position right' and 'position left' are a useful shorthand for a particular combination of aids. 'Position right' means that you have your right leg on the girth with more weight on the right knee and right seat-bone than on the left, your left leg being behind the girth. Think of stretching your right leg

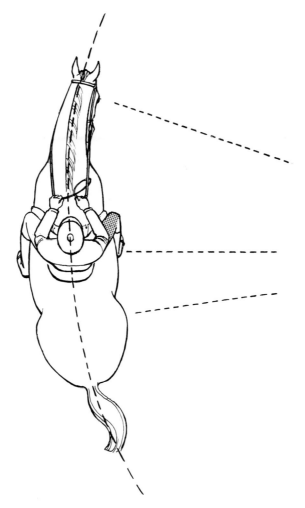

Figure 6.2 *'Position right'. The contribution of the rider to the development by the horse of the correct bend for a turn to the right. The rider puts more weight on his right seat-bone and right knee than on his left, but continues to sit upright, facing straight ahead, and without leaning over to the right. His right leg is maintained on the girth while his left lower leg is moved backward to a position behind the girth. The horse responds by bending his spine sideways. (In practice, apart from the bend in the neck, nearly all the bending of the horse's spine occurs in the lumbar region.) There should be no twist in the rider's spine, because this would interfere with the bracing action that is needed to drive the saddle forward for the maintenance of impulsion. When riding on a circle, the transverse axes (dotted lines) of the horse's withers, of the horse's hindquarters, and of the rider's shoulders and hips, should all meet at the centre of the circle round which the horse is progressing.*

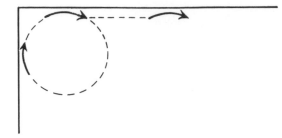

Figure 6.3 *Track to prepare for 'shoulder-forward'. After a small circle in the corner of the arena the horse is asked to proceed along the long side without losing the bend. The heavy arrows are schematic plan views of the horse to show the bend. In 'shoulder-forward' the horse's shoulders are slightly further from the wall than the hindquarters (see Figure 6.7) so that forefeet and hindfeet move on overlapping tracks.*

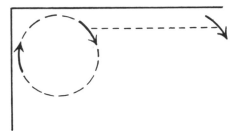

Figure 6.4 *Track to prepare for 'shoulder-in'. After a small circle in the corner of the arena the horse is asked to move out* after *the forequarters have already left the long side but while the hindquarters are still on the outside track. The horse proceeds along the long side of the arena with forelegs and hindlegs following distinctly separate tracks. The horse is bent* away from *the direction of progression. (Compare with Figure 6.5.)*

downward as though to push your heel well below your toe, without at the same time actually putting any more pressure on the stirrup. Although you are putting more weight on the right side to give this positional signal to the horse, you must be careful to keep your body centrally placed over the horse's midline, as in *Photo 2.10c*, and to sit facing squarely forward. If you allow your body to slip to one side, the horse will feel it and this will alter the signal that you are trying to convey to him through the saddle.

Many riders, including even some highly successful competitors, unintentionally allow their weight to move out of the midline when they are attempting lateral movements. This may be why they apparently have such difficulty in persuading their horses to bend properly.

Let us now look briefly at the different lateral movements in turn, and consider how the horse may be introduced to them, before analysing each of the individual movements in more detail.

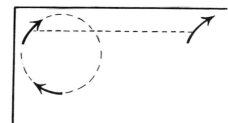

Figure 6.5   *Track to prepare for 'travers'. The command to leave the small circle in the corner of the arena is given* before *the hindquarters have reached the long side. The horse proceeds along the long side with the forelegs and hindlegs following distinctly separate tracks. The head is toward the wall and the body is bent* toward *the direction of progression. (Compare with Figure 6.4.)*

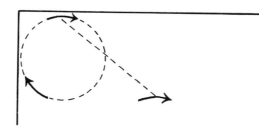

Figure 6.6   *Track to prepare for a half-pass along the diagonal. (Compare with Figure 6.4.)*

Shoulder-forward

To introduce this manoeuvre, start by making a small circle on the right rein in a corner of the arena, entering the corner from the short side, as in *Figure 6.3*. You will be sitting in 'position right' and you will be keeping the horse's head bent slightly to the right, using both hands in the direct-rein position, with your left hand a little in front of your right. Both your legs are inactive except when you need them to correct a tendency for the horse's haunches to wander from the true circle. You keep up the impulsion by applying your seat aid whenever necessary.

The aim now is to leave the circle where it touches the long side of the arena and to continue on a straight track without losing the bend. As you pass the corner, warn the horse to pay attention, by making a half-halt with seat and reins. Then, as you come onto the track along the side of the arena, move both hands briefly to the left, giving left opening rein and right indirect rein in front of the withers, but keep up the tension in both reins so as to hold the horse's head steady in its bend to the right. The horse should step off the circle with his forelegs. As soon as he does this, return your hands to the direct rein position and use your legs to keep the haunches following straight along

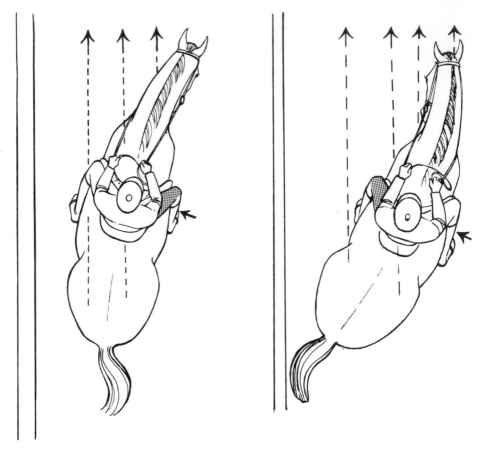

Figure 6.7   *(left) 'Shoulder-forward', top view. The right hindleg follows the left foreleg on overlapping tracks. (Compare with Figure 6.9. See also Figures 6.11 and 6.12.)*

Figure 6.8   *(right) 'Renvers', top view. The horse proceeds on two tracks, bent toward the direction of progression, exactly as in 'travers', except that in renvers the haunches are toward the wall while in travers it is the head that is toward the wall. If the same manoeuvre is carried out somewhere other than along a wall, it is referred to as a 'half-pass' (see Figure 6.6.)*

behind the forelegs (*Figures 6.7 and 6.11*). The horse should now proceed straight along the long side of the arena while his head remains turned to the right, with the rider continuing to sit in 'position right'.

Because of the bend, the horse has his left shoulder ahead of his right. The manoeuvre is therefore called 'shoulder-forward'. Forelegs and hindlegs follow overlapping tracks.

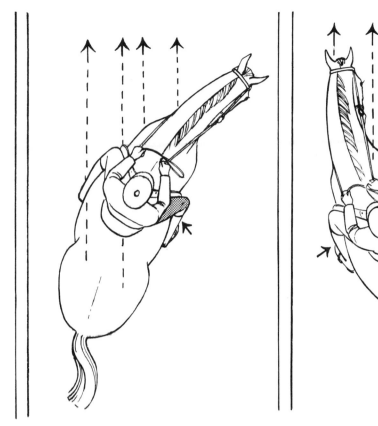

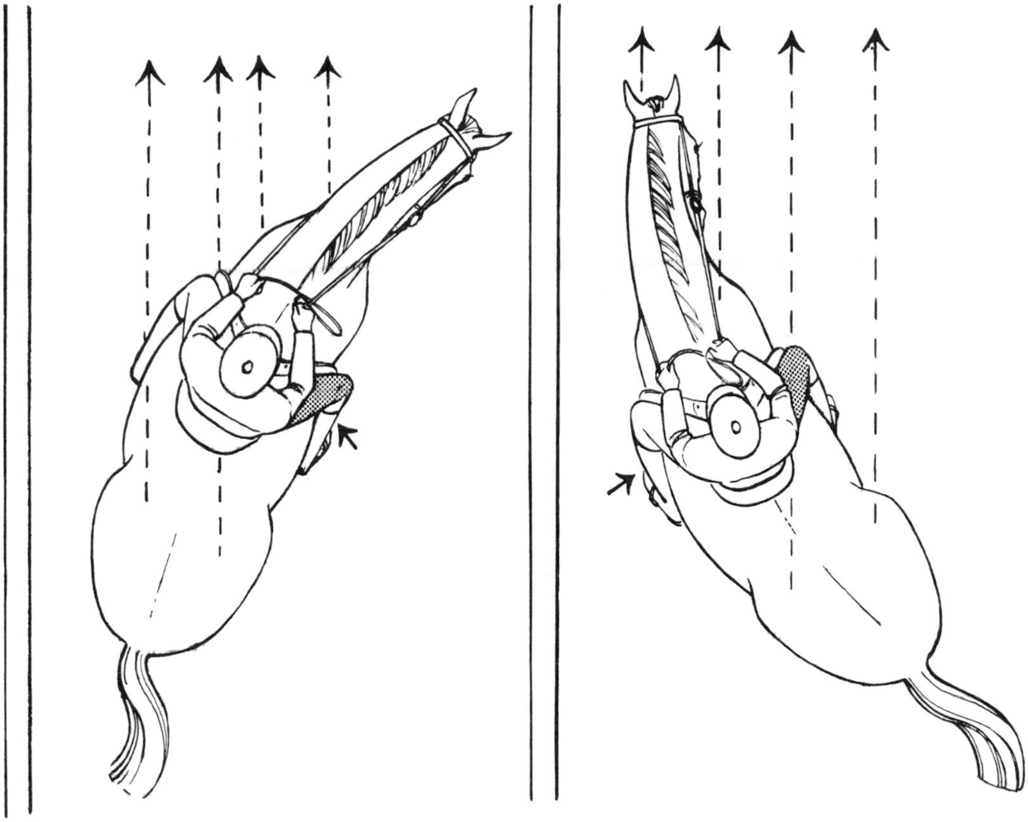

Figure 6.9 *(left) 'Shoulder-in', top view. Forelegs and hindlegs follow separate tracks, the track of the forelegs being nearer to the centre of the arena, i.e. the forelegs follow the 'inside track' along the side of the arena. (See also Figure 6.12. Compare with Figure 6.7.)*

Figure 6.10 *(right) 'Travers', top view. The horse proceeds on two tracks, bent toward the direction of progression. (Compare with Figure 6.9. See also Figures 6.12 and 6.13.)*

Shoulder-in

The preparation for the manoeuvre called 'shoulder-in' is similar to that for 'shoulder-forward', but this time the horse leaves the circle a little later. The half-halt is given as the horse reaches the long side of the arena and the commands for the horse to leave the circle are given after the forequarters have moved out onto the circle but while the hindlegs are still on the side track (*Figure 6.4*).

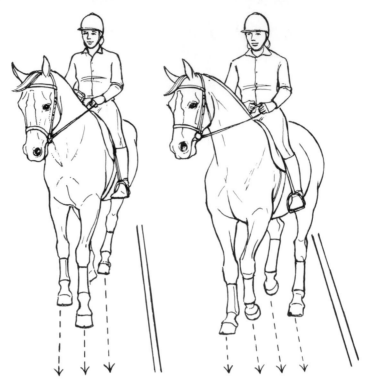

Figure 6.11 *(left)* *'Shoulder-forward', front view. Hoofprints form three tracks. (Compare with Figure 6.12.)*

Figure 6.12 *(right)* *'Shoulder-in', front view. Forefeet and hindfeet follow four distinctly separate tracks. (Compare with Figure 6.11. See also Figures 6.7 and 6.9.)*

Here again, both hands are moved briefly to the left while keeping up the tension in the rein to preserve the bend. The left hand gives opening rein and the right gives indirect rein, this time behind the withers, to encourage the hindlegs as well as the forelegs to step sideways. The right leg is strongly active on the girth to initiate the lateral progression as for the full pass. The left leg is held ready behind the girth to correct any tendency for the haunches to swing too far over to the left. The seat keeps up the impulsion, driving the horse forward into the bit to preserve the bend. As soon as the horse has stepped off the circle, the left hand returns to the direct-rein position, while the right hand continues to give indirect rein behind the withers. Forelegs and hindlegs follow distinctly separate tracks (*Figures 6.9 and 6.12*) parallel to the long side of the arena. The horse remains bent toward the inside of the arena, so that he is facing away from the direction of progression. In *Figures 6.9 and 6.12* he is on the right rein with his right shoulder in. This movement is called 'shoulder-in to the right' although the horse is actually moving to the left.

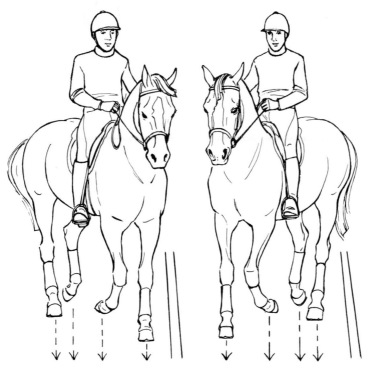

Figure 6.13 *(left) 'Travers', front view. Forefeet and hindfeet follow distinctly separate tracks, with the body bent toward the direction of progression. (Compare with Figure 6.14.)*

Figure 6.14 *(right) 'Renvers', front view. The movement is the same as for travers except that the haunches are toward the wall. (See also Figure 6.12, shoulder-in, where the bend is away from the direction of progression.)*

Travers

If the command to leave the circle is given before the horse has reached the long side of the arena (*Figure 6.5*), the horse will proceed on two tracks to his right instead of to his left. He is still bent toward the inside of the arena but this time his head is facing toward the direction of progression instead of away from it.

The warning half-halt is given as the horse approaches the short side and the commands to leave the circle are given as the horse reaches the corner. The right hand gives opening rein and the left gives indirect rein behind the withers. The outside leg is applied strongly behind the girth, as for a full pass. Instead of continuing round the circle onto the long side of the arena, the horse steps sideways, cutting across the circle with his hindlegs. The rider's right hand returns to the direct-rein position as soon as the horse has started stepping to the side, while the left keeps up the indirect rein behind the withers (*Figure 6.10*). The right leg is clear of the horse's side but it is held ready to check any tendency for the horse to swing his haunches to the right (*Figure 6.13*).

Half-pass

If all the commands just described for initiating the travers are applied later in the circle, when the horse has already reached the long side of the arena, this will make him move sideways diagonally across the arena (*Figure 6.6*). He will be bent to the right and his long axis will be parallel to the long side of the arena. This movement is called a 'half-pass'. It differs from the travers only in the direction of progression. The movement is called 'travers' when the horse's head traverses along the long side of the arena or along the wall of an enclosed school. In the open, away from the wall, the movement is referred to as a half-pass. Notice that both in travers and in half-pass the horse is bent toward the direction of progression while in shoulder-in he is bent away from the direction of progression.

Transitions in lateral work

There are three types of transition between the various movements on two tracks. In the first place one may change the inclination of the horse's body to the direction of progression while preserving the same bend throughout, passing, for example, from shoulder-in to the left through shoulder-forward to a half-pass to the left (*Figure 6.15*), or from half-pass to the right to shoulder-in to the right, and so on. Alternatively, one may keep the horse facing in the same direction and with the same bend while changing the direction of progression as in performing the counter change of hand (*Figure 6.16*), changing from a half-pass to the left through shoulder-forward to shoulder-in to the left. Yet another possibility is to change the bend while continuing on the same line of progression and without changing the inclination of the horse's body (*Figure 6.17*), changing from half-pass to the right through leg-yielding to the right and finishing with shoulder-in to the left. Or we may pass from shoulder-in through leg-yielding to the half-pass.

Thus we may start with the horse's head to one side or the other of the direction of progression and bent either to the right or to the left. Thereafter we may change the way the horse is facing, or change the direction of progression, or change the bend. Furthermore, each of these transitions can be executed either at the walk or at the trot. Even greater variety is available if we include progression at the canter (*Chapter 8*).

Figure 6.15 *Change of inclination without change of bend, proceeding in the same direction throughout.* **(a)** *Shoulder-in to the left, shoulder-forward, and half-pass to the left.* **(b)** *Half-pass to the right, shoulder-forward, shoulder-in to the right.*

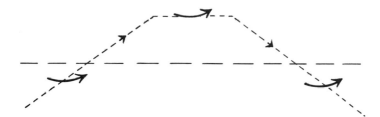

Figure 6.16 *Change of direction of progression with change of inclination, but without change of bend. Half-pass along a diagonal to the left, shoulder-forward parallel to the long side of the arena, shoulder-in to the left along a diagonal to the right, as in the counter change of hand. The axis of the horse's body remains parallel to the long side of the arena and he is bent to the left throughout.*

Figure 6.17 *Change of bend while continuing along the same track without changing the inclination of the horse's body to the direction of progression. Half-pass to the right, leg-yielding to the right, followed by shoulder-in to the left.*

Renvers

After practising the various transitions in lateral work we may arrive at the position shown in *Figure 6.8*. Here the horse is progressing along the long side of the arena, both bent and facing in the direction of progression, and with his haunches toward the wall or to the outside of the arena. This movement is called 'renvers'. So far as the horse is concerned, it is a version of the half-pass, like travers, but this time with haunches to the wall instead of head to the wall (*Figure 6.14*). It differs from shoulder-in (*Figure 6.12*) in that the horse is bent toward the direction of progression rather than away from it. The renvers movement differs from all other types of lateral movement in that it cannot be developed from the circle. It is produced either by a change of bend from straight ahead along the wall, or from an incompleted turn on the haunches executed with the hindlegs on the outside track alongside the wall (*Figure 6.18*).

When working on the long side of the arena, either in travers or in renvers,

Figure 6.18 *Development of renvers from a half-turn on the haunches executed alongside the wall.*

the long axis of the horse's body makes only a small angle with the direction of progression. Accordingly, because of the bend, the horse's forequarters remain more or less square-on to the track and the forelegs move directly forward while the hindlegs step diagonally to one side. When performing the half-pass in the open, it is possible to increase the angle between the long axis of the horse and the direction of progression until the forelegs as well as the hindlegs are stepping diagonally out to the side. This is achieved by moving the inside rein across to act, momentarily, in front of the withers, while the outside rein continues to act behind the withers. Meanwhile the outside leg remains strongly active behind the girth. (Here 'inside' and 'outside' relate to the bend of the horse.) Then, in a fully developed half-pass to the right, the horse may begin to cross his legs, the left feet (fore and hind) stepping across in front of the corresponding right feet.

Competitive dressage

The various movements on two tracks and the transitions between them provide excellent opportunities for developing one's skill in communicating one's wishes to the horse and for practising one's alertness to what the horse is about to do at each stage. It should be pointed out, however, that it is very difficult for a rider to appreciate on his own what kind of image he presents to an onlooker. When you enter for a competition you will be entirely in the hands of the judges. The art of marking dressage competitions is handed down by oral tradition and no amount of verbal definition can eliminate the subjective element of the personal impression made on the judge. Accordingly, if you wish to compete, it is essential to enlist the help of an experienced judge who knows what to look for and who can point out to you aspects of your performance that are visible to the onlooker but of which you yourself may be unaware. It is only after your attention has been drawn to a particular movement or habitual posture that you can start on remedial work.

It is instructive to read over the 'Object and General Principles' section in the official BHS Dressage Rules. The aim is that the horse should achieve perfect balance and extreme lightness in all his actions. He should give the impression of doing of his own accord what is required of him. Accordingly the aids given by the rider should be, so far as possible, imperceptible to the onlooker. Such perfection is achieved only after diligent practice.

The progressive series of official dressage tests do not include lateral work until a fairly advanced stage. The Preliminary, Novice, and most of the Elementary tests are concerned only with steering and with changes of gait or of speed, the emphasis being on the smoothness with which the horse performs what is asked of him.

The schooling whip

The horse has to be taught how to respond to unsymmetrical leg aids. This is a fairly straightforward task when you are making the turns from the halt, either on the forehand or on the haunches, but problems may arise if you have taught yourself to be inconspicuous with your aids before your horse has been introduced to lateral work. He may not understand what is required of him when you use your leg aids to produce lateral movement at the same time as you are also using the leg aids for steering the forward progression.

One way to resolve the difficulty without having recourse to exaggerated rein aids is to use a schooling whip. This is a very flexible whip, something over a metre long, with a very short lash. It is used discreetly to draw the horse's attention to a particular leg by gently tapping the appropriate leg as low down as possible. On no account should the whip be used with any vigour, because the horse will easily become alarmed and he will no longer be in a suitable frame of mind to absorb instruction. Once he has been introduced to the whip he will pay attention to the whistling sound of the lash moving through the air as well as to the sight of the movement itself and there will be no need for the whip actually to make any contact at all with his body. It is, of course, always very important when using a whip not to jerk the bit.

You may prefer to keep the reins in one hand, using the whip with the other hand. In which case, the modified grip (*Figure 6.19*) may be preferred to that shown in *Figure 1.21*. The spare portions of both reins lie together over the forefinger. It is a simple matter to shorten rein without disturbing the bit. One simply pulls on the loop of spare rein with the other hand. If one rein needs to be shortened more than the other, you shorten both and then allow the appropriate rein to slip a little.

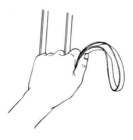

Figure 6.19 *Modified single-handed grip on the rein. The two reins lie side by side, emerging over the forefinger together, where they are gripped by the thumb. Separation for steering is provided by the second, third and fourth fingers.*

┌7┐ AIDS IN COMBINATION

We are now in a position to resume our detailed study of the actions of the aids in combination, starting with some examples of the actions of the indirect rein.

Example 1 – Turn on the forehand

Start with the horse at the halt, maintaining a fair amount of impulsion by combining your seat aids with restraining hands, and set the horse's head to the right. Move your left hand to the position for indirect rein in front of the

Photo 7.1a-d *Rein aids in combination, with the horse's head to the right, after building up a certain degree of impulsion. (a) (left) Right indirect rein behind the withers, hand active and restraining. Left indirect rein in front of the withers, hand inactive and restraining. The horse executes a turn on the forehand to the right. (b) (right) Right opening rein, hand active and restraining. Left indirect rein in front of the withers, hand active and restraining. The horse executes a turn on the haunches to the right.*

withers and continue to restrain but don't allow the rein tension to fluctuate. At the same time move your right hand to a position about half-way between the direct-rein position and the horse's midline (*Photo 7.1a*). This is the position for indirect rein behind the withers. The line of the rein should point to the horse's left hip. Now make the right hand active while continuing to restrain. The horse will step out to the left with his hindlegs, starting to make a turn on the forehand to the right and pivoting on his right foreleg. Reinforce the request for a turn with a leg aid behind the girth on the right. Let your left hand yield momentarily to allow the horse to make a small step with the forelegs, placing the right foreleg, after this step, in the same place as before. Do not ask for a second sideways step until the horse has lifted and replaced the leg on which he is pivoting, otherwise he is liable to twist this leg and strain it.

Example 2 – Turn on the haunches

Start as above, with the horse at the halt, with the horse's head to the right, and with a good deal of impulsion. Again bring your left hand to the position for

(c) *(left) Right opening rein, hand active and yielding. Left indirect rein behind the withers, hand active and yielding. The horse executes a half-pass to the right, stepping out diagonally forward and to the right.* *(d)* *(right) Right indirect rein in front of the withers, hand active and yielding. Left opening rein, hand active and yielding. The horse executes a right shoulder-in, stepping out diagonally forward and to the left, with the head still bent to the right.*

indirect rein in front of the withers but this time make it active as well as restraining. Move your right hand to the opening-rein position, making it also active and restraining (*Photo 7.1b*). The horse will step to the right with his forelegs, and will start to make a turn on the haunches, pivoting on his right hindleg. You complete the turn by supporting the rein aids with a leg aid on the girth on the left side. Again you need to make sure that he makes a step with his pivoting hindleg before asking for a second sideways step with his forelegs.

Example 3 – Half-pass

For this example, have the horse moving freely forward with his head to the right. Move your right hand to the opening-rein position, as in the previous example, but this time allow it to yield as well as making it active. With your left hand give indirect rein behind the withers, and make this hand active and allow it to yield (*Photo 7.1c*). The active yielding hands, in combination with the impulsion from the seat aids, encourage forward progression. The horse responds to the position of your hands by stepping out diagonally forward and to the right, with all four legs in the appropriate sequence, in a half-pass. You can encourage the movement by applying your leg aid on the left behind the girth.

Example 4 – Shoulder-in

Here have the horse again moving freely forward with his head turned to the right. This time move your left hand to the opening-rein position, make it active and allow it to yield. At the same time move your right to the indirect-rein position in front of the withers, and make it also active and yielding (*Photo 7.1d*). The horse will step out diagonally forward and to the left with all four legs in sequence. As the head is to the right, this is the start of a shoulder-forward or a shoulder-in to the right. It is usual to reinforce the request for this movement by active leg aids, with your right leg on the girth and your left leg behind the girth, to encourage the horse to bend his spine to the right.

Strictly speaking, if he makes a lateral movement without bending his spine, the movement should be classified as merely 'leg-yielding', rather than half-pass or shoulder-in, no matter to which side the horse has bent his neck.

Bends

Exercise in the lateral movements can play an important role in the horse's athletic development. For example, in right shoulder-in, where the horse moves diagonally forward and to the left, he has to step to the side with his left legs and he has to bring his right legs across under his body. To get the full benefit from the exercise, he should, at the same time, bend his spine to the right, in the way he would naturally bend it when making a small circle to the right.

Photo 7.2a-b *The bend in the horse's spine during attempts at renvers. The direction of progression is indicated by the dotted arrow. **(a)** (left) The rider is relying too much on the reins and, in consequence, the horse's neck is strongly bent, while there is virtually no bend at all in the horse's trunk. **(b)** (right) The bend in the horse's trunk is indicated by the dotted lines.*

The meaning of 'the horse's bend'

In the context of lateral work, the expression 'bend' is used to refer to what the horse is doing with his trunk. A bend of the neck alone is of much less interest (*Photo 7.2a*). The presence of the rib-cage greatly restricts the amount of lateral bending that can occur in the chest region, so the bend we are concerned with is that taking place in the horse's lumbar region, behind the saddle (*Photo 7.2b*). The effect of this bend is to turn the haunches to one side, enabling the horse to reach forward with the inside hindleg when executing a turn. He will also tend to reach forward with his outside foreleg, so that his outside shoulder will be further forward than his inside shoulder. Since the shoulders are not articulated with the spine, he can move his shoulders without bending his spine. This movement of the shoulders does contribute, however, in conjunction with the movement of the haunches, to the apparent bend, as seen by an onlooker.

If you have not been in the habit of attending to the way your horse bends his spine, you may find that he very often doesn't seem to bother. The corresponding habitual lack of suppleness in the horse's back can cause problems with other manoeuvres, especially those to be described in the next chapter. He may, for instance, obstinately strike off on the wrong lead when you call for a canter, or he may be awkward to manoeuvre round the tight turns involved in a jumping competition.

Let us look now at some routines that will help you in developing your horse's suppleness. All these routines can be executed at walk, trot, or canter. The walk allows more time for the rider to study the horse's reactions and to pay particular attention to the precise timing of the aids, but the horse may find some of the movements easier at the trot.

Bending routines

First of all, you need to establish smooth forward progression, without the hindlegs wandering from the track of the forelegs. You can do this best when riding a large circle. Take care to ride a true circle all the way round. Make sure there are no straight portions and avoid making an oval. It is better to work on a circle instead of just riding round the arena, since, on a circle, you will not have to adjust the steering and it is therefore easier to develop an uninterrupted steady rhythm. When you are satisfied that this has been achieved, make a definite shift to a new circle of smaller diameter, say one metre inside the original circle. Again pay attention to riding a true circle. Keep going steadily forward on the new circle until the horse has settled to the new rhythm, then move in again onto an even smaller circle. Then alternate between sequences of diminishing circles and sequences of circles of increasing diameter.

The horse may tend to go forward more slowly in the smaller circles and you have to be on the look-out for signs of flagging and to take prompt steps to maintain the forward speed.

Because the BHS Dressage Rules call for the wearing of spurs for all tests of Medium standard and above, many riders, once they have attained this standard, get into the habit of using their spurs all the time for the routine maintenance of impulsion. Another habit that sometimes develops at this stage is that of allowing the knee to come off the saddle, ostensibly to maintain better contact of the lower leg with the side of the horse. If you fall into the trap of developing these two habits, you will find that they combine to introduce undesirable uncertainty into the tracking by the horse's hindquarters. This may show up in the irregularity of the circles.

The reason for this complication is that, inevitably, the spur acts behind the girth. It will come about, equally inevitably, that the action of your spurs is not quite the same on the two sides because, since you do not have the security of constant knee contact at your disposal, you have to use your lower legs to help maintain your balance. The horse, of course, cannot distinguish those movements of your legs that are intended as signals from other movements that are merely part of your struggle to keep your balance. When going forward, the horse responds to any inequality in the leg aids behind the girth by moving his haunches away from the more emphatic signal, particularly if this is being reinforced with the spur. It is no surprise, therefore, that those riders who have adopted this way of applying their leg aids find it hard to obtain much of a distinct bend either in shoulder-in or in half-pass. Both manoeuvres come out as indistinguishable from leg-yielding, apart from the bend in the horse's neck. They may also find that an attempt at a turn on the haunches comes out as a spin, with the horse stepping out sideways with the outside hindleg.

It is preferable to keep your knees in light contact with the saddle at all times and to use the seat aids rather than the leg aids to maintain the impulsion. The seat aids do not give rise to problems of lateral uncertainty. Your lower legs are then available to give delicately adjusted unilateral signals, and any tendency the horse may have to wander sideways with his hindlegs can be promptly corrected. The leg aid with the inside leg should never be reinforced with the spur, since what is required here, to maintain impulsion at the same time as encouraging the bend, is a leg aid *on* the girth, rather than one *behind* the girth. The vertical form of the leg aid, pressing down on the stirrup with the inside foot, does not carry the same risk of misinterpretation by the horse.

During a sequence of diminishing circles it will be natural for the horse to bend his spine more when making the smaller circles. You encourage this with unsymmetrical leg aids, with your inside leg on the girth and your outside leg behind the girth. When applying these leg aids, put a little more weight on your inside seat-bone. This puts you in an unsymmetrical position in the saddle (see 'Position right', *Figure 6.2*). In spite of this asymmetry, you should be careful to keep your head and shoulders facing forward along the line of the horse's axis.

The horse feels the effect of your posture through the contact of the saddle with his back, and he comes to associate this feel with the bending of his own spine. By maintaining the unsymmetrical leg aids and the unsymmetrical position of your seat in the saddle, you encourage the horse to maintain the bend in his spine even when the circles are made larger again. Then, each time the circles are diminished, the horse is prompted to increase his bend. You should ride concentric circles, both diminishing and increasing, repeatedly, and on both reins, until the circles are all perfectly round. This gives you practice in accurate tracking. Here you may find the assistance of a helper on the ground to be useful. He can tell you whether the footfalls of the hindfeet fall precisely on the same circle as the footfalls of the forefeet. When you have achieved this precision on the circles, you can intensify the exercise by riding the circles in the haunches-in position.

The horse now proceeds round the circle on two tracks, the hindlegs following a slightly smaller circle than the forelegs. The pirouette is just an extreme example of a very small circle ridden on two tracks in the haunches-in position. The track of the hindlegs at the pirouette may be a circle as small as about half a metre in diameter or even less.

The object of these circling exercises is to develop the flexibility of the lumbar part of the horse's spine. There is no virtue in riding round crab-wise without a definite bend and there is, in fact, a particular disadvantage in allowing the horse to form a habit of drifting inward with his quarters when not being specifically asked to move on two tracks. If the inward drift of the hindquarters were to occur when riding a circle in a dressage test, it would be marked down as a definite fault.

As the circles get smaller, the horse, being in the haunches-in position, is constrained to increase his bend, and you can become accustomed to the consequent change in the 'feel' in the saddle. The horse gives the appearance of bending round the rider's inside knee. The small circle with haunches-in is a clear demand for a good bend. Accordingly, these exercises are worth a good deal of repetition, working on left rein and right rein alternately. Only when the bend has been established on the circle, will it be time to try to improve the precision of your lateral work.

Routine for encouraging the bend in lateral work

Start by riding 10-metre circles on the left rein at the walk. Then, when you arrive at a position on the circle where you are facing the long side of the arena, make two steps of left shoulder-in. This will take you two steps to the right onto a new track (*Figure 7.1a*). Continue on the new 10-metre circle. When again facing the long side after completing the next circle, make two steps of half-pass to the left, returning to and continuing along the original circle (*Figure 7.1b*). After repeating this sequence a few times, ride a figure-of-eight to change the rein to a new 10-metre circle, and perform the same routine on the other rein: when facing the long side, take two steps of right shoulder-in, and continue on a circle displaced to the left; then, after completing the circle, and when next facing the long side, take two steps of half-pass to the right, continuing on the original circle; and so on, repeating on one rein then on the

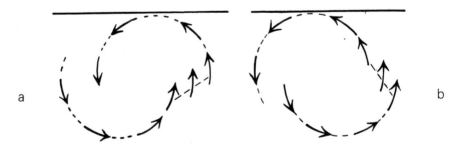

Figure 7.1 *Track to encourage the bend in lateral work by shifting the circle. The heavy arrows are schematic plan views of the horse to show the bend. (a) During the approach to the side of the arena while riding a 10 m circle on the left rein, two steps are executed at left shoulder-in, to displace the circle toward the right. (b) Two steps half-pass to the left, executed during the approach to the side of the arena, shift the 10 m circle to the left. Care is taken to preserve, during each of the lateral movements, the bend in the horse's spine that is natural to the circle.*

other. All the bends are those appropriate to the circles.

When you are using one leg to call for a lateral movement, it may help if you move the other leg out of contact with the horse's side for a moment. This emphasises the asymmetry in the leg aids. Your knees will need to be kept in light contact with the saddle throughout. The bend should be retained during the lateral steps, which should be carried out with the horse continuing to face the same direction throughout. He should not start to veer again until he is put onto the new circle.

When riding on the right rein with the horse bent to the right, it will be natural for you to adopt 'position right' (*Figure 6.2*) because of the way you are applying your leg aids. Similarly you will be in 'position left' when riding on the left rein. A change in bend thus calls for a change in your position in the saddle. After some practice this association begins to operate in reverse; a change in your position in the saddle now indicates to the horse that you want him to change his bend. Here is a routine to help in establishing this command.

Routine to practise changing the bend

Walk round the arena on the right rein. When you emerge from the corner after one of the short sides, ride right shoulder-in for five steps (*Figure 7.2*). Straighten the horse while retaining the inclination to the track, and proceed in leg-yielding to the left for five steps. Change to position left to produce the left bend and proceed in renvers to the left for five steps. Again straighten the horse

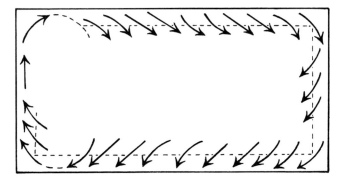

Figure 7.2 *Track for practising the change of bend without change of inclination to the direction of progression. On the right rein throughout: start at the top left-hand corner of the figure and execute, in sequence: a corner, right shoulder-in, leg-yielding to the left, renvers to the left, leg-yielding to the left, right shoulder-in, corner, right shoulder-in along the short side, change of direction without change of bend, travers to the right, leg-yielding to the right, left shoulder-in on the right rein, leg-yielding to the right, travers to the right, corner, emerging along the short side in travers to the right. The pattern may be repeated. Alternatively, after a half-volte and change of hand, a corresponding pattern may be ridden on the left rein.*

while retaining the inclination, and proceed in leg-yielding to the left for five steps. Change to position right and ride right shoulder-in until the corner. Continue in right shoulder-in along the short side. At the next corner, make a change of direction without change of bend and proceed in travers down the long side for five steps. Straighten the horse, retaining the inclination to the track, and proceed in leg-yielding to the right for five steps. Change to position left and ride left shoulder-in (facing the outside of the arena) for five steps. Straighten the horse, retaining the inclination, and proceed in leg-yielding to the right for five steps. Change to position right and proceed in travers to the right to the next corner and along the short side, emerging in right shoulder-in along the long side. Repeat as above. Eventually, ride a figure-of-eight to change the rein and ride the corresponding pattern on the left rein.

The aim here is to make clearly marked distinctions between the bends for shoulder-in and for half-pass. Notice that the diagonal progression is *away from* the bend in shoulder-in and *toward* the bend in half-pass, while leg-yielding is executed without significant bend to either side.

Distinctions between lateral movements

There are several manoeuvres in which the horse progresses diagonally forward and to one side (*Figure 7.3*). These are distinguished according to the nature and direction of the bend of the horse's spine. When the horse bends his spine to one side in these manoeuvres, he also holds his head turned slightly to that side.

A diagonal progression without significant bend is referred to as leg-yielding (*Figure 7.3f*). Where the horse is bent *toward* the direction of progression, this is a half-pass (*Figures 7.3a-c*), while in shoulder-in (*Figure 7.3d*) and shoulder-forward (*Figure 7.3e*), he is bent *away from* the direction of progression.

Travers, renvers and half-pass are all identical movements so far as the horse is concerned. Travers is a half-pass along the side of the arena with the head toward the outside of the arena (*Figure 7.3a*). Thus, on the right rein, travers is a half-pass to the right. Renvers is also a half-pass along the side of the arena, but with the haunches to the outside (*Figure 7.3b*). On the right rein, renvers is a half-pass to the left.

In right shoulder-in along the side of the arena on the right rein, the horse is bent, and faces, to the right, and progresses diagonally forward and to the left, with the forelegs on the inner track (*Figure 7.3d*).

The distinction between shoulder-in and shoulder-forward (*Figure 7.3e*) depends on the inclination of the horse's axis to the direction of progression. For appropriate steering you adjust the position of your right hand and alter the intensity of your leg aids on one side or the other as occasion demands. In the shoulder-forward manoeuvre (*Figure 7.3e*), the bend of the horse makes it possible for his hindquarters to move forward along the outside track while his forequarters, on an inner track, move diagonally forward and to the left. The

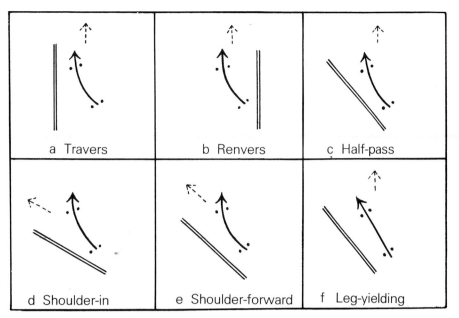

Figure 7.3a–f *Relationships between lateral movements: schematic plan views of a horse (heavy arrows), bent to the right in (a)–(e), straight in (f). The direction of progression (dotted arrow) is inclined at 30° to the horse's axis, except in (e). In (a), (b) and (c) the horse is bent toward the direction in which he is moving. In (d) and (e) the horse is bent away from the direction in which he is moving. The proximity of a long side of the arena (wall) is indicated by the double lines.* **(a)** *Travers (head to wall), on the right rein.* **(b)** *Renvers (tail to wall), on the left rein.* **(c)** *Half-pass to the right (along the diagonal from K to M).* **(d)** *Right shoulder-in, on the right rein: hindlegs and forelegs follow four separate tracks.* **(e)** *Shoulder-forward on the right rein: the inside hindleg (R) follows the same track as the outside foreleg (L).* **(f)** *Leg-yielding to the right, along a diagonal: no significant bend.*

footprints form three tracks. For shoulder-in, the forequarters are brought further away from the outside track, and the hindquarters as well as the forequarters move diagonally forward and to the left. The footprints form four tracks (*Figure 7.3d*).

Combined aids for the individual lateral movements

To achieve full precision in the execution of the various lateral movements you will need to combine the actions of aids with your seat, with your weight, with your legs, and with your reins. It is essential in all this work that you should first ensure that you have built up adequate impulsion by driving the saddle forward with the seat-bones, while at the same time using your reins with carefully restraining hands until the horse is clearly eager to surge forward as soon as your rein signal permits. In a well-trained horse, a simple half-halt will be sufficient reminder of what is required.

The basis of all lateral movements is the horse's response to the application of an unsymmetrical leg aid. You make a succession of nudging movements with your lower leg on one side while your other leg is comparatively inactive. The horse moves away from your active leg.

The simplest of the lateral movements is leg-yielding, in which the horse moves diagonally forward and to one side, away from the rider's active unilateral leg aid, without bending his spine. He may turn his head to one side or the other, or he may continue to face straight ahead.

The aids for **leg-yielding to the right** are as follows (*Figure 7.3f*):

- The rider sits symmetrically, both legs on the girth, and both reins in the direct-rein position.
- The rider gives the seat aid to call for a half-halt.
- The middle fingers of the left hand are gently closed on the rein to produce a slight increase in rein tension on that side while the right hand yields, inducing the horse to turn his head slightly to the left.
- The rider's left leg applies active nudging movements on the girth while the right leg, also on the girth, is inactive but is held in readiness either to encourage forward progression or to restrain any excessive movement to the side.
- Both hands, in the direct-rein position, are active and yielding to encourage forward progression.
- To initiate the movement, the left hand may move momentarily to give indirect rein behind the withers, thereafter returning to the direct-rein position.

Note that, if the rider's left leg is allowed to slip back, and particularly if, at the same time, his weight is allowed to slip over to the right, the horse will make a normal turn to the right instead of moving diagonally forward and to the right without changing the direction in which he is facing.

For **leg-yielding to the left** interchange 'left' and 'right' above.

In all other lateral movements, the horse is required to bend his spine in the same way as he would spontaneously bend it in making a turn. The bend is induced by the rider adopting an asymmetrical posture in the saddle, referred to as 'position right' or 'position left' as the case may be (page 162). For *position right*, the rider puts more weight on the right seat-bone and right knee and moves his left leg backward to a position behind the girth while keeping his right leg on the girth. The horse responds by bending his spine (*Photo 7.2b*). The rider at this stage adjusts his posture to keep his shoulders square to the axis of the horse, which for this purpose may be taken to run from the centre of the horse's withers to the centre of his hindquarters. This combination of changes in the rider's posture alters the feel of the saddle on the horse's back and it is this signal that induces the horse to bend his spine as required.

The aids for a **half-pass to the right**, **travers on the right rein**, or **renvers on the left rein** are as follows (*Figures 7.3a, 7.3b, and 7.3c*):

- The rider gives the seat aid to call for a half-halt.
- The rider gently closes the middle fingers of his right hand to produce a small increase in rein tension on that side, while yielding with the left hand. This induces the horse to turn his head slightly to the right.
- The rider adopts 'position right', with weight on the right seat-bone and right knee, and with the left leg back behind the girth and the right leg on the girth.
- The rider applies active nudging movements with his left leg behind the girth, while his right leg is maintained on the girth, inactive but held in readiness either to encourage forward progression or to restrain any excessive movement to the side.
- The left hand initiates the movement by giving indirect rein behind the withers with the hand active and resisting.
- The right hand maintains an appropriate balancing rein tension to preserve the bend in the horse's neck and gives opening rein at the beginning of the movement, thereafter direct rein, moving toward opening rein or toward indirect rein in front of the withers as necessary for steering. The hand is active and yielding.

For **half-pass to the left**, **travers on the left rein**, or **renvers on the right rein**, interchange 'left' and 'right' in the sequence above.

The aids for **right shoulder-in** are as follows (*Figure 7.3d*):

- The rider gives the seat aid to call for a half-halt.
- The rider gently closes the middle fingers of his right hand to produce a small increase in rein tension on that side, while yielding with the left hand. This induces the horse to turn his head slightly to the right.
- The rider adopts 'position right', with weight on the right seat-bone and right knee, left leg back behind the girth, right leg on the girth.
- The rider makes active nudging movements with his right leg on the girth, while his left leg behind the girth is inactive but is held in readiness either to encourage forward progression or to restrain any excessive movement to the side.
- The rider's right hand initiates the movement by giving indirect rein in front of the withers with the hand active and resisting.
- The left hand maintains an appropriate balancing rein tension to preserve the bend in the horse's neck and gives opening rein at the beginning of the movement, thereafter direct rein, moving toward opening rein or toward indirect rein behind the withers as necessary for steering. The hand is active and yielding.

Right shoulder-in is usually performed along the sides of the arena, either on the right rein (tail to the wall) or on the left rein (head to the wall). It may also be performed elsewhere in the arena. The manoeuvre is still called 'shoulder-in', referring to the bend in the horse's spine, rather than to the centre of the arena.

For **left shoulder-in**, interchange 'left' and 'right' in the sequence above.

Whether the resulting movement is a shoulder-in or a shoulder-forward (*Figure 7.3e*) depends on your steering.

8 CANTERS AND JUMPS

Canter and gallop

The gait used by the horse when travelling at his maximum speed is the gallop. The action will be familiar to anyone who has watched horses in a race. There is a marked bending and stretching of the back, with associated up-and-down movements of the head, but the horse's body flows along very smoothly with comparatively little obvious vertical movement, allowing the jockey to remain balanced on his knees with his seat well out of the saddle.

In each cycle there is a single unsupported phase during which the horse bends his back and reaches forward with his hindlegs, lowering his head as he does so (*Figure 8.1*). He then lands on a single hindleg which makes a strong backward sweep against the ground. Similar strong sweeping movements are then made one at a time by the other three legs in turn with only brief periods when there is more than one foot on the ground. The effect is like that of a waggon-wheel, where the weight is taken successively on adjacent spokes. While the two hindlegs are making their drive, the pelvis is also rotated, like the hub of the waggon-wheel. At the same time, the horse strongly extends his back and reaches forward with his forelegs to cover as much ground as possible between footfalls. He is still bringing his head down at this point to help in delaying the footfall of the front legs. When the front legs do come to the ground, this may be in the same order as the hindlegs, transverse gallop (*Figure 8.1*), or in reverse order, rotatory gallop. While the two front legs are on the ground in turn, the horse strongly lifts his head and this helps to draw his hindlegs up under him ready for the next unsupported phase, during which he starts to lower his head again, draws his hindlegs forward, and bends his back.

From this analysis it is seen that, in the gallop, the horse takes off from the forelegs. This is in marked contrast with the gallop of many other animals, like antelopes, where the take-off is from the hindlegs in a series of leaps from each of which the animal lands on the forelegs. Sprint specialists, like the cheetah and some dogs, use a form of galloping which has two unsupported phases in each cycle, one with the body at full stretch as in the gallop of the antelope, and one with the legs bunched together under the body as in the gallop of the horse (*Figure 8.2*).

The canter is a less energetic mode of progression than the gallop. It involves

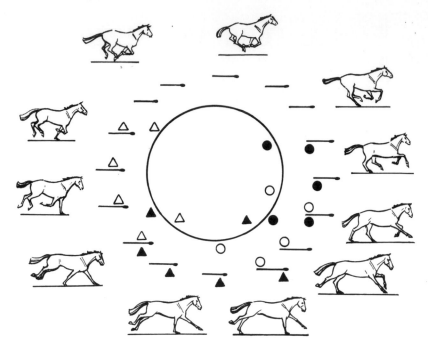

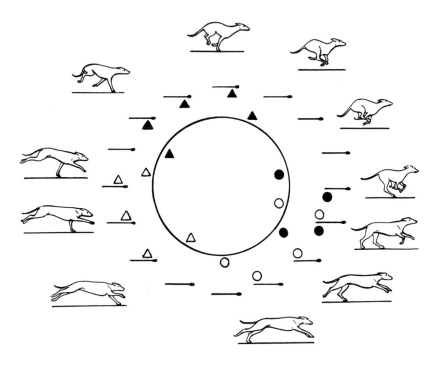

Figure 8.1   *(left) Cycle of leg movements and support patterns at the gallop. (Symbols as in Figure 1.16; clockface as in Figure 1.19; side views from Muybridge (1893), retouched.) The second hindleg comes to the ground before the touch-down of the diagonally opposite foreleg.*

Figure 8.2   *(below left) Cycle of leg movements and support patterns in the gallop of the dog. (Symbols as above.) The sequence of movements is similar to that in the gallop of the horse (Figure 8.1) but there are here two principal unsupported phases, one after the take-off by the forelegs, with the legs bunched together as in the gallop of the horse, and the other after the take-off from the hindlegs, where the body is at full stretch as in the gallop of the antelope.*

Figure 8.3   *(below) Cycle of leg movements and support patterns in the canter. (Symbols as in Figure 1.16; clockface as in Figure 1.19; side views from Muybridge (1893).) Note that the footfalls occur in the same order as in the walk (see Figure 1.20) but they are here grouped together in time, to leave a single unsupported phase. (Notice also the similarity between the action of the legs of the right diagonal pair in this diagram and in that of Figure 3.2 for the trot.)*

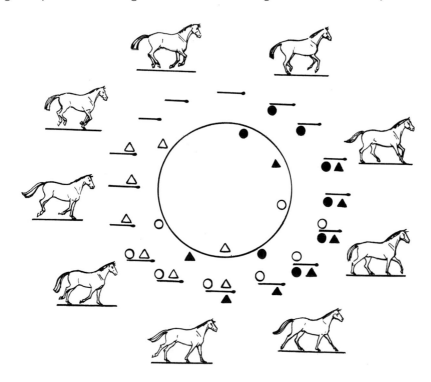

much less extensive bending and stretching of the back. The horse lands on a single hindleg and takes off from a single foreleg, as in the gallop, but in between there are stages when he has three, or even all four, feet on the ground at once. It is convenient to think of the main support during the canter as being on a single diagonal, assisted first by the hindleg on which the horse has landed from the unsupported phase, and assisted later by the opposite foreleg, which will be the take-off leg (*Figure 8.3*).

During the unsupported phase, the horse reaches forward with the hindlegs, as in the gallop. At the same time he lowers his head and this produces a pitching motion of the trunk, the shoulders rising and the haunches falling. During the support phase, the thrusts of the legs produce a pitching in the opposite direction because the hindlegs lift the haunches before the forelegs are available to lift the shoulders. The horse also throws his head up at this time, to be ready for the next unsupported phase.

The pitching motion of the trunk is characteristic of the canter. The motion can be quite pleasant for the rider. Indeed, this is how the gait gets its name. It is the gait preferred for rapid but comfortable long-distance travel, as for pilgrims on their way to Canterbury. 'Canter' is short for 'Canterbury gallop'. It is also the gait usually adopted by cowboys in Western films.

When you watch a cantering horse you will see that, for most of the time, he holds one foreleg well out in front of the other. This leg is called the 'leading leg'. Actually this is the last of the four legs to touch down at each stride and it is also the last to leave the ground. From the saddle you can easily distinguish which is the leading leg by paying attention to the movement of the shoulders. You will see the shoulder of the leading leg lifting more prominently and moving forward during the later part of the unsupported phase. The horse seems to point his leading leg and shoulder in the forward direction. If he is about to turn to the right, he will usually lead with the right foreleg, and he will lead with the left foreleg into a left turn. We use this information to work out how to indicate to the horse that we want him to canter, and on which leg.

Transition from trot to canter

In the trot, the horse springs from one diagonal pair of legs to the other, making two bounces to a stride. In the canter there is only one bounce to each stride and the single unsupported phase correspondingly lasts longer than either of the two unsupported phases of the trot. A stronger thrust is needed to launch the weight of the horse's body into this longer-lasting unsupported phase. In preparation, the horse sinks a little further onto the diagonal that is to be the main support in the canter. At the same time he brings down the opposite foreleg earlier than he would for a trot stride. This makes three legs available for the upward throw. Meanwhile he can reach forward with the other hindleg and delay putting it down till he is ready to land on it after the unsupported phase of the first canter stride.

Starting the canter

The horse changes naturally to the canter when he wishes to cover the ground more rapidly than at a fairly relaxed trot. He may canter on either lead. However, if we are to ask him to change into the canter, we need first to make up our mind which lead is to be used, because each lead calls for a different set of aids. To resolve the ambiguity, we make our early attempts to initiate the canter while the horse is already turning in a circle. As already mentioned, he will lead naturally with the inside leg on a circle, that is, with the right foreleg when turning to the right and with the left foreleg when turning left.

Suppose we start with a circle to the right at the sitting trot. The circle should not be too large; 10 m diameter will do very well. First make sure that the horse is trotting forward freely, with a regular rhythm. When you first turn into the circle, your left leg will be a little behind the girth, but when the turn is well established, your leg may return to the girth. The horse's head is turned a little to the right so that you can just see the corner of his eye. Your hands are in the direct-rein position, the left having given a little more than the right.

Practise changing the speed over the ground, alternately driving forward with your seat for a few strides and then surreptitiously shortening rein for a few strides while you increase the pressure on the bit. Make sure you can produce noticeable changes in the speed over the ground. The rhythm of the footfalls should remain unchanged, but you need not worry too much about this at this stage. Now start to build up impulsion by keeping up the rein pressure instead of at once giving with the rein when you start to drive forward with the seat. The horse needs to be 'wound up' between the drive of your seat and the restraint of your hands. The aim is to reach a stage where he surges forward as soon as you relax the pressure on the rein a little.

You are now ready to give the aids for the canter. Pay attention to the movements of the horse's shoulders so that you are clear in your mind which diagonal is being used for support at each bounce. Remember that it is the outside diagonal that forms the principal support at the canter. For a canter on the right lead, the outside diagonal consists of the left foreleg and the right hindleg. At the point of transition from the trot, you want the horse to reach forward with his left hindleg. The appropriate aid for this will be to apply your left leg behind the girth. What remains to be settled is the question of timing.

Just as in the transition from halt to walk and from walk to trot, it is necessary to proceed in stages. First build up alertness and impulsion, next give a warning of your intention, and then at the 'moment of decision' apply simultaneously the appropriate aids with seat, legs, weight-change and reins. The warning for the canter is given by drawing your outside leg back, without at this stage applying any extra pressure to the horse's side. This draws the horse's attention to his outside hindleg. The 'moment of decision' for a canter on the right lead occurs just as the horse is about to land on the outside diagonal. This is why you have to have already made up your mind which diagonal is which. Then, just as you are coming down for the bump on the outside diagonal, you brace your back to thrust the seat-bones forward against the saddle, squeeze with both legs, and at the same time momentarily ease the pressure on the rein. It helps to think of squaring your shoulders. Do not attempt to urge the horse forward by leaning forward yourself. This is likely to have the effect of moving the saddle backward instead of forward and the forward urge of the saddle produced by bracing your back is probably the most important single component in the complex of movements collectively referred to as 'the aids for the canter'.

If it should happen that your horse strikes off with the wrong leg, that is to say leading with the left foreleg on a right hand turn, at once change back to the trot. Relax your legs, take up the pressure on the rein and give a few brief pulls, sitting well down into the saddle and squaring your shoulders. Remember that it is unrealistic to expect the horse to change from trot to canter on the correct leg within a single stride without previous warning. Make sure your warning indication with the outside leg is definite and early enough. If the trouble persists, use a larger circle, say 20 m diameter, for the preliminary preparation, practising the changes of speed and building up impulsion, and then turn in onto a smaller circle for the transition to canter. You will naturally use your outside leg to signal the turn. Bring it on again as a warning about halfway round the small circle and then give your main drive for the canter command just as you are coming out of the small circle and back onto the track of the larger circle (*Figure 8.4*). If you are working in an enclosed school where you can ride close to the wall, you can make your small circle into the

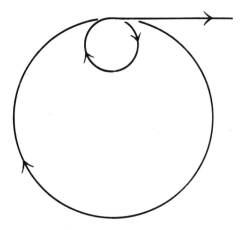

Figure 8.4 *Track for starting the canter on the correct lead (here the right). Prepare by building up impulsion at the trot on a large circle. Turn into a smaller circle and give a warning to the horse with your outside leg. Drive on into canter as you rejoin the larger circle. The turn into the small circle ensures that the horse will strike off on the inside leg. Do not turn in so sharply that the horse has to slow down, and be especially careful if conditions are at all slippery.*

corner. Apply your canter command as the horse passes the corner itself, and canter on along the side of the school.

You will find that the movements of the horse's head at the canter are very different from those made at the trot. When a horse gallops in a race the hands of the jockey execute quite extensive forward and backward movements. These movements are needed to maintain a steady contact with the horse's mouth. In the canter, just as in the gallop, the horse makes a swinging movement of his head at each stride, bringing his head down to help in reaching forward with the hindlegs and throwing his head up again when the forelegs are on the ground. You need to be very careful with your hands at the onset of the canter because, if you are not ready for it, this surging movement of the head can pull the rein taut with a snap, and this will feel to the horse like an urgent command to stop. If a horse feels a jerk on the bit every time he starts to move off in a canter, he will become more and more reluctant to canter with a rider on his back. It is this effect, in conjunction with the inherent difficulty of hitting off the timing correctly, that is responsible for most of the problems that beginners complain of in getting their horses to canter.

You should have no difficulty if you first make sure you are able to build up sufficient impulsion at the trot so that the horse accelerates with a forward surge as soon as you relax your pressure on the rein. When you are ready for the canter, you can let the horse accelerate on the inside diagonal just as you are about to give the canter command with your seat and legs. Practise starting the canter on both leads, always first turning to the appropriate side so that the horse leads with the inside leg.

Wrong lead

The reason for emphasising the correct lead is that, when the leading foreleg is on the ground, the diagonally opposite hindleg is already reaching forward. If the horse is bent toward the side of the leading leg, the hindleg will pass forward freely. But if the bend is toward the other side there is a possibility that the hindleg may trip over the foreleg, with the risk of injury, a stumble or even a fall. It is thus important that the horse should be bent toward the leading leg. He will usually do this for himself if you ask for the canter while he is turning. However, if he is going straight, you may have to look after it for him. This is only fair because he is cantering to your command. He would not get his legs mixed up if left to himself.

Disunited

There is another situation in which injudicious commands by the rider may lead the horse into difficulties. If your horse strikes off on the wrong leg, do not attempt to force him over at once onto the correct leg while he is still cantering. He may respond by changing the sequence of his forelegs while continuing with the hindleg sequence unchanged. Suppose that he has struck off, wrongly, on the right lead. The sequence of footfalls after each unsupported phase is then: left hind, left fore and right hind almost together, then right fore. You force him to change the lead and he may go: left hind, right hind and right fore together, following with left fore. This sequence works satisfactorily at the gallop − it is referred to as the 'rotatory gallop' − but it leads to difficulties in the canter.

The reason is that at the canter the trunk has to pivot over the pair of legs that come to the ground together. In the correct canter, this is a diagonal pair, and the body can pitch comfortably forward. With the rotatory sequence of footfalls, the corresponding pair of supporting legs is a lateral pair. This produces lateral rolling in place of the normal fore-and-aft rocking motion. The action tends to be jerky. The horse is said to be 'going disunited'. In the rotatory gallop, the movements of the individual legs are more spaced out in time and the same problems do not arise.

Change of lead

Accordingly, at any rate during the early stages of training, always return to the trot if your horse canters on the wrong leg. In some dressage tests you are expected to go right down to the walk before asking for a canter on the opposite leg.

Changes of speed

After practising the transition from trot to canter on a circle both to the right and to the left, you will be ready to try the transition while the horse is going straight. Make up your mind which lead you want and then go through the following stages: build up impulsion at the trot; ask for the appropriate bend with 'outside' leg back and a little more weight on the 'inside' knee; give with the rein as you come down on the inside diagonal; then, as he starts to accelerate, drive with your seat and both legs just as you are coming down for the next, outside, diagonal. In this description, 'inside' means the side on which you want the horse to lead, because he needs to be bent to that side. After a few strides at the canter, come back to the trot and try again.

The practice routine of alternating faster and slower progression at the trot can now be extended to include periods at the canter. This provides an opportunity to become accustomed to the feel of the rein when the horse changes his gait. It is important to develop independence between hand and shoulder. Your hand should move forward and backward with the movements of the horse's head, keeping the same light tension on the rein all the time. Your shoulders will also be moving forward and backward with the rocking motion imparted to your body by the saddle. But the timing of your shoulder movements is not the same as that of the movements of the horse's head and your arm must be supple enough to absorb all the changes in relative position.

If you encourage the swinging movements of the horse's head by pulling a little while his mouth is moving toward the saddle and relaxing a little when his head is moving forward, the effect on the horse will be that he will lengthen his stride. You may see hints of this action when a racing jockey is urging his horse toward the finishing post. Do not make the mistake of overdoing it, as some beginners do, urging their horses on by flapping their elbows. All too often the effect of such exaggerated movements is just to jerk the reins and thus to unsettle the horse. If you execute your encouraging movements smoothly the horse will gradually move into gallop.

Collected canter

To get the horse to shorten his stride at the canter apply rhythmic pulls on the rein with a different timing. First, gently resist the forward movement of the horse's head and then relax the tension in the rein at the moment when the horse's mouth is moving back toward the saddle. You need to be careful not to allow the rein to go completely slack. During the periods of increased rein tension you can tell the horse to pay more attention by rapidly repeated clenching and unclenching of the fingers while keeping up the same gentle pull. This is a rather sophisticated action with the rein as the periods of increased tension do not last very long at each stride.

The effect of this rein action, working against the natural swing of the horse's head, will be to make the horse drop back from gallop to canter and even to a trot unless you actively keep the canter going, by bracing your back at each stride and driving forward with your seat-bones every time your weight comes down onto the saddle. If, at the same time, you sit up and square your shoulders you should, after a little practice, be able to develop a short, bouncy, canter for a few strides, with the horse making only a very little ground forward at each stride. You may have seen show-jumpers edging forward like this in front of a fence that calls for particular care in the approach. They cautiously bring their horses up toward the point they have selected beforehand as the start of their run-up.

By judiciously balancing the vigour with which you drive forward with your seat against the restraint or encouragement of your hand, you can adjust the length of stride and make the horse cover the ground either faster or more slowly while still keeping in the canter. For the apprehensive rider it is a great help in building up confidence to spend some time in practising these changes of speed at the controlled canter.

Stopping a runaway

Many horses enjoy a good canter and if they happen to be feeling rather lively they may take advantage of the inexperience of the rider to accelerate forward into a full gallop. They may then easily get so excited that they forget to pay attention to the bit. If the rider pulls at the reins, the horse just puts more weight on the bit as though in an attempt to pull the reins right out of the rider's hands. The rider may even be pulled forward out of the saddle. It may be useful here to recapitulate some of the advice given earlier about how to deal with a runaway.

A common reaction to being carried away faster than expected is for the beginner to try to hold on by wrapping his legs round the horse's belly. Unfortunately, this just makes matters worse, because the horse interprets the bouncing contact of the rider's heels against his side as an encouragement to gallop on even faster. The rider's best strategy is to adopt what was earlier described as the 'safe position for the beginner'. The first rule is: heels away from the horse, and forward rather than back. This brings the knees firmly against the saddle to give the rider lateral stability. The next rule is: fold forward at the hips to bring your elbows in front of your knees. This takes some of the weight off the seat-bones and provides a shock-absorbing mechanism to make it less likely that the rider will be bounced out of the saddle. The hands are now in a good position to take hold of the mane or of the neck strap if there is one. The feet should be held out and forward, rather than back. This helps to stiffen the knee to reinforce the lateral stability, and it also allows the rider to use the stirrups if the horse should swerve or if he should decide to stop suddenly. A relaxed or bent knee is of no use here. It just increases the chance of casually banging the horse's side with the rider's boot.

The third rule is: steer for the open spaces and gradually turn your horse into a circle. If you have enough room you can just let the horse run himself out. If he is strong and fit this may take a couple of miles and you will need to keep well clear of obstructions such as trees and gateposts. Going round and round in a big field will be reasonably safe. Try very hard not to be taken onto a tarmac road as this is the worst possible place for a gallop. There is a very high risk of the horse slipping, and a fall onto such a hard surface could easily prove fatal.

After the initial shock of dismay that things are beginning to get out of hand, you should make yourself think firmly about stopping rather than about parting company with your horse. Remember the importance of telepathy. Growing confidence in the security of your position will help. You can also now start taking positive action with the reins.

You will already be leaning well forward with your elbows in front of your knees. You can therefore work your hands well down the reins toward the horse's mouth. Suppose you have decided to steer him to the right. Take a firm grip on the reins with your hands as far forward as you can go. Slide your left hand up the side of the horse's neck and across to the right side so that you can put your weight on to your left wrist where it lies against the horse's crest. The left rein should then be taut and firmly gripped in your left fist, which presses into the right side of the horse's neck. Now pull outwards and downwards with the right rein using a succession of brief strong pulls. Aim to bring the horse's nose right round to your knee. The simultaneous blocking action of your left hand is necessary to keep the bit from being pulled right through the horse's mouth. He will not want to dash forward so impetuously if you get his head round far enough.

If you are unlucky and the bit does manage to slip through his mouth, all is still not quite lost. You may be able to get one hand onto the cheekstraps of the bridle just below the ears, taking a firm grip on the mane with the other hand. Slide your hand down the cheekstrap of the bridle and pull his head round with the noseband. Remember to keep your breastbone over the midline of his neck and push your feet well forward to stop yourself being pulled out of the saddle. All this may sound rather heroic, but, after all, we are talking about an emergency situation here, and if you know in advance what to do this will make it very much easier to cope with.

An alternative routine which works well with some horses, and which perhaps does not sound quite so alarming, is to shorten rein as before, as far as you can go, then put both reins in one hand well up by the horse's poll. Use the other hand to pull in the slack until each rein is taut. Then grip the reins very firmly so that they cannot slip through your fingers. Gradually work the fist that holds the reins little by little down the horse's neck, taking advantage of every moment when the horse relaxes, and blocking firmly when he pulls. He will finish up with his nose right in against his chest. He needs to swing his head to keep up the gallop and if you can, by this trick, manage to check the swinging movements of his head, the effect will be to check the urgency of the forward progression. You may even be able to bring him right down to the halt.

Regarding the runaway horse it should be emphasised that here prevention is much easier than cure. The more often you practise the stops, the more accustomed your horse will become to obeying your instructions and, correspondingly, the less unlikely he will be to disregard your commands, even when he is excited. Do not deceive yourself with the notion that if you let him have his head, his lust for speed will become satiated. This is very far from being likely. He will just become confirmed in his habit of making off at the slightest opportunity.

It is true that some horses have been cured of galloping off by driving them on, but plenty of space is needed for this. For example, you may need to force the horse to continue galloping for a further mile or two beyond the point where his natural enthusiasm for galloping has begun to flag. Such forcing may be necessary; otherwise he will get the impression that he can do as he likes, making off when he wants to and slowing up only when he feels like it.

The reason for adopting the folded posture in the saddle, with the elbows in front of the knees and with the feet pushed well outward and forward, is that this brings your centre of gravity low down over the withers. It is here that the ride is smoothest, with the minimum of jolting from the movements of the horse's legs and from their impact with the ground. The posture is like that of the racing jockey, apart from the effect of the difference in the length of the stirrup leathers. (It is, in fact, an exaggerated version of the jump seat described in Chapter 5.)

Jump seat and drive seat at canter and gallop

When you first practise the transition from trot to canter, it is essential to start by building up impulsion. For this you need to be in sitting trot, bracing your back in the 'drive-seat position'. You can continue in this position at the canter, squaring your shoulders and allowing the suppleness of your back to absorb the impact when your weight comes down into the saddle at each stride. After you have become accustomed to the motion you will find that your seat-bones no longer part company with the saddle at each stride, although the pressure is very slight for a moment just after take-off.

For a prolonged canter you may prefer to move forward into the jump seat. Bring your elbows and shoulders forward and your seat-bones will naturally rise out of the saddle. You will find it very easy to balance on your knees at the canter. So long as your ankles are supple and you do not let your feet get out of position, you can just float along. With a little coaxing with the rein, encouraging the horse to swing his head freely, he will change imperceptibly into the gallop, particularly on rising ground in open country. All you need do to get him to go full out is to give the occasional squeeze with your legs.

Although your horse will be obviously enjoying himself at the gallop, do not ask too much of him unless you are sure that he is really fit. It is all too easy to persuade your horse to over-exert himself. In former times it was not uncommon for horses to be ridden to death.

The distinction between canter and gallop is seen more readily by the bystander than by the rider. At the gallop the four legs are brought to the ground one at a time, whereas at the canter the legs of the support diagonal touch down almost simultaneously. There is, consequently, a difference in the rhythm of the footfalls and the rider may spot this if he is riding alone. Otherwise all he has to go on is the increased involvement of the horse's back as he reaches forward with hindquarters and forequarters alternately in the gallop, in contrast to the rocking motion of the whole body at the canter.

The jump seat is appropriate to relaxed conditions. When you need precise control of the horse you should move into the drive seat so that you can give indications through the saddle by bracing your back. Normally, your horse will slow up at the gallop as soon as you sit down into the saddle and start taking up the reins. If he doesn't do this you may need to treat him as a runaway.

The drive seat is essential for the half-halt with which you prepare the horse for any transition that is to be executed with precision. It is also the natural seat when riding at the canter without stirrups.

It is useful to practise changing between jump seat and drive seat at the canter. You may find that, when you sit down into the drive seat, the horse slows up, as though expecting a transition down to the trot. Watch for this and feel for the way he responds to the variations in the position of your weight and to changes in your pressure on the rein. Practise bracing your back quite strongly just after sitting down into the drive seat so that, instead of slowing up at this point, the horse actually accelerates forward. Also practise taking up the rein and increasing the pressure on the bit while you are cantering in the jump seat. Then put these two manoeuvres together into an alternation between accelerating forward in the drive-seat position and slowing into a collected canter while staying up in the jump-seat position. This alternation is fundamental to the preparation for jumping.

Transitions

At this stage in the training of horse and rider a period of consolidation is appropriate. The changes of speed should be practised at the walk, at the trot, and at the canter on both leads, together with all the possible transitions from one gait to another, including halts from each gait and starts at each gait directly from the halt. Each of the transitions involves the judicious application of forward drive of the seat-bones against the saddle, by bracing the back, carefully balanced against restraint or encouragement of the horse's head movements by the action of the reins. At each stage the rider must be alert to feel the changes in the horse's muscles that indicate what the horse is about to do. The aim should be to produce the transitions so smoothly that the onlooker is given the impression that the horse is doing it all for himself. Be particularly on the look-out for those little jumpy movements that the horse makes when you take him by surprise, as by a too sudden or too vigorous application of the legs.

All of this work can be practised without stirrups, and it is natural to combine it with exercises in steering along the various tracks in the dressage arena (*Figure 3.7*). Remember that where the track involves a change of rein, it will be necessary, at the canter, also to change the lead. This means that you have to drop back to the trot, or even to the walk, in plenty of time before the cross-over point. If you need an incentive for detailed practice of this kind, there are several official dressage tests that call for not more than steering, changes of speed, and changes of gait.

The simple transitions have been described already: walk on from halt; trot from walk; canter from trot; gallop from canter; halt from walk; walk from trot; trot from canter; halt from trot; halt from gallop.

The more demanding transitions are built up from the same components as the simple transitions. The first need is to develop adequate impulsion, so that when you do give the necessarily strong indication for the transition itself, the horse does not jump right out of his skin.

Trot from halt

To persuade the horse to start directly at the trot from the halt, you need to hold in a little at first so that he doesn't walk on before you have built up enough impulsion. Start by calling the horse to attention by tickling the bit. Watch for his response. When he moves his ears, raises his head, and begins to play with the bit, progressively increase the pressure on the bit and start a series of brief squeezes with your legs. You will feel him tensing himself ready for moving off. Then give an extra squeeze with the legs, brace your back to drive the saddle forward, and relax the rein. You will need to practise so that the horse gets the chance to come to understand what you want and so that you can judge just how much preparatory winding-up is needed. If you overdo it before he has worked out what to do, he will just get excited and start throwing his head about and generally playing up. If this happens, abandon the exercise and try again on another day, being a little more tactful the next time.

Walk from canter

The direct transition from the canter to the walk, without any intervening trotting strides, calls for considerable alertness on the part of the rider. You have to know just when to relax the onward drive with your seat that maintains the canter in the face of the progressively increasing restraint that you are exerting with the reins. As soon as the canter breaks, you must immediately start the alternating leg aids for the walk; otherwise the horse will either go into the trot or will stop altogether. It will help the horse to slow up if you raise your hands for a moment just as you are giving the final increase in the pressure on the rein. Then, as you feel the change in the horse's action, start to give alternating pulls on left and right rein, to initiate the lateral sway of the horse's head appropriate to the walk.

You will find that precise work at the collected canter is much easier if you have already persuaded your horse to hold his nose in. You may need to spend some time consolidating this before trying more ambitious moves.

Canter from walk

The transition into the canter from the trot, as usually practised by beginners, relies to a large extent on the natural tendency of the horse to change gait when he wishes to increase his speed over the ground. The technique based on this type of training does not lend itself to precise timing of the transition. If you want to improve the precision, in order to be able to strike off exactly at a marker in a dressage test, it is preferable to concentrate your practising on the transition into the canter from the walk.

At the walk, the four feet come to the ground in turn at approximately equal intervals, each landing before the opposite foot is lifted, in symmetrical fashion.

This symmetry has to be disturbed during the transition into the pattern for the canter stride, where the two legs of the non-leading diagonal are brought to the ground more or less simultaneously.

The nature of the adjustments that the horse has to make in this transition can be deduced from a comparison of the sequences of support patterns for the two gaits as set out in the cyclic gait diagrams of *Figures 1.20 and 8.3*. Looking at these two figures you will see that the open triangle which represents the moment of placing of the left forefoot, is at the bottom of the circle in each case. You will also see that most of the support patterns for the canter in *Figure 8.3* also occur in the lower part of the diagram in *Figure 1.20* for the walk. It is this similarity that provides the basis for an understanding of what the horse has to do during the transition, and it also tells us what aids will give the best chance of achieving a transition precisely on cue.

During the transition from walk to canter, the horse has to adjust the timing of his leg movements and, at the same time, he also has to prepare for the extra thrust that will be needed for the take-off into the unsupported phase of the canter. The pattern of the nodding movements of the head also has to be altered. At the walk, the horse lifts his head twice in each cycle, timing these liftings to correspond with the liftings of the hindlegs. At the canter, there is only one up-and-down movement of the head, and it here corresponds with the lifting of the leading foreleg.

You tell the horse which lead you want by moving your leg back behind the girth on the side opposite to the one on which you want him to lead, at the same time raising your hand on the leading side. Thus, for a canter on the right lead, you bring your left leg back behind the girth and raise your right hand.

The command that indicates the actual moment at which to take off is given by squeezing with both legs and driving the saddle forward with the seat-bones while at the same time slightly easing the rein tension for a moment. After you have given the warning indicating that it is the right lead that is wanted, by moving your left leg behind the girth, the horse responds to the 'take-off' command by gathering himself for the extra push against the ground that will be needed to launch his body upward into the unsupported phase of the canter stride.

He prepares by allowing his weight to sink slightly onto the support triangle provided by the left hindleg together with the left diagonal pair of legs. He allows his head also to sink a little at this stage. He then surges his body forward over the left diagonal onto a new triangle made up of the right foreleg together with the left diagonal pair, and it is this triangle that provides the platform for the take-off thrust. During this forward surge, he reaches forward with his left hindleg while the feet of the left diagonal pair remain on the ground a little longer than they would at the walk. He throws his head upward strongly just before the time comes for him to lift his right foreleg, and this upward movement is continued into the take-off for the canter stride, which is achieved by springing upward from the three legs that are still on the ground at this time. The feet now come to the ground in the pattern appropriate to the canter: first the left hind, then the left fore and right hind in rapid succession, and finally the right fore. From this point on he is fully into the canter pattern.

You must give your warning to the horse at least two strides ahead of the moment at which you want him to break into the canter. This will give him time to rearrange the timing of his leg movements and to get his legs ready for the extra thrust that he needs to develop in order to launch his body into the unsupported phase of the first canter stride. He needs one stride for the adjustment of timing and one stride for the extra push for take-off.

A transition of this kind calls for a good deal of impulsion and, without this, you are unlikely to have much success in avoiding the untidiness of spurious intermediate steps. If you are not confident about the degree of impulsion at any stage, the way to test it is to move your hands forward a couple of centimetres or so for a moment. The horse should instantly respond by surging forward and immediately taking up the rein tension by his own head movement. He should give the appearance of always seeking the bit, without at any time leaning too heavily on it. This is the condition known as 'being on the bit', and 'light in the hand'.

Canter from halt ('Canter depart')

In the transitions into the canter, either from the trot or from the walk, the horse is moving forward all the time. His task during the transition consists solely in the adjustment of the timing and forcefulness of the limb thrusts. In the transition from the halt, he has, in addition, to accelerate the mass of his trunk forward from rest directly into a speed over the ground that will be appropriate to the canter stride. This acceleration has to have been accomplished before either of the hindfeet can be free to leave the ground. If he is to achieve this, he must first be brought to a high state of impulsion.

He can then react to the command of the rider's seat aids and leg aids by first lowering his weight a little, by bending his legs, and then surging his body forward over his feet. At the halt, his two forefeet will be roughly side by side, but he can extend his platform of support by making a small step forward with one foreleg. This prolongs the time during which the leg thrusts can act effectively to develop forward acceleration. The asymmetry of your leg aids and hand position tells the horse which leg to advance. If your left leg is behind the girth, the horse will advance his right foreleg. Then, as the horse's weight passes over his left diagonal, he can give the extra push needed to launch his body into the unsupported phase of the first canter stride. The feet then leave the ground in the usual sequence, starting with the left hind. The transition is initiated by the advance of the leading foreleg, the right. The right forefoot is also the last foot to leave the ground before the unsupported phase, as is appropriate to a canter on the right lead.

You should be able to achieve any desired lead in the transition from halt to canter if you ensure that the horse knows well in advance which lead you want. If you have trained your horse to bend his spine sideways in response to a change in your posture in the saddle, you can use this signal to indicate the desired lead. Thus, if you adopt position right, he will know you will be asking for a canter depart on the right lead and he will be ready for you when you apply your take-off signal with your seat aids and leg aids.

The routine that follows will give you practice in the canter depart and at the same time helps in building up impulsion.

Routine for developing impulsion for the canter depart

Suppose you want to start the canter on the right lead from the halt. Put your weight on your right seat-bone and stretch down with your right leg. Apply right opening rein and left indirect rein in front of the withers, both hands active and

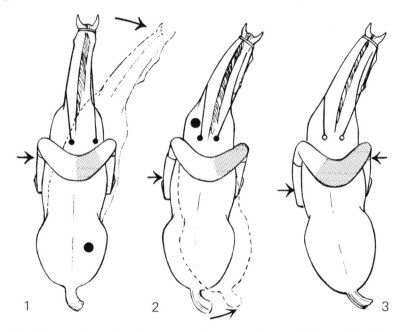

Figure 8.5 *Preparation for the canter depart on the right lead. (1) Pivot on the right hindleg (right turn on the haunches, one step). Weight on the right seat-bone. Left leg active on the girth. Right hand gives opening rein. Left hand gives indirect rein in front of the withers. Both hands are active and restraining. (2) Pivot on the left foreleg (left turn on the forehand, toward the bend, one step). Weight on the right knee. Left leg active behind the girth. Right hand gives indirect rein in front of the withers. Left hand gives indirect rein behind the withers. Both hands are active and restraining. (3) Canter depart. Weight on right knee and right seat-bone. Left leg behind the girth and right leg on the girth. Both legs active with simultaneous forward drive with both seat-bones. Both hands active with momentary easing of the rein tension as the signal for take-off.*

restraining. Nudge the horse's side with your left leg over the girth. This asks the horse to make a right turn on the haunches, pivoting on the right hindleg. Make one step only, and halt (*Figure 8.5:1*). Then, keeping the horse's head turned to the right and keeping your right leg stretched down, put your weight on your right knee and apply right indirect rein in front of the withers and left indirect rein behind the withers. Nudge the horse's side with your left leg, this time behind the girth, to make a left turn on the forehand, pivoting on the left foreleg. Make one step only, and halt (*Figure 8.5:2*). Note that in this turn the horse moves his haunches *into* the bend. This increases the degree of bending. At this stage your left leg is already behind the girth in the correct position to prompt the horse to strike off on the right lead. Now give the strike-off command for canter depart right, using both legs and driving with both seat-bones (*Figure 8.5:3*) while at the same time momentarily easing the rein tension. Canter on for a few strides, and halt. Rein-back two strides, and halt. Prepare for another canter depart, this time on the left lead. Make a left turn on the haunches, one step only, and halt. Then, keeping the horse's head turned to the left, make a right turn on the forehand, one step only, and halt. Strike off in canter depart left. Canter on for a few strides, and halt. Rein-back two strides, and halt. Repeat the canter depart several times on alternate leads.

This exercise is particularly valuable in helping your horse to acquire the habit of associating the feel of your position in the saddle with striking off into a canter with the appropriate bend for each lead. It also has the effect of thoroughly waking up the horse so that he develops considerable impulsion. When you can do the canter depart at will on a specified lead and with the appropriate bend, and provided that your horse changes his bend well, in response to a change in your position, you should thereafter have no problem with transitions into canter from the walk on a desired lead or with the flying changes at the canter.

Your horse will also be able to perform the counter canter, retaining his bend in spite of being steered into a course away from his bend, and will continue in counter canter until you change your position in the saddle.

Counter canter

It has already been emphasised that the horse's body should, at the canter, always be bent toward the leading side. This bend is natural when the horse is making a turn toward the side of the leading leg. The bend has to be maintained also when the horse is going straight. Up to this point we have insisted that a change of rein, for a turn away from the leading leg, must be preceded by a change of gait. The horse is first asked to drop back from the canter to the trot and thereafter a new canter is initiated on the other lead. Sometimes it may not be convenient to go through the whole of this routine, particularly if the change of rein is to last for only a short time. The appropriate manoeuvre here is the 'counter canter'.

It is important to distinguish between the counter canter and the canter on the wrong leg. In the counter canter, the horse continues to be bent toward the leading leg while moving on a curve toward the other side. For example, the horse may be asked to turn to the left while cantering on the right lead and remaining bent toward the right (*Figure 8.6*). If the bend is not maintained, the horse will be cantering on the wrong leg. The manoeuvre is practised with shallow serpentines, and you need plenty of space.

First, establish the canter on a fairly large circle (about 20 m diameter), say to the right, making sure that you emphasise the bend by keeping the horse's nose turned slightly to the right and sitting firmly in 'position right' with left leg

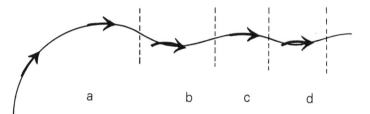

a   b   c   d

Figure 8.6 *Track for introducing the horse to the counter canter. Establish the canter in a large circle, here to the right. Then occasionally veer to the left slightly for a few strides taking great care not to lose the bend. Distinguish between counter canter and 'wrong lead' (in which the horse leads with the outside leg, e.g. with the right leg on a curve to the left with a left bend). In the counter canter the horse leads on the side to which he is bent, even though he is travelling along a path that is curved to the opposite side. (**a**) Canter right; (**b**) counter canter; (**c**) canter right; (**d**) counter canter.*

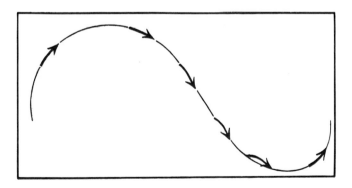

Figure 8.7 *Developing the flying change of lead from the counter canter (see text overleaf). Canter right on a large circle; straight canter along a diagonal; counter canter as you approach the long side; ask for canter left as you enter the turn for the corner. Change from 'position right' to 'position left' at the moment when you want the horse to change lead.*

back, weight on the right knee, urging him on in collected canter. Now, *without changing the position of the horse's head* or altering your position in the saddle, apply opening rein with the left hand and indirect rein in front of the withers with the right. At the same time pat him on the girth with the right leg. He should swing away to the left of the circle. After a couple of strides bring your hands across to the right and discontinue the activity of the right leg, so that the horse moves back onto a curve toward the right, parallel to the original circle. Take great care that he doesn't lose his bend to the right, and at first make only small sways to the left of the straight line. Repeat on the other lead, starting from a circle on the left rein.

When you are confident that you can keep the bend the way you want it, you can gradually increase the distance covered at the counter canter and you can try turning a little more sharply. Always be on the look-out for a collapse of the bend and, if this happens, at once steer strongly toward the leading leg to avoid confirming the horse in the habit of cantering on the wrong leg.

Flying change of lead

There are some circumstances in which it is convenient to be able to change from one lead to the other at the canter without interrupting the flow by dropping back to the trot. Such occasions often arise when negotiating a sequence of jumps in a restricted area. In these conditions it is appropriate to execute what is called a 'flying change'.

The horse is to be persuaded to change from one lead to the other while in the air during a single stride. To develop this manoeuvre, start with the counter canter (*Figure 8.7*). Here the canter is first established on the right lead, circling to the right. The horse is then steered on a gentle curve to the left, maintaining the bend to the right in counter canter. Decide upon the place where you want to execute the flying change and be prepared then to do several things at the same time. The object is to ensure that the horse completes his move precisely on cue. To do this several unambiguous indications have to be given simultaneously at the beginning of the stride during which we want the horse to execute the flying change.

During the preparatory counter canter you will be sitting firmly in 'position right' with a good deal of collection and with the horse bent to the right. The warning to the horse telling him that he is to do something different takes the form of a half-halt, or emphasis of the collection. Both hands are in the direct rein position at this stage and the horse's nose is turned slightly to the right, although he is moving on a gentle curve to the left. The right hand may be raised slightly as part of the indication for the half-halt. After the change of lead you are going to steer strongly into a left turn. By itself, this turn to the left is an indication that the horse should be cantering on the left lead. This will mean that you should then be sitting in 'position left'.

The change in your position in the saddle is the most important single indication for the change of lead. You move your weight over from right knee to left knee, bring the left leg forward onto the girth, and move the right leg back. At the same time move the horse's nose over from right to left, by pulling the left rein a little and giving a little with the right; move your left hand to the opening-rein position with the hand raised, and apply indirect rein in front of the withers with the right hand at the regular height, steering firmly to the left. The horse should change his bend and strike off on the left lead.

If you build up to the flying change in this way, the horse should have no doubt about what is required of him and you should have no problems. Naturally, you both have to practise before everything gets synchronised smoothly. Thereafter you can try asking for the change of lead while cantering on a straight line. Be on the look-out for a sloppy change in which the horse alters the sequence of movements of the forelegs without changing the hindlegs. This leads to the disunited canter, which should be scrupulously avoided.

After the horse has learned to do a neat flying change when cantering on a straight line, you can ask him to change again after a few strides. Thus you can ride in succession six strides on the left lead, flying change, six strides on the right lead, another flying change, and so on. Then you can ask for the change after four strides, or after two, and finally the horse will be able to perform a flying change at each stride. He skips along, leading with left and right foreleg alternately. If you can manage this without throwing your weight about too violently in the saddle, the effect can be quite spectacular. It will be a good idea to have a friend to watch while you are practising so that he can draw your attention to any untidy and unnecessary movements that you may be making without being aware of them. This helps you to avoid building up bad habits. You should also ask him to watch out for any tendency for the horse to become disunited by failing to make one of the changes with hindlegs as well as with forelegs.

Lateral work at canter

While working on counter canter and flying changes, you will become accustomed to feeling for the bend in the horse, correcting and encouraging it as necessary. You can now experiment with half-pass and shoulder-in at canter. The aids for these are, in principle, the same as those you have already used for lateral work at the trot. At the canter, however, you have to be particularly careful to preserve the correct bend. It will be important to maintain a good deal of impulsion with the horse well collected. Make sure also that he is truly 'on the bit' so that he is able to appreciate what you are telling him through the reins.

After practising all the manoeuvres described up to this point you will be beginning to feel some confidence in your ability to get your horse to do what you want. However, the training of horse and rider cannot be regarded as complete until some facility has been acquired in the art of jumping.

Preparation for jumping

It is sometimes said that the horse is not a natural jumper. I do not believe this, because I have observed that, when at liberty, horses will jump hedges and ditches quite freely either to obtain food or to rejoin companions from whom they have been separated. On the other hand, it is clear that the presence of a rider on his back makes the novice horse somewhat unsure of himself when he is faced with an obstacle. Novice riders also approach obstacles with some trepidation, and this feeling is inevitably communicated to their mounts. In addition, the novice rider tends to rattle about in the saddle when going over a jump and this must contribute to unsettling the horse. Accordingly it is appropriate to prepare both horse and rider before embarking on the actual jumping.

The first requirement is that the rider should be able to regulate the speed of his horse. He should be able to control the canter and keep a firm grip on the steering while riding in the jump-seat position. He should also be able to produce smart acceleration from the drive-seat position on the word of command. It is essential to have firm control of speed and steering both at the trot and at the canter.

Horses that have already been trained to jump will often carry novice riders over jumps successfully for a time. The problem is that, in the absence of the accustomed confirmatory indications from the rider, the horse may begin to have doubts about what is intended. He has, after all, to know whether what is in front of him is an obstacle that is to be jumped or is a gate which has to be approached gently so that it can be opened. Occasionally he will be asked to jump a gate. If he does not know what is intended he may just drift into the obstacle without actually jumping and thus bang his legs. Alternatively, he may get into the bad habit of refusing at the last moment, putting his head down and ducking out to one side while his rider sails gracefully on, to land with a crash on top of the fence. Systematic preparation avoids these hazards.

Trotting-poles

A point to remember when assembling the equipment for jumping is that the horse will not necessarily bother to lift his feet over anything that looks no thicker than his own leg. He will expect to be able to crash through, either breaking the obstacle or brushing it aside. You may have noticed that in a steeplechase the horses do not attempt to clear the brushwood fences completely but charge happily through the top fifteen centimetres or so of the obstacle. Similarly they do not expect strands of wire to present a serious obstruction. They treat wire with the contempt appropriate to brambles. They may thus easily be brought down. One must not attempt to jump gaps in a hedge where there may be a strand of wire. Poles to be used for practice jumps should be at least 8−10 cm thick and 3−4 m long.

Competition jumps are usually painted in bright colours, so you might like to paint your practice poles similarly. As well as the poles, you will need some supports. For many purposes oil drums do very well, or you can use the plastic crates made for handling bottles by the dozen. Wooden packing cases are not suitable as they are easily broken and then present dangerously sharp pieces. You will also need one or two markers, such as half-bricks or paint cans, but remember to clear these out of the way when not in use, so that the horses do not trip over them.

Another aid that is almost indispensable is a willing assistant who can watch where your horse is putting his feet and who can move poles about or rebuild jumps when needed.

To start working over trotting-poles, trot steadily round and round in a fairly large circle, giving your horse a chance to get settled. Ask your assistant to lay one pole across the track while you continue to trot round, stepping over the pole without breaking the rhythm. Your assistant now carefully watches the horse's feet as they pass over the pole and judges where he can safely put down a second pole. When your horse has learned to adjust his stride to clear a single pole smoothly, the assistant can add a second pole about 1.5 m away from the first, the distance being judged in terms of the horse's natural stride. The position of the second pole may need to be adjusted when you see where the feet come down, and this is where the aid of an assistant is so vital.

When the horse has learned to negotiate two poles, a third can be added, and then a fourth. If several horses are working together it may be necessary to arrange the poles in a fan so that each horse can be ridden on a track that crosses the poles at the distances appropriate to the stride of that particular horse.

With two or more poles, the rider should move into the jump-seat position. Then, as the horse rises to clear each pole, the rider should give a little squeeze with his legs. If he has his stirrups on the ball of the foot, as he should have, his legs will be moving upward slightly over the horse's side while his body is being carried upward by the horse's movement. The leg squeeze then has a sort of lifting action. This encourages the horse to lift his feet well up as he passes over each pole in turn. At the same time the rider begins to get the feel of the horse 'coming up under him'.

One may be tempted to leave the poles lying, with the idea that they will then be ready to be ridden over on a later occasion. This doesn't work well in practice. The length of the horse's stride is not constant; indeed you have already seen how you can adjust the stride by varying the balance between the forward drive of your seat and the restraint of your hands. It turns out, however, to be much more difficult to adjust the horse's stride to suit the poles than it is to set the poles to suit the horse while he is being maintained in a steady rhythm. It is for this reason that it is so difficult to set the poles satisfactorily if working alone and having to dismount to make each adjustment. If the horse is forced to make an alteration to his stride because the poles are not quite at the natural spacing for the pace he happens to be using, the effect is to disturb his rhythm, and much of the benefit of the exercise is lost. The aim is to get the horse used to passing freely over the poles with no disturbance, and to encourage him to respond to the presence of the poles by making his action more springy, throwing his weight up higher at each stride. Continue for some time with this exercise, riding most of your circle in sitting trot and moving forward into the jump seat as you come to the poles, ready to give your lifting aid with the legs.

Cavalletti

For the next stage it is convenient, though not indispensable, to have a few poles fitted with wooden crosses at their ends to hold them a little way above the ground. The actual height can then be varied by rolling the crosses over (*Figure 8.8*).

When the horse has settled down and passes smoothly over three or four trotting-poles without changing his rhythm, have the assistant place a small jump (say 50 cm, or one of the cavalletti at its full height) at a distance from the last pole about twice that between adjacent trotting-poles (*Figure 8.9*). Now that the horse has learned to pay attention to the poles, he will probably accept the small jump without hesitation. He should, however, notice that the last pole presents a different kind of obstacle from the poles on the ground. To make sure of this you need to make the jump high enough. If it is too low, the horse may attempt to treat it as another trotting-pole, and he may stumble over it instead of making a definite jump.

On no account be tempted to build higher obstacles by piling cavalletti one on top of another. This can lead to serious accidents. If the horse were to collide with such an obstacle, either by failing to clear it or in the course of a refusal, he could get his legs tangled up in the muddle of tumbling poles and fall awkwardly, perhaps even breaking a leg. There is also a very serious risk to the rider in such a fall.

Transition from trot to jump

The rhythm of the horse's movement over a jump is quite different from the rhythm at the trot, but the rider should at this stage not make any deliberate adjustments in his own posture. Just ride straight through in the jump-seat

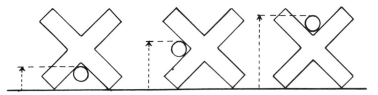

Figure 8.8 *Cavalletti rolled over to provide obstacles of different heights.*

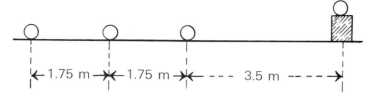

Figure 8.9 *Arrangement of three trotting-poles followed by a small jump. Suggested distances: 1.75 m, 1.75 m and 3.5 m. Adjust the distances to suit the stride of the horse.*

position as though the jump were, in fact, just another trotting-pole. Pay attention, however, to the feel of the horse's movement and make sure that your hold on the reins is sufficiently springy so that, if he stretches his neck suddenly, the rein will not jerk the bit in his mouth.

The horse has to make several alterations to his stride when negotiating a jump. Instead of tossing his weight from one diagonal pair of legs to the other in the trot, he has to reach forward over the jump with both forefeet together, holding them curled up under his chest, and he has to use both hindfeet together to propel his body upward and forward over the jump. Just as it is an advantage to a golfer, when he wants to drive his ball as far as possible, to take his club back in a preparatory back-swing, so also is it an advantage to the horse, in preparing to take off in a jump, to lower his quarters and bend his hindlegs. In this way he not only develops a stronger push against the ground, but he also gives himself more time for the thrust to act on the body before the feet leave the ground. These two factors together ensure that the horse's body is projected up and over the jump with the greatest possible momentum for the amount of effort put out by the muscles. As well as lowering his haunches, the horse also raises his forequarters so that the trunk is tipped back like a javelin ready for launching.

In making these various adjustments the horse uses the momentum of his head in a sequence of strong up-and-down movements. The head is relatively heavy so that, when the neck muscles pull the head upwards, they also have an important effect upon the trunk, tending to lift the hindquarters. This action has already been described in relation to the nodding of the head that occurs in brisk walking. When the head is pulled upwards, the body tends to pivot forward over the support of the forelegs. Thereafter the forequarters can be lifted in their turn, by pulling down on the head to transfer its upward momentum to the body.

The sequence of events in the transition from trot to jump is illustrated in *Figure 8.10*. In this case the obstacle to be jumped is so placed that, if it were merely another trotting-pole, it would be straddled by the horse's right diagonal. The horse has to have made up his mind to jump while this same right diagonal pair of legs is coming down to the ground in the previous stride.

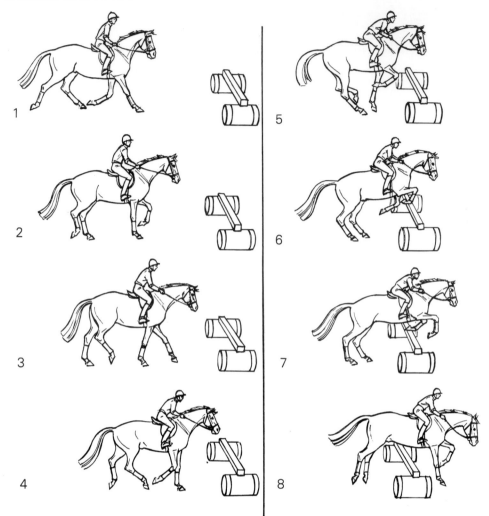

Figure 8.10 *Stages in the approach to a jump from the trot. The right hindleg reaches forward to be set down close behind the left foreleg. The horse takes off from the two hindlegs. The sequence is continued in Figure 8.11. (The interval between frames is one-eighth of a second.)*

The first stage of the horse's preparation for the jump is a slight exaggeration of the normal tossing movement of the head associated with the rhythmic tossing of the body from one diagonal pair of legs to the other during the trot. He allows his head to sink a little more than usual at the moment when the legs of the right diagonal are beginning to take the weight, and then he throws his head up a little more forcibly than usual. In this way the head develops extra upward momentum that is used during the succeeding unsupported

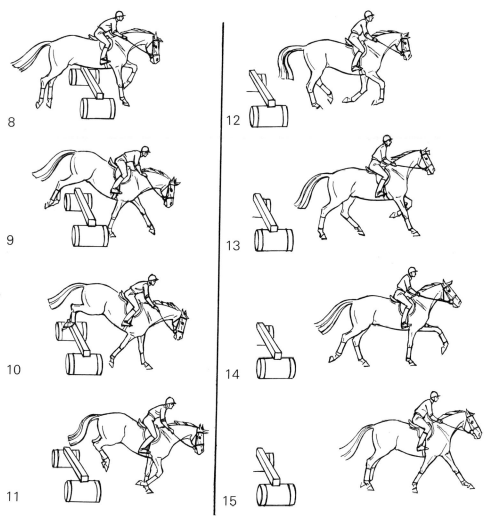

8

9

10

11

12

13

14

15

Figure 8.11 *Stages in the landing after a jump (continuation of the sequence shown in Figure 8.10). The forelegs are used one at a time to absorb the impact. The hindlegs come down later in the rhythm of a canter stride (see Figure 8.3). (Interval between frames: one-eighth of a second.)*

phase to modify the steps performed by the left diagonal pair of legs.

By pulling down on the head in this unsupported phase the horse can reach forward with his right hindleg so that it will land just behind the left forefoot. Instead of moving in time with the left foreleg, the right hindleg now doesn't touch down until its diagonal foreleg has almost completed its support phase. The delay in the support to the hindquarters has the effect that the foreleg upthrust on landing at this stride tends to tip the trunk backwards.

While the left foreleg is on the ground, the head is thrown up again very strongly. The effect on the trunk of the action of the neck muscles to lift the head enables the horse to bring his left hindfoot forward so that he can set it down close beside the right hindfoot, in the position needed for take-off. The extra upward momentum of the head is then used to lift the forequarters, both forelegs being folded up under the chest ready to clear the obstacle. The trunk is thus positioned ready to be launched upward and forward over the jump by the combined thrust of the two hindlegs.

The rider can observe the exaggerated up-and-down movement of the head and he can also feel the haunches sinking under him just before take-off. Because the body is also moving up and down, the head movements are not so noticeable from the side as they are from the saddle. Indeed, from the side one gets the impression that the head remains at almost the same height above the ground while the horse's withers move up and down. One can, however, deduce the relative movement of the head from the attitude of the neck as seen in side view.

As well as getting the horse used to negotiating small obstacles without fuss, this exercise with a few trotting-poles followed by a jump gives the rider an opportunity to accustom himself to the feel of the various stages in the jump itself. After some practice he will be able to anticipate the horse's movements and he can then start to work on the timing of his command to jump. As explained above, if the horse is to jump an obstacle which he would meet on the right diagonal, he needs to start his preparations while the same right diagonal is coming down to the ground in the previous stride. This means that the command to jump must be given a little before this.

One virtue of the use of trotting-poles in front of a small jump is that there is some control over the relationship between the footfalls and the take-off point for the jump. The horse arrives at the jump either on the left diagonal or on the right diagonal according to which diagonal is used for the first trotting-pole. There is no occasion for the horse to put in an additional short stride or to make any other kind of adjustment to his rhythm. With three trotting-poles (*Figure 8.9*), the diagonal on which the jump will be met is the same as the diagonal that straddles the first pole. The horse comes down on the same diagonal again when the rider's body is over the third pole. The appropriate moment at which to give the command to jump has to be just a little earlier than this, that is to say, during the upward spring after crossing the second pole. This gives the horse a chance to start his preparatory head movement during the half-stride over the third pole.

When practising with trotting-poles alone, the rider gives an encouraging squeeze with the legs during each upward spring of the horse when he is tossing his weight from one diagonal to the other. The timing for the command to jump is the same as the timing of one of these 'lifting' squeezes. To make a distinction that the horse will recognise, use a double squeeze and apply it during the spring between the second and third poles.

Seeing a stride

One of the main problems with jumping is for the rider to choose the correct moment for his command to jump. With the trotting-poles in place, the position of the footfalls is determined, and the rider is left only with the decision as to which is the right stride during which to give his command. In the more usual situation the rider also has to position the horse, and to adjust his stride length, so that he enters the 'preparatory zone' in front of the jump with his feet in the right places. Otherwise, when the horse actually arrives at the jump, he will not be at the correct distance from it. He will take off either too late or too early, or he will try to put in an extra stride. In any such case, the rhythm of his preparation for the jump will be upset. This may not matter for small simple jumps because the horse can make many adjustments in the course of a single stride. In a competition, where the nature of each obstacle has been adjusted by the course-builder to present particular difficulties in order to sort out the better performers from the less good, every departure from precision carries the penalty of an increased risk of failure.

The exercise with three trotting-poles and a small jump may be used to help the rider to develop the ability to 'see a stride', as it is called. A rider is said to have this ability when he can present his horse to a jump in such a way that the horse approaches and takes off smoothly without having to make any last moment adjustments in his stride. The crucial task here is to pick a spot on the ground directly in front of the jump and three strides away from it, and then to adjust the horse's approach so that, when the rider is directly over this spot, the horse is landing and taking off for one of the bounces in a steady stride pattern.

Three strides are needed for horse and rider to work together in harmony in tackling the obstacle. In the first stride, the rider consolidates his aiming of the horse at the centre of the obstacle and indicates his intention to jump by a number of subtle adjustments of weight distribution, posture, and feel on the rein which are the unconscious consequences of 'making up his mind to it'. During the second stride the rider urges the horse forward, to confirm that this is an obstacle to be jumped and not a gate at which to pause while the fastening is manipulated, and this is when he gives the actual command to jump. The third stride is needed by the horse so that he can make his own preparations, without interference from the rider. He can then get his feet organised and wind up his muscles ready for take-off.

It is not a very straightforward matter to measure off three strides in front of the jump because the stride length is not a fixed distance. Each horse has his own preferred stride length for a particular gait. To some extent this depends on the conformation, temperament and training of the horse, but there is also an important element that depends on the mood of the moment and on the degree of collection, so that part of the skill in seeing a stride lies in the rider's ability to gauge the way his horse is reacting to the situation at the crucial moment in question. In the exercise with the trotting-poles as described above, the spacing of the poles has been selected by the assistant to suit a steady rate of striding which is being maintained by the rider as he trots calmly round and round on his circle.

If you are going to practise with a jump that has separate supporting uprights, start your trotting-pole exercise with a single pole set on the ground between the uprights just under the place where you will later put up a pole for jumping. Have your assistant put down the second and third trotting-poles on the approach side of the pole that is lying between the uprights, adjusting the half-stride spacing to suit the horse. Now have your assistant move the first pole to the approach side of the other two with the same spacing, and then move the second pole back also, to finish in the pattern of *Figure 8.9*. This procedure ensures that all the distances will be correctly adjusted to suit the horse with half-strides between the poles and a full stride between the last pole and the jump.

After the rider has got used to giving his double squeeze for the command to jump at the moment when he is passing over the second pole in *Figure 8.9*, both this pole and the third pole can be removed, leaving only the first in position. When he comes round again the rider now continues his sitting trot over this remaining pole, gives his jump command at the place where the second pole used to be, and then goes forward into jump-seat position for the actual take-off. The horse's rhythm for the trotting circle should remain unchanged throughout.

Jump seat over a jump

It is important to be in the jump-seat position when the horse gives his main thrust with the hindlegs at take-off. If the rider's seat-bones are in contact with the saddle at this point, he is liable to be thrown strongly upwards and it will be difficult to predict where he will land. For any but a very small jump the rider should fold right forward at the hips and reach out with his hands beside the horse's neck and with his elbows in front of his knees. Keep your head slightly to one side to avoid being hit in the face by the horse's neck (*Figure 8.12*). You may notice, when watching top-level show-jumpers coming in at the end of a round, that the front of the rider's jacket often shows signs of having been in contact with the horse's neck.

When you are approaching a jump, make sure that each of your stirrups is safely under the ball of your foot, so that the springiness of your ankle is available to you. If you neglect this precaution, and particularly if you also allow your feet to move back from their normal position over the girth, there is a risk that, when the horse rises suddenly to take off for the jump, you will be catapulted upward and forward out of the saddle. Then, when the saddle catches up with you a little later on, the rein will come tight suddenly, jabbing the horse in the mouth.

The importance of moving the hands forward briskly cannot be too strongly emphasised. As the horse passes over the obstacle he throws his head well forward as part of the effort to lift his forequarters (*Figures 8.13 and 8.14*). If the rider does not give with his hands at this point, it is inevitable that the horse will feel a jab in the mouth. If this happens repeatedly, it is only to be expected that the horse will become less eager to jump. Moving the hands forward doesn't necessarily mean letting the rein go slack, as you can see in *Figure 8.13*, where the rider's hands have moved well up the horse's neck. A light contact will be needed for steering out of the jump on landing.

There is an advantage in allowing the feet to come forward a little as you are coming down to land (*Figure 8.14*). With the stirrup on the ball of the foot to take advantage of the springiness of the ankle-joint, this provides additional shock-absorption for the impact of landing. Most of the rider's weight on landing should, however, be taken on the knees and one should not allow oneself to become dependent upon the stirrups. It is very easy for one foot to come out of its stirrup during the preparation for a jump and then it is sometimes advisable to quit the other stirrup also because, if the rider's weight were to come down on one stirrup alone, this would almost certainly tip him sideways and he might be thrown off. Another hazard of depending upon the stirrup is that, if the stirrup slips back under the arch of the foot, the cushioning action of the ankle is lost. The weight then comes down on the stirrup with a severe jolt which may break either the stirrup or the leather and, again, the rider risks being thrown off to one side.

If the rider's feet are allowed to move back when he is over the jump, he is in danger of losing contact with the horse during the descent. It is then possible that when he lands he will not be over the midline of the saddle, and if this happens he is liable to be thrown to one side. Do not be tempted to excuse yourself for letting your feet go back on the grounds that many successful show-jumpers also do this. Remind yourself that many prominent show-jumpers have been competing successfully from a very early age. They owe their success partly to natural balance and acrobatic flair. They may never have thought it necessary to pay much attention to style. Lesser mortals get on better with more orthodox techniques. It is noticeable that horse-trials competitors, who have to contend with dressage tests and cross-country obstacles as well as with show-jumping, often ride in a more orthodox style, as shown in *Figures 8.12, 8.13 and 8.14*.

Landing after a jump

After taking off from the hindlegs, the horse lands on the forelegs. During the descent the horse's body acquires a great deal of momentum and substantial forces are needed to absorb this momentum on landing. The horse solves this problem in dynamics by using the springiness of his muscles to make a very soft landing in which the work of arresting the downward movement of the trunk is spread out over a comparatively long time. The forelegs are used one at

Figure 8.12 *Experienced rider just after take-off.*

Figure 8.13 *Experienced rider at the top of the jump.*

a time, the footfalls being well separated as they are in the gallop (*Figure 8.11*). The hindlegs come down later, sometimes after the forelegs have already left the ground. The forelegs then come down again to form with the hindlegs a support phase like that of a canter stride. It is, accordingly, natural for the horse to continue in canter after a jump.

Figure 8.14 *Experienced rider preparing to land after a jump.*

The forelegs contain several special shock-absorbing mechanisms that are important in landing from a jump. In the first place the pastern is set at an angle to the cannon bone, so that it is only the foot itself that has to be stopped suddenly. When the foot strikes the ground the leg bends at the fetlock, pulling on the springy tendons at the back of the leg. Sometimes a horse may land awkwardly with the fetlock straight so that the jolt of landing is transmitted up the whole leg. The pastern bone may be broken in such an incident. Laboratory tests show that the pastern bone of a steeplechaser can support a compression of nearly seven tons before giving way. This gives some idea of the stresses involved in catching the weight of the horse as it comes down after a jump.

Another shock-absorbing mechanism is found in the zig-zag arrangement of the bones at the shoulder and elbow joints. Here again the joints fold up during the impact, stretching the muscles that work over these joints. Lastly, the horse's shoulderblade is not firmly attached to the skeleton of the trunk. There is no collarbone, and the weight of the trunk is slung from the shoulderblades by long bands of muscle which can stretch like springs.

The rider's contribution to the jump

At this point it will be convenient to review all the various tasks that the rider should set himself to perform during a jump. An important component is the rider's determination to pass cleanly over the obstacle without striking it. If the horse senses that the rider is uncertain or that he is not secure in the saddle, this will lead to uncertainty in the mind of the horse and this will inevitably affect his performance. A crash against the poles will undermine the horse's confidence and it may take a great deal of patient training to get him back to form. The moral here is: do not put your horse to a jump unless you are sure not only that you really mean it but also that the horse is being given a reasonable chance to clear the obstacle. Drifting casually into jumps has a very unsettling effect on the horse and he is unjustly punished when he bangs his legs on the poles after the rider has not played his part properly. Always do your best to prepare the horse for the jump and be quite unambiguous in your commands.

Your first task after deciding to attempt a particular obstacle is to select the point at which you are going to start your three-stride run-in. Adjust the approach so as to be facing the middle of the jump and to be exactly at the bounce of a stride as you arrive at the selected spot. Then steer straight for the jump and make sure that the horse feels your determination to get over it. Once you have presented the horse to the jump correctly, and once he has made his own decision to jump in response to your 'asking' command, your most important task is to avoid interfering with his execution of the jump itself.

You no longer need to look at this particular obstacle. Indeed if you continue to gaze too intently at it during the later part of the approach, the horse will sense that perhaps there is some nasty concealed hazard that he has not yet seen for himself and he will start to worry about it. It is preferable to look straight ahead over your horse's ears at something on the far side of the jump so that he comes to regard the immediate obstacle as merely a minor triviality on the way to a desirable and eagerly sought goal a little further off. With this mental attitude he will sail easily over the obstacle as though jumping at liberty.

To get used to picking the right spot for the run-in, have your assistant set down a marker for you to aim at and ask him to watch and tell you whether you are arriving early or late. A good time to start this exercise is as a continuation of the work with three poles and a jump. After the second and third poles have been taken away, the remaining pole continues to control the placing of the horse's feet in relation to the approach to the jump. The assistant puts down the marker one full stride ahead of this pole. Thus, if the poles were 1.5 m apart, with the jump 3 m from the third pole, the marker will be 3 m before the first pole, or 9 m from the jump. The exact distances will, of course, be dependent upon the length of stride that the horse has chosen for the steady trot round the circle that keeps bringing him back to the jump.

When the assistant is satisfied that he has the marker in the right place in relation to the remaining pole, that pole can then be removed. The whole of the approach to the jump is now in the hands of the rider. Because the exact track round the circle will naturally vary a little each time, the horse will not always arrive with a bounce at precisely the same place. The rider has to adjust the horse's stride, by reining in or urging on, during the few strides before he reaches the marker, in such a way that the bounce occurs exactly as the rider's body passes the marker. Thereafter all he needs to do is to steer, urge, ask, and fold. The horse does the rest.

Indications by the horse

During the run-in, the rider should be alert for the rhythm of the horse's movements. He should watch for the up-and-down movement of the horse's head and he should feel for the moment when the horse lowers his haunches to reach forward with the hindlegs. He will also be able to feel the change in the horse's muscles as he braces himself for the extra effort required for the jump. If these indications are present, the rider knows that the horse has decided to jump, and all will be well. If the indications, or some of them, are absent, there is the chance that the horse has not yet made up his mind. If the rider is quick enough, an extra squeeze may save the day.

Refusals

The rider should be particularly wary if he feels the horse is not surging forward into the jump. Instead of increasing the up-and-down swing of his head, the horse may be inclined to lower his head and keep it there. He may throw his head forward to try to pull the reins out of the rider's hands. The next thing the rider knows is that, instead of the horse lifting his forequarters and reaching under himself with his hindlegs, he suddenly puts both forelegs straight out in front of him and comes to a dead stop with his head right down. The horse then swings briskly away to one side, leaving the rider with nothing to hold on to.

It is important to avoid giving the horse a chance to practise the technique of refusing a jump. If he stops a second time, try a different jump, or have someone give you a lead over the jump and follow closely behind, leaving about two horse's lengths clear. Horses usually jump freely in company and follow one another without hesitation. If your horse refuses this also, get someone else who is a strong rider to take him over a couple of times for you. Then go back to the beginning again. Make sure you can control the speed, getting him to go faster or slower at will. Repeat the work with the trotting-poles and re-introduce the jump only after the horse has accepted the trotting-poles without any disturbance of the rhythm of the trot.

Horses at liberty usually approach a jump at the canter rather than at the trot and, so long as they do not get jabbed in the mouth, they will often canter over small jumps quite freely even when ridden by a novice. This may give the misleading impression that the novice rider is already reasonably competent. Care is needed in deciding whether the rider has passed the stage of needing instruction. Problems will arise as soon as the horse finds himself slightly out of position for a smooth take-off. The horse will then make his own adjustments, but the change in his rhythm may unsettle the rider. In the course of regaining his balance the rider makes involuntary movements which the horse takes as commands, particularly if there is a jerk on the reins. The rider then complains that his horse has suddenly developed the habit of making mistakes. He will be tempted to chastise the horse, whereas the proper remedy is for the rider to discipline himself to accept further instruction. Although to approach a jump at the trot is a more demanding exercise for the horse, because he has to pay attention to what he is doing, it is a more instructive exercise for the rider than the uncontrolled approach at the canter, and there is less chance of unintentional jabs on the horse's mouth.

During the run-in to the jump build up a fairly firm pressure on the rein and maintain the impulsion by driving forward with your seat. Do not on any account allow the reins to jerk. Very often the cause of the trouble is that the rider's hands are not sufficiently springy. It is not that the rider is deliberately jerking the reins, just that because the rider's shoulders don't move in quite the same way as the horse's mouth, the rein occasionally goes slack and then snaps taut again. Be on your guard against any tendency for the horse's nose to deviate to one side or the other. Correct this at once so that the horse knows you are not going to tolerate any attempt to run out to one side.

If the horse succeeds in ducking out to one side, immediately bring him to a halt and turn him back toward the jump. If he has run out to the left, turn him to the right, and so on. Do not let him get the idea that you will allow him to turn whichever way he pleases. Remember that the problem is most likely to be one of the horse misunderstanding your commands, or not being certain what you want him to do. Accordingly there is little point in chastising him. This only serves to make him more reluctant to submit to the ordeal of being put to a fence. He comes to associate the nearby presence of the poles and uprights with the unpleasant experience of being beaten.

When you do succeed in getting him over the jump, be sure that you let him have the rein completely free while he is in the air and reward him at once with effusive praise and caresses. He will be happy to have discovered the solution to his problem.

Arm exercises over the jump

It does not require very much effort for a horse to pop over a small jump from the trot. All the problems arise in the timing and from unintended jerks on the rein. For the rider to learn about the timing he needs to practise jumping. Meanwhile the horse must be protected from having the bit jerked about in his mouth. A routine that helps is to jump without reins. You will need an alternative means of steering.

Some horses will jump any obstacle that is offered, but it usually helps if there are larger obstacles on either side to define just where the horse is intended to go. In the show-jumping arena the uprights supporting the poles are extended sideways in short fences called wings, often with the top rail sloping up toward the jump. What is needed for the present exercise is an extension of the wings to form a lane about two or three strides long on the approach side of the jump. It is often convenient to use the wall of an enclosed arena as one side of the lane. Poles and drums, or a couple of spare cavalletti, can form the other side of the lane. The rider steers into the start of the lane and then drops the reins before reaching the jump itself. Tie a knot in the rein so that, when you let go, there are no long loops of rein dangling down for the horse to catch his foot in.

Start without any obstacle in the lane. Get used to riding through at sitting trot, dropping the rein as you enter the lane and taking it up again as you emerge. Make sure you have plenty of impulsion, driving the seat forward each time until the horse gets the idea that he is to accelerate through the lane. Have your assistant put down a single pole at the far end of the lane where the jump will be eventually. Ride through two or three times, moving into jump seat as you pass over the pole. Then have the assistant raise the pole about 60 cm, or replace it with one of the cavalletti, and continue round as before. Approach at the sitting trot, then, as you enter the lane, drop the reins and urge the seat forward. Ask for the jump by giving your double squeeze with the legs at least one full stride ahead of the jump. Then move into jump-seat position and fold forward from the hip when you feel the horse gathering himself for the take-off. This will happen when his nose is almost at the pole.

The arm exercise described below is intended to confirm the distinction between the drive seat for the approach and the jump seat for the take-off. As soon as you are ready to drop the reins at the opening of the lane, bring your arms up to shoulder height. Have your upper arms straight out to the sides, level with your shoulders, elbows bent forward, hands in front of your shoulders just below your face. This posture helps you to square your shoulders and straighten your back while you are driving your seat forward into the saddle during the 'urge' phase of the approach. Just after the 'ask' command, move forward into jump-seat position and throw your fists and shoulders as far forward as they will go, alongside the horse's neck, folding forward from the hips as you do so and also bringing your feet forward a little. This forward thrust of the fists should coincide with the take-off so that, as you feel the horse rising under your knees, your shoulders should come forward to meet them. The effect of this is to make your body feel very springy to the horse. Your body gives as the horse pushes the saddle up under you. He feels that he doesn't have so much weight to lift. In consequence he jumps more freely and easily. This is a very good exercise for training horse and rider to move in harmony over the jump.

Jump from canter

When you are confident that you can keep your balance in the saddle over small jumps approached at the trot, and can be reasonably certain that you will not jerk the bit in the horse's mouth, it will be time to get used to approaching the jump at the canter. The jumping lane is very useful here. Again start with no obstacle in the lane. Ride through the lane at the canter, sitting well down in the drive seat for the approach and moving forward into jump seat as you near the end of the lane. Practise altering the horse's speed over the ground, holding back while in jump seat going round your circle, and urging forward when in drive seat as you come toward the lane. Make sure you can get a definite acceleration just as you enter the lane.

You are now ready for your assistant to put up the small jump, or one of the cavalletti, at the end of the lane. If you are accelerating into the lane, the horse will almost certainly take the jump in his stride, apparently without any change in the movement as you feel it in the saddle. In these conditions he jumps without needing any definite action on your part. Move into jump-seat position as you approach the pole and fold briskly forward when you see the pole about to pass under the horse's nose. You can see this without actually looking directly at the pole. Indeed, as mentioned earlier, it is better to look straight out ahead of you between the horse's ears and not to look down at all. If the horse shows any reluctance, or slows down in the lane instead of accelerating, take the obstacle away and go back to practising the changes of speed until you can rely on the horse surging forward as he comes to the lane.

Transition from canter to jump

Although it feels to the rider that the horse will take a small jump at the canter without changing his rhythm, there are, in fact, some adjustments necessary in the movements of the individual limbs. The ordinary take-off in the canter is from the forelegs and the horse lands on his hindlegs after the unsupported phase. For the jump he has to take off from the hindlegs and land on the forelegs.

To make the transition, the movements of the support diagonal are spread out in time (*Figure 8.15*). Instead of these two legs landing almost simultaneously, as they do in the canter, the hindleg lands early and the foreleg is held up and stretched forward over the jump. The two hindlegs thus land close together in time, and provide some of the thrust for take-off. As well as reaching forward with the foreleg of the support diagonal, the horse also reaches over the jump with the leading foreleg, ready to make a landing, after the jump, on the two forelegs just as in the jump from the trot. These adjustments are sufficient for a small jump. For a larger jump the two hindlegs may put in an additional short stride, coming to the ground before the haunches have begun to rise so as to be able to develop a long strong thrust to accelerate the body upward for take-off.

To make these adjustments at the right time, the horse must be warned, during the take-off for the previous stride, that the rider wishes him to make a jump. It is also necessary for the rider to take care to adjust the horse's stride during the approach, so that the last three strides before the jump may be taken at an accelerating pace without interference from the rider. The same rules apply as for a jump from the trot. Select the start point for the run-in and adjust the stride so that the bounce occurs as your body passes the selected start point. Then aim, urge, ask, and fold, just as for a jump from the trot.

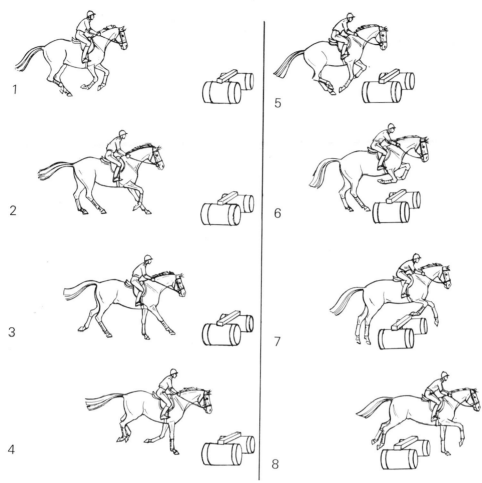

Figure 8.15 *Stages in the approach to a jump from the canter. Instead of taking off from the forelegs as in a normal canter stride (see Figure 8.3), the take-off is from the hindlegs. To achieve this, the forequarters are first thrown up at the end of the last full canter stride before the jump, and the hindlegs are then drawn well forward to give an extra thrust for the actual take-off. (Compare frames 4 to 7 in this sequence with frames 11 to 15 in Figure 8.11). (Interval between frames: one-eighth of a second.)*

Casual jumps

Horses usually enjoy jumping, provided they are not repeatedly and unjustly punished by being hit in the mouth by improper movements of the rider's hands, or by getting tangled up in the poles and banged on the legs because they have been ridden into the jump with inadequate impulsion or without sufficiently unambiguous commands. Once the rider has been introduced to jumping by careful systematic preliminary work over small jumps, his later development is largely a matter of practice.

A problem with many eager youngsters is that they are keen to jump everything in sight without having the patience to spend adequate time on the early stages of training. Because their ponies are at first clever enough to take them over the jumps whatever the rider does, they get the impression that they 'know everything' and they become resistant to advice. Meanwhile they gradually undermine the earlier training of the pony and assiduously practise whatever bad habits they happen to have acquired. Instead of improving steadily and continuing to enjoy their riding, they are liable to run into a phase of refusals and knockdowns unless they are very lucky. They tend to put the blame on the pony and start to beat him unmercifully. This only upsets the pony and leads to a further deterioration in performance, until eventually the rider gives up and the pony is sold at a loss.

A parent who buys a pony for his child will avoid many disappointments and greatly enhance the value of his gift if he is firm enough to insist upon laying a proper foundation for his child's training as a rider. It is not sufficient just to pack the child off to a riding school for a few lessons. Riding-school ponies behave very differently from family pets. Because they work daily with an instructor, riding-school ponies come to respond to the instructor's voice rather than to the rider's signals, so that one may get the impression from his performance at the riding school that the child is reasonably expert. When he gets home, however, the situation is suddenly very different.

When horse and rider have developed mutual understanding by practising in a jumping lane, the next stage is to set out several small jumps in the practice area at various positions so chosen that they can be jumped independently. Cavalletti do very well here. For each jump the rider should select a suitable start point. He then rides round at trot or canter, turning this way and that, and every so often takes in one of the jumps. In each case, he rides carefully over the selected start point so as to be directly in line with the jump for the approach, and he then urges forward with determination and unambiguous commands. This is usually a most enjoyable stage for both horse and rider.

The opportunity can now be taken of jumping any suitable obstacle, such as a fallen tree-trunk or a ditch, that may happen to present itself during a cross-country hack. One may even venture out with the hunt. Remember that 'the hunt' is a society with a long tradition of strict ceremonial, and you will not be welcome unless you are prepared to adhere to all the rules, written and unwritten. You will need to pay close attention to all the guidance given you by the friend who introduces you. Horses tend to get very excited when galloping along in company and it is as well to confirm from time to time that your horse still remembers how to stop. Most hunting accidents arise from riders being carried over-enthusiastically into awkward situations that are beyond the competence of that particular combination of horse and rider. Look ahead, be on your guard, take care — and enjoy yourself.

When riding through woodland remember that your horse may not bother to leave enough room for you. He will pass without hesitation under a low branch that just clears his withers and he will leave less than a couple of centimetres between his shoulder and a tree-trunk. The low branches you must steer round. Sometimes you can get through by lying forward over the withers with your head right down beside your horse's neck, but you may still be in trouble if the hood of your anorak catches in the tree; so go through very slowly. Steering will also help to save your knees, and you can use your leg aids to increase the clearance, provided you have trained your horse in leg-yielding.

Crossing water

Horses differ a good deal in their reaction to ditches and streams. This is largely a matter of what they have become accustomed to. Some horses enjoy splashing about and will paw the water with enthusiasm. Some like to roll in water and the rider must be on his guard and urge the horse on strongly as soon as he shows the slightest inclination to bend his knees with his head down. The preparation for a roll is not quite the same as just putting his head down to drink. Usually, before actually bending his legs to go down for the roll, the horse will shuffle his feet to bring the hindfeet closer than usual behind the forefeet. To prevent the roll, pick his head up with a few brief strong pulls on the reins, urge the saddle forward with your seat, and drive on strongly with both legs and the whip.

Other horses are very reluctant to put a foot into water. It may be necessary to dismount and lead them in. Wade in yourself to show the horse that the footing is sound. Splash about a bit and get him used to the feel of the water splashing against his legs. You may need to talk to him and reassure him with caresses until he realises there is no danger. Finally, turn away and lead him across the water while a friend urges him on from behind by throwing small pebbles aimed at his rump just beside the tail. Pebbles are better than a stick here as they are less likely to provoke kicking.

To get the horse used to ditches, you need to start with small dry ditches with good firm banks. Bring him to the edge and urge on with your legs. Resist any attempt he may make to turn his head to one side. It may be helpful to be given a lead over the ditch by a friend on another horse. Alternatively you can use the pebble trick mentioned above. The normal 'startle reaction' to the impact of the pebbles is a sudden bending of the hindlegs. This is just what you need in the preparation for take-off. The startle reaction may have the effect of overbalancing the horse into the ditch and his natural response will be to jump it. A jump from a standing start is a very sudden movement. It is essential that you should let his head go forward freely without the reins jerking tight. You will need to be careful, as no doubt before the jump you will be holding the reins pretty firmly to prevent him from turning out to one side. It helps to have a neck strap to hang on to.

Types of obstacle

As confidence begins to be built up, the severity of the obstacles can be gradually increased. The cavalletti may be arranged in pairs instead of singly. The distances should be chosen carefully. With about 4 m between cavalletti, the horse will bounce once without taking a stride. The assistant should watch to see that the second obstacle is placed as near as possible halfway between take-off and landing for the second jump.

To leave room for one stride between the cavalletti they need to be about 7.5 m apart. For two strides, leave about 10.5 m. With these distances in mind, you can build up sequences of cavalletti, and you can then use such a sequence to lead up to a slightly higher jump. In the early stages watch carefully to see that the distances suit the horse so that he does not become unsettled through meeting one of the obstacles awkwardly. You can then go on to individual obstacles of different shapes and sizes, but there is no point in going much over 1 m in height except for competition purposes. If your horse jumps 1 m smoothly, he will not need to adjust his technique much, even for the biggest obstacles that he can manage.

In the show-jumping arena you will be faced with jumps of many different kinds. Course-builders employ much ingenuity in providing variety in the appearance of obstacles, but basically there are two main types: uprights, in which the emphasis is on the height, as in a wall or a gate; and spreads, where the horse has to jump for distance as well as height. An example of a spread fence is the 'oxer' which consists of a hedge with poles in front and behind. Often two poles are set up on separate supports, one behind the other, with no hedge in between. Or there may be a group of three or four poles, each with its own supports, set at progressively increasing heights one behind the other, like a staircase.

The space below the top poles in some of these jumps may be filled by other poles, either parallel or sloping to form a cross, or by planks or stout wooden boxes painted with bold geometric patterns or made to look like brickwork, stone arches, or the like. The individual jumps may be grouped into combinations such as a spread followed by an upright, or an upright followed by a spread, and there may be three obstacles in a combination. Where obstacles are not more than 12 m apart they together rank as a single obstacle.

The art of the course-builder consists partly in the selection of the sequence and heights of the obstacles, but perhaps more importantly, in the placing of the obstacles in relation to one another and to the boundaries of the arena, particularly where the distances between obstacles are less than about 25 m, so that the landing from the first influences the stride with which the horse meets the second. Obstacles that interact in this way are said to be 'at related distances'.

All the obstacles in a show-jumping competition must be capable of being knocked down. In contrast, the obstacles in a cross-country course are solid and immovable. The fences are often combined with banks, ditches, and water. In some horse-trials courses, competitors are offered a choice of route over a complex obstacle, such as a pair of long post-and-rail fences meeting at a narrow angle. Where there is some variation in the spacing of the elements along their length, as in this example, one may elect either to aim for a place where the fences are close together so as to jump two elements as one spread, or by taking a different track, one may take the two elements separately with a stride in between.

Competitive jumping

In order to perform well in any jumping competition it is essential to be able to select the best possible track between the obstacles. The competitor's defence against the wiles of the course-builder is to plan carefully while walking the course before the start of the competition. Here one has the opportunity to measure the distances between obstacles by pacing them out, and one can also work out where to make any necessary turns in order to leave a just adequate distance for the run-in to the next obstacle.

One can turn quickly after a jump, but it is a mistake to attempt a sharp turn during a run-in. On the other hand, many jumps can be negotiated safely when approached at an angle. Where the time to complete the course is important, as in a jump-off against the clock, it is usually better to ride carefully over the shortest possible track than to rush on madly and consequently be forced out into wide turns.

In preparation for competitive jumping one should set up practice obstacles of different kinds to accustom your horse to those you expect to meet in the next competition. Thus you will need spreads as well as uprights, and you should arrange some of them as combinations. Also, when you have worked out the distances your horse prefers, get used to measuring these distances in terms of your own paces. It is this kind of measurement you will have to rely on in competition. Remember that your horse uses different stride-lengths for different types of jump. You approach an upright with short bouncy strides, while a spread calls for longer strides and more speed over the ground. When dealing with combinations, the natural distance for a spread followed by an upright will be longer than that for an upright followed by a spread. The distances between the obstacles you meet in a competition will almost certainly be slightly different from the distances that are 'natural' for your horse. You should be on the look-out for this when walking the course so that you will know beforehand where you need to lengthen the stride and where to hold back.

To get used to adjusting the stride between jumps, start with obstacles set up, say, 14 m, 17 m, and 20 m apart, or whatever distances near these values suit your horse. Work on these for a while, then move one of the obstacles a metre or so one way or the other and ride the combination again with the appropriate aids to adjust the stride. Again, pace out the new distances so that you will be able to anticipate the kinds of adjustment that are effective for the various distances.

Rushing fences

Some horses get so excited when they see a set of jumps that it is hard to hold them back. In this excited state they often do not judge the approaches to the jumps correctly and they will make many mistakes. To persuade them to take things more calmly, keep them down to a walk. Move in and out among the obstacles without jumping them. Occasionally walk right up to a jump and halt, as though it were a gate. When your horse has begun to settle, take him quietly into one of the jumps at the trot and at once bring him back to a walk and continue moving among the jumps as before. Eventually he will come to realise that, when he sees one of these contraptions with painted poles and so on, he is not necessarily expected to jump it right away, and he will be content to wait for your command.

It is also important to train him not to go rushing on like mad after landing from a jump. In a competition it may be vital to be able to slow up promptly in order to turn toward the next obstacle. It will help your horse considerably if you yourself start looking toward the next fence as soon as you are over the last one. He will feel the change in the distribution of your weight and this will tell him which way to turn even while he is still in the air. He can then adjust his landing to suit the direction of the next turn.

One effect of over-enthusiasm on the part of the horse is that he may tend to get too close to the jump before taking off, particularly if he is comparatively inexperienced. To help him to learn the proper distance for take-off you can put a pole on the ground in front of the jump. The distance between this pole and the jump should be about equal to the height of the jump.

Further development

It is not appropriate in a book of this kind to go into too much detail about the finer points of advanced competitive work. Once you are launched into competitions you will find yourself learning rapidly by experience, provided you have taught yourself the fundamentals correctly and do not have too many bad habits to handicap your development. You will also inevitably come into contact with other competitors, with their trainers, and with judges. You will not lack for advice. Your problem is more likely to be that of selecting which advice is relevant to your own case. Do not change just because someone else has a different technique from yours. By all means try out other people's ideas, but decide what suits you and what suits your own horse. Once you have established an understanding with your horse, it would be a shame to disturb it for a casual remark by a stranger not familiar with your own special problems.

9 SPECIAL MOVEMENTS

Preparation

A rider who has mastered the movements described in earlier chapters will be well prepared to start competitive work in any of the equestrian arts that he may choose, from Pony Club games and gymkhanas to show-jumping, dressage, and horse trials for combined training ('eventing'). There are, however, certain interesting additional movements that are called for only in the more advanced dressage tests and which can be regarded as 'display items', rather than as part of the basic training of the horse and rider. These movements − the pirouette, the passage, and the piaffe − present a particular challenge to the rider's skill. Even if one never intends actually to offer these movements in competition, one can still derive a good deal of entertainment and pleasure from attempting them.

An essential preliminary to these special movements is that the horse should have been trained to work on the bit, keeping his nose well in without being 'overbent' and without leaning on the bit (*Figure 9.4*). The rider should have practised urging his horse on by the action of his seat-bones, preferably without at the same time squeezing with the legs. The combined effect of this preparatory work is that the rider can obtain substantial impulsion without using his legs and with only a very light touch on the rein. The horse is ready to respond enthusiastically to the least indication by the rider's hand or leg.

The reason for practising the independence of seat and legs is that the legs will be needed for control of the horse's hindquarters. It is an advantage to be able to maintain the impulsion without confusing the horse by using the legs for forward drive at the same time as you are trying to give delicate indications for lateral movement. Practise bracing your back and driving forward with your seat-bones while at the same time holding your lower legs away from the horse's sides. As a further refinement, try reducing the pressure of your knees against the saddle while urging on with your seat, the lower legs still being held away from the horse's sides. The aim is to drive the horse forward into the bit. He does not actually accelerate forward because you are continuing to restrain him with your pressure on the rein. You should feel him ready to surge forward instantly the moment you give a little with the rein.

Also practise lateral work (*Chapter 7*), particularly the turn on the haunches and the half-pass. It is an advantage to be able to perform both the half-pass and the shoulder-in at the collected canter as well as at the trot.

Spurs and double bridle

The BHS Dressage Rules prescribe that spurs are obligatory for all tests of Medium standard and above, while they are permitted for other tests. The double bridle is forbidden at Preliminary and Novice standard, optional for Elementary and Medium, and obligatory for tests at Advanced standard and above. It should be clear from these provisions that the spurs and double bridle are instruments for fine control such as are needed for producing movements of extreme precision. They are definitely not weapons for violent coercion, despite the rather terrifying appearance of some of the specimens that have come down to us from the Middle Ages.

Before attempting to use spurs, the rider must be absolutely certain that he can keep his heels well away from the horse. Accidental application of the spurs can produce sudden violent reactions and may even cause injury to the horse. In preparation, the rider should get used to riding with rather long stirrup leathers. He should still be able to have his heel below the line of the sole of his foot and his knee can be nearly straight. This is the natural leg position when riding without stirrups; it is not an appropriate leg position for jumping. With this attitude of the legs it is possible to use the spur very gently, just stirring the hairs of the coat. There are now several places where your lower body can act against the horse: seat-bones, knee, inside calf, and spur. Each gives a different kind of message.

The spur is used to add emphasis to the leg aids, particularly when these are used with the 'lifting' action like that used when riding over trotting-poles. The effect is to encourage the horse to lift his hindleg higher on the side indicated by the spur. It is sometimes necessary to judge the timing of the application of the spur rather carefully to produce the best effect.

When you first start to use the double bridle, it will be sensible to leave off the curb chain. This gives the horse a chance to get used to the feel of the extra bit in his mouth and it gives the rider the opportunity to get used to handling two pairs of reins without any risk of overdoing the action of the curb.

There are two systems for holding the two sets of reins.

The 'Fillis' system is based on the idea that a tilt of the hand, thumb forward or back, will produce a corresponding tilt of the cheekpiece of the bit (*Figure 9.1*). The curb rein is accordingly passed under the little finger while the snaffle rein lies over the fore-finger and is gripped by the thumb (*Figure 1.21c*). Thus the free parts of the two reins cross the palm of the hand in opposite directions.

In the 'English' system the curb rein is held above the snaffle rein, being gripped with first and second fingers only, while the snaffle rein is in the normal position below the third finger. The two reins are separated by the ring

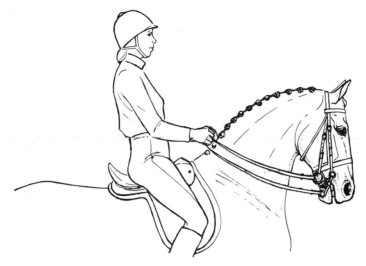

Figure 9.1 *'Fillis' system for managing the reins to a double bridle. 'The reins should occupy the same respective positions in the hand as the snaffle and curb do in the mouth, namely, the snaffle reins should be above the curb reins.' Fillis himself advocated using all four fingers to separate the reins (as in Figure 1.21). Here the rider is using the modified grip of Figure 6.19, the curb rein below the little finger and the snaffle rein between second and third fingers. The horse should be feeling the bit and contributing to maintaining a slight tension in the rein. The slack rein here indicates that the posture is not produced by pulling with sheer force on the rein.*

Figure 9.2 *'English' system for managing the reins to a double bridle. The curb rein is above the snaffle rein. The finger movements for controlling the snaffle bit are thus the same as when using a snaffle alone.*

finger, or by the ring finger and little finger together (*Figure 9.2*) if not too much force is going to be needed on the rein. The free parts of both reins run forward together over the forefinger where they are gripped by the pressure of the thumb.

If the curb rein is held above the snaffle rein, the finger movements that the rider has learned when using the snaffle alone will still work as before. When additional curb action is needed, this can be produced by turning the hand in the horizontal plane to bring the fingernails nearer to the rider's chest. This is a fairly natural movement to make in response to a situation calling for firmer control of the horse's head. In the Fillis system, by contrast, a completely new set of finger movements has to be learned for the management of the double bridle because those fingers that formerly played upon the snaffle rein now bear against the curb rein instead.

When the reins are to be taken together into one hand, the forefinger of that hand is used to separate the curb and snaffle reins received from the other side. The two curb reins are now adjacent, separated only by the middle finger, the two snaffle reins being to the outside, one on each side, separated by the whole width of the hand. The rider can steer with the snaffle rein by moving his hand so that the thumb is carried either further forward or further back; and he can increase the curb action by rolling his hand so as to bring his knuckles nearer to his chest, thus pulling equally on both curb reins.

In this movement, the hinge at the wrist allows the hand to pivot about an axis through the centre of the fist. (You can imagine the position of this axis as that taken up by a pencil held in the fist.) The two snaffle reins, gripped in the centre of the fist, slide over the outside edges of the hand during the rotation, so that the bridoon bit remains unaffected, Meanwhile, the curb reins are pulled upon because they are gripped between the fingers at a point which is a little way away from the axis. This rotation of the hand can produce a movement of the curb reins of as much as three or four centimetres without changing the tension in the snaffle reins.

By this stage in the rider's development he will have become quite used to adjusting the relative position of his hands on the rein, allowing the rein to slide a little through the fingers, or taking up rein, as required. It should not take him long to get used to the extra rein and to adjust the two reins in his fingers to give more purchase on the snaffle or more on the curb, according to the needs of the moment. The curb chain can now be fitted. Be sure that the chain is correctly twisted so that all the links lie flat against the horse's chin, and adjust the length so that the chain is drawn tight when the cheekpieces of the bit are at about 45° to the line of the horse's mouth.

Most of the control of the horse by the rider's hands is produced with the snaffle rein. The curb rein is used occasionally to remind the horse to keep his nose well in so that the snaffle rein can work at the most effective angle, across the line of the horse's jaw. The curb can also be used to ask the horse to pay attention when he is day-dreaming. It should not be used with excessive force because this will just stimulate the horse to resist and his mouth may be bruised in the ensuing battle.

Overbent in the double bridle

When you first come to use the double bridle, you may be tempted to use the combined reins together as though you were still using a single rein. What may happen, if you are not wary, is that you adjust the two reins in your fingers to give an approximately equal tension in bridoon rein and curb rein, and thereafter apply your rein aids with the whole hand, making no distinction between the effects on the two reins. The horse may then tend to become overbent because he is responding to the continued pressure on the curb bit. You may try to correct this overbending by raising your hands, in the hope of persuading the horse to lift his head. This attempted remedy does not work because the action of raising your hands puts unwanted additional pressure on the curb bit. There is a risk that the horse may soon come 'behind the bit', and it will become increasingly difficult for you to develop impulsion.

The solution to this common problem is to make a habit of always leaving a little more slack in the curb rein than in the bridoon rein unless you really want to use the curb for some specific purpose.

An overbent horse can be persuaded to take up a contact with the bit, and eventually to hold his nose a little further out, by the following routine. Use the bridoon as a simple snaffle, with the curb rein lying inactive on the horse's neck. Encourage the horse to walk briskly forward, using a light rein contact with both hands active and alerting. Then make a series of turns, first to one side and then to the other, indicating the turn in each case by yielding with the outside hand while maintaining a steady tension with the inside hand. Keep up the impulsion by vigorous seat aids and leg aids so that the horse does not slacken speed as he makes the turns.

After some repetitions, and provided that you maintain the activity of both hands with continual slow variation in finger pressure, the horse will start to 'seek the bit', moving his mouth forward to take up the tension whenever you yield with your outside hand. He may even start to stretch his neck, moving his head forward and downward and pulling on the rein. When you feel the horse responding in this way and taking an interest in the bit, reward him immediately by voice and caresses. You can then start to take up rein little by little. If all is going well, and the horse is keeping up his pressure on the bit, you can now start to raise your hands, a little at a time, first on one side and then on the other. Any slackening in the horse's forward progression has to be met at once by increasing the vigour of your seat aids and leg aids. This combination of manoeuvres is what is intended by the phrase 'pushing the horse's head up with the rider's legs'.

The aim is to develop an elevated head-carriage with arched neck and with the profile of the horse's face just a little in advance of the vertical, the poll being the highest point of the neck. When you have achieved this, you can take up the curb rein again, always remembering to leave a little more slack in it than in the bridoon rein. If the horse starts to lift his head higher than you want, you can correct this quickly by a brief touch on the curb rein.

Adjusting rein with the double bridle

Some riders find that the bridoon rein tends to slip more easily through the hands than the curb rein, and that this can happen without their noticing. They may set out with the desired amount of extra slack in the curb rein and then discover, after riding on for a few minutes, that the tensions in the two reins have unintentionally become equalised again so that there is more tension than intended in the curb rein. Continual readjustment with two hands would be liable to catch the judge's eye in competition, so it is preferable to make one-handed readjustments surreptitiously. Since there will be no occasion for applying the curb in these circumstances, you can hold the curb rein, temporarily, with your ring finger alone, gripping this rein between your middle finger and your ring finger. The bridoon rein passes from below your little finger to be gripped between thumb and forefinger in the position normal for a single snaffle rein. You can then use the single-handed rein-shortening routine set out in *Figure 1.14* to take up the appropriate tension in the bridoon rein, as required, on each side in turn, returning afterwards to the orthodox grip.

Pirouette at walk

The track of the footfalls in the pirouette is the same as for the turn on the haunches. The horse pivots on one of his hindlegs and his forelegs move laterally, the outside foreleg crossing in front of the inside foreleg. The turn on the haunches is performed from the halt, one step at a time. In contrast, the pirouette is performed in the course of a forward progression without interruption of the cadence of the footfalls. It can be performed at walk, trot, canter, or piaffe. It is permissible for the hindfeet to move slightly to the side, instead of pivoting precisely, but if they do, they must move on a very small circle in the same direction as the forefeet (*Figure 5.8*).

Because of the marked change in the speed over the ground at the start of the turn, it is essential to have plenty of impulsion in order to preserve the rhythm of the footfalls. For this reason it is not appropriate to check the forward motion simply by pulling on the reins. What is needed is an increased drive with braced back, as in the half-halt. The horse is driven into the restraining hand so that his weight is thrown more onto the haunches. The rider assists this shift of weight by moving his shoulders back slightly and raising his hands.

As soon as the horse shortens his stride, the rider carries both hands over toward the side to which the horse is to turn. Thus, if the horse is being asked to pirouette to the right, the rider gives opening rein with the right hand and indirect rein in front of the withers with the left hand. The horse's nose is moved slightly to the right and the rider applies his left leg over the girth to encourage the lateral movement of the forelegs. The rider's right leg is held in readiness to check any tendency for the horse to step sideways with the inside hindleg.

If the horse shows signs of stepping back, both legs are brought on and the seat-bones urge the saddle forward, while the tension in the reins is relaxed for a moment and then taken up again. Throughout the whole manoeuvre the rider has to be supremely alert to gauge at what moment, and in which direction, the horse is beginning to shift his weight over his feet, and to judge just when he is about to move each of his legs. The indications that the rider makes with his hands and with his legs are brief and very precisely timed so as to influence each stage of the horse's movement individually.

The first attempts at the pirouette can be made at the walk. Ride a 10 m circle in collected walk, urging the horse forward with seat and knees rather than with the lower leg. Bring a little of your weight onto each knee in turn to emphasise the natural swing of the shoulders. Work with the rein against the forward and backward swing of the head but encourage the lateral swing. This should produce short steps with the feet lifted well up at each step. Draw the outside leg back and give indirect rein behind the withers with the outer hand, the left if the turn is to the right. These aids should produce the 'haunches-in' position with the hindlegs tracking on a smaller circle than the forelegs.

Eventually, of course, you will be asking the horse to make a larger movement to the side with his forelegs than with his hindlegs. The object of starting with the inward movement of the haunches is to ensure that the horse is not tempted to step outward with his hindfeet; this would lead to a spin instead of to the pirouette aimed at. Once he gets used to the manoeuvre, the emphasis on the initial haunches-in can be reduced until the pirouette is finally performed by moving the forehand alone.

After establishing the haunches-in, bring the left hand over a little further to give indirect rein in front of the withers, give opening rein with the right hand, and bring the left leg forward again onto the girth. The horse should now be stepping into the circle slightly with his forelegs, making a half-pass but continuing round the circle. The rein aids to move his forequarters to the right should be given just as he is lifting his right foreleg and again just as he is lifting his left foreleg. The action of the rider's left leg is to ask the horse to step diagonally toward the right with his left hindleg. The rider may need to keep readjusting the point where he applies this leg aid, moving his leg forward or back according to the response he feels in the horse.

Moving inward in half-pass gradually reduces the size of the circle. Do not attempt too much all at once because this is a difficult exercise for the horse. With patience and much practice you will eventually be able to bring the circle right in until the horse is pivoting on the inside hindleg, the hoof being replaced on the same spot after each step. When both rider and horse are

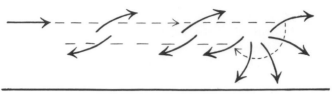

Figure 9.3 *Developing the half-pirouette against the wall. Renvers on the left rein about one horse's length from the wall. Half-halt and turn in toward the wall. Emerge into travers on the right rein.*

familiar with what is required you can start to ask for the pirouette from a straight progression at the walk. For this stage it helps to have a high solid fence or a wall to work against, like the wall of an indoor riding school. Walk a straight track parallel to the wall (*Figure 9.3*) and move into the renvers position, that is to say, a half-pass with the haunches toward the wall, at about one horse's length away from the wall. Then give a half-halt and turn in toward the wall in a half-pirouette, coming out into travers along the wall.

When the half-pirouette against the wall is being executed smoothly, either to the right or to the left, you can ask for a full pirouette during a straight walk without the support of the wall. The point of using the wall in the early trials is that it prevents the horse from moving forward after you have started the turn, and this gives you a chance to concentrate on the indications for the lateral components of the manoeuvre.

In particular you need to be very tactful in your management of the hindquarters. If you are too energetic with your left leg and not quite quick enough with your right, the horse will move his hindlegs to the side, producing a full pass instead of a pirouette. If, on the other hand, you are too energetic with your right leg, the horse will spin, the hindquarters moving to the left while the forequarters move to the right. The horse finds it much easier to spin than to perform the pirouette correctly. If you once allow him to make a habit of it, you may later find this habit extremely hard to eradicate.

In practising difficult manoeuvres like the pirouette it is essential to avoid confusing the horse. This means that you should not spend too much time repeating the same thing over and over again in the same session. If you do so there is the risk that the horse may be learning the wrong things, practising his mistakes as well as the moves you want him to make. Reward him with caresses and by making much of him whenever he does any part of the manoeuvre correctly. Then go on to do something quite different, leaving the horse time to forget those wrong moves of his which you did not reward.

Your own technique for influencing the movements of the individual limbs of the horse can be developed by further practice of the step-by-step turn on the haunches and of the rein-back balance. Both of these contain elements that are used in the pirouette. Also use these manoeuvres to practise 'tuning in', so to speak, to the feel of the movements of the horse's muscles as he shifts his weight and prepares to lift one leg or another.

For competitive dressage purposes all the aids have to be given very discreetly so as to be barely visible to the onlooker. It is also required that the same cadence of the footfalls shall continue throughout the manoeuvre without any interruption or hesitation in the rhythm.

The current set of schedules for the higher-level dressage tests call for pirouettes at the walk and at the canter, but not at the trot. However, the pirouette at the trot can provide useful practice as part of the preparation for the passage and piaffe.

Pirouette at trot

The preparation for the pirouette at the trot is essentially similar to that for the pirouette at the walk except that even more impulsion is required to keep the trot going when the circles are getting smaller. The rein aids for the lateral movement of the forequarters are applied as the horse is rising on the right diagonal (for a turn to the right). The horse then moves his right foreleg out sideways while it is in the air, and the consequent shift of weight has the effect that the next thrust of the left foreleg will push the forequarters to the right. At the same time the rein gives a slight check to the forward movement to make sure that the right foreleg goes out to the side rather than forward. Meanwhile a leg aid on the left encourages the horse to reach forward with his left hindleg.

When the horse is rising on the left diagonal, you relax the rein pressure slightly as well as giving the indication to move the forequarters to the right. This asks the horse to reach over with the left foreleg to cross in front of the right foreleg. The pressure of the rider's left knee and leg encourages the lateral movement of the forequarters so that after the right hindleg has been lifted it will be set down again on the same spot.

Care has to be taken here again to balance the vigour of the leg aids on the two sides so as to avoid letting the horse go into a spin. It will be preferable to accept a small amount of forward progression with the inside hindleg rather than to permit any lateral movement away from the point on which the horse is supposed to be pivoting.

As before, start with the half-pass in decreasing circles, then try the half-pirouette toward the wall, and finally the full pirouette during a straight-line progression without the aid of a wall. The pirouette at the trot presents a considerable challenge to the rider's skill, particularly as he may need to use 'lifting' leg-aids to maintain the trot while at the same time using his legs to control the lateral movement of the hindquarters.

Pirouette at canter

The canter pirouette is the most spectacular as well as the most satisfying manoeuvre that can be performed by the ordinary rider without recourse to the highly-specialised training routines needed for Haute École or for the circus repertoire. The first requirement is a very active collected canter. This is obtained by the combination of a strongly braced back with a carefully adjusted rhythmic action on the reins.

The rider should 'sit deep' into the saddle, driving on with his seat rather than with his legs. The rider's back has to be kept supple to absorb the impact as his weight comes down into the saddle at each stride. The seat-bones are thrust forward just as you begin to feel the increasing pressure against your seat. The legs are relaxed with the knees gently touching the saddle. The shoulders are squared back to open the chest and the head is held erect. The rein action is quite subtle. In the first stages of collection, the hands are working against the swing of the horse's head, without at any time allowing the rein to go slack. As the horse responds and brings his nose in, the rider increases the pressure on the reins and begins to encourage the head swing again, this time lifting his hands a little at each stride and putting particular emphasis on the phase where the horse's nose is moving toward the saddle.

The aim of this action of the rein is to ask the horse to arch his neck and to lift his head without at the same time poking his nose out. This movement of the horse's head alters the horse's balance to throw more weight on the hindquarters and to lighten the forehand. The continued urge of the rider's seat also encourages the horse to reach forward with his hindlegs so that he rounds his back and bounces higher and higher at each stride while making less and less ground forward.

When you have achieved a really bouncy collected canter, turn in to ride a 10 m circle. With your outside leg ask the horse to bring his haunches in and then move your hands over to get him to make a half-pass round the circle. It may help if you lift your outside hand a little higher than your inside hand. With the half-pass you gradually decrease the size of the circle. Do not be in too much of a hurry or the horse will get excited and begin to resist.

In the early stages, before he has worked out what it is you want him to do, the horse is liable to try something he has done before, like a full pass, a spin, or even a rear. You must be careful to give him no opportunity to learn that one of these unwanted movements is rewarded by a relaxation in the vigour of your commands. It is better for you to stop short before he has completed his manoeuvre, and to allow him to relax at a moment of your own choosing, rather than to persist until he breaks away and then to let him get away with it.

Another disadvantage of attempting too tight a turn too early at the canter is that the horse may not have learned to lift his feet neatly. He can strike one leg against another and cut himself. This will be an irrelevant punishment which will interfere with the smooth progress of his training. Uncertainty leads to excitement, particularly if the rider is obviously trying to say something emphatic and the horse doesn't understand what it is that is being asked of him. Horses do not learn quickly when they are excited. They keep trying moves that have been appropriate in previous moments of excitement and they do not pay too much attention to the rider's commands; they just try frantically to escape from the tense situation by one means or another. Naturally any move that allows them to break free and relax will be tried again on future occasions when the rider is trying to teach something new.

After the decreasing circles, try the half-pirouette toward the wall, first on one hand and then on the other. You should then be able to produce a full pirouette at the canter on a straight line without the help of the wall. Ask a friend to watch the horse's hindlegs carefully and to tell you if the horse is not pivoting accurately. Steer the lateral movement as necessary by adjusting the position at which you apply your outside leg. Bring the leg forward to encourage the sideways movement of the forelegs and move the leg back behind the girth to regulate the movement of the hindquarters. Use the inside leg to restrain the horse from stepping into the turn with his inside hindleg.

Passage and piaffe

After you have succeeded in keeping the trot and canter going while the speed of forward progression is gradually being reduced for the start of the pirouette, you will have taught yourself most of the commands needed for the passage and piaffe. These movements are closely related to the collected trot. The horse tosses his weight from one diagonal pair of legs to the other, just as in the trot. The difference from the trot lies in the height of the spring at each step. At passage and piaffe the horse springs so high, and consequently spends so long in the air at each step, that he has time to make elegant display movements with his feet. When the feet are first lifted, the hooves are tucked right up, with strongly bent fetlocks and pasterns (*Figure 9.4*). Then, before the descent proper, the hooves are pointed at the ground with a sort of hesitation. The horse appears to be hanging in the air at each step before the legs are extended in the preparation for landing.

The expression 'piaffe' is used for this specially elevated and collected trot, with the characteristic display movements of the feet, when it is performed on the spot, without forward progression. If the horse moves over the ground, with the same elevated gait, the movement is referred to as a 'passage'. This very elevated springy trot, with arched neck and head tucked in, is part of the natural display behaviour of the horse. Often one will see high-spirited horses displaying to one another in this way when they are first let out from stable to paddock on a bright spring morning. They appear to be proudly showing off their vigour and their feeling of well-being. From time to time they hoist their tails like pennants, make snaking movements with head and neck, and suddenly take off in short, high-speed sprints and chasing games. It is a most exhilarating sight. They are so obviously enjoying themselves.

To produce the elevated action of passage and piaffe the rider must sit deep in the saddle with a supple back so that he can urge the saddle forward at each step to keep up the impulsion. His hands are very still, but with some

Figure 9.4 *Piaffe: an elevated, springy trot, without forward progression. The raised feet perform elegant display movements.*

encouragement to the lateral sway of the horse's head by curling and uncurling the fingers on the two sides alternately, tightening one rein a little while relaxing the other, and then changing over at each stride in time with the horse's natural head movement. The rider's legs hang at their full length, either with long stirrup leathers or without stirrups altogether. Spurs may help. The springy action of the trot is encouraged by using 'lifting' leg aids. In addition, an extra tickle is given with the spur on each side in turn just as the hindleg of that side is beginning to develop its thrust. The tickle tells the horse to push a bit harder with that hindleg so as to have time to lift the leg higher, this being the natural response to any leg aid. The timing is rather crucial and the rider may need to experiment a little before he gets it right. He will feel the difference when the horse lifts his feet properly because of the play of the muscles when the horse is making the additional pointing movement with his feet that distinguishes the passage from the ordinary collected trot.

The various lateral movements described earlier (*Chapter 7*), such as the shoulder-in and half-pass, can all be performed at the passage, as can the rein-back. Indeed the piaffe can be regarded as a balance between forward progression and rein-back. Turns on the spot can be executed at piaffe – turn on the forehand, turn on the haunches, and finally the pirouette.

When the rider has taught himself, and his horse, all these various manoeuvres, he will have the great satisfaction of knowing that he can feel what the horse is telling him through the muscular adjustments that precede every movement, and that he can also indicate to the horse just what movements to make at any given moment. Both horse and rider will derive long-continued pleasure from the intimate relationship that develops through such an interchange of messages, which is truly a conversation between friends.

APPENDICES

Introductory note

There are several questions that arise in discussions related to riding where it is hard to give fully satisfying explanations without going into a good deal of highly technical detail. However, it does help when formulating practical advice to have a sound idea of just what it is that is going on.

In the following appendices I deal with two of these questions: what is involved in maintaining our balance without falling over; and how we come to be able to do certain things without thinking about them.

In relation to balance I should warn you that some of the ideas that may be familiar to you from school physics turn out to be rather misleading. This is because they are based on simplifications that conceal factors which prove to have crucial significance in our understanding of the real world. For example, there is no such thing in the real world as a rigid body with the whole of its mass concentrated at its centre of gravity. Such a notion is simply a convenient fiction. Real objects are not like that.

In my explanations, I have tried to steer a middle course between misleading simplification and obsessively careful detail. If you are not clear about some of the terms involved, you will find explanatory notes in the third appendix.

APPENDIX 1

Balance and Related Ideas

'Staying on while the horse is moving is a matter of balance'. What does this mean? And how can it be achieved?

Requirements for balance

Balance is a fairly familiar idea but, like many English words, it is used in several different senses, often without a clear understanding of the distinctions between them. The word itself comes from the Latin name ('two scale-pans') for a device used for comparing weights. In a beam-balance, the beam pivots about a point just above its centre of gravity. When the weights in the two scale-pans are equal, the beam see-saws slowly before coming to rest in the 'balanced' position. The weights in the two scale-pans tend to tilt the beam in opposite directions. In the 'balanced' condition, with the beam at rest, the two opposing tendencies to tilt are equal in magnitude. This leads to the basic meaning of 'balance' to indicate the equality of opposing tendencies.

When the beam of the balance is swinging, the movements of the beam itself have to be taken into account. If the left-hand scale-pan moves downward, this moves the centre of gravity of the beam toward the right of the pivot. The support force exerted by the pivot then tends to tilt the beam toward the right and this counteracts the displacement from the rest position. This is what happens to anything that is hung from a support that is above its centre of gravity, such as a stirrup suspended by the stirrup leather from the stirrup bar of the saddle, or a coat hanging on a peg.

Any situation in which a displacement from a particular condition generates forces that tend to reduce the displacement is referred to as a state of 'stable equilibrium'. [The word 'equilibrium' ('equal weight') is just another word for balance.] The contrast here is with an 'unstable equilibrium', such as that of a pencil stood up on its point where, even though the pencil may be in balance for a moment in the rest position, any displacement, however small, generates forces that tend to increase the displacement further so that the pencil falls. An intermediate condition, that might be referred to as one of 'precarious balance', arises where an object stands on a support that is below the centre of gravity and where the available area of support is relatively restricted. An example is the case of a coin stood up on its edge. So long as the centre of gravity of the coin remains vertically above the area of contact, the coin is in stable equilibrium and will stay upright. But as soon as the coin is displaced beyond the vertical projection of the edge of the area of support, the condition becomes unstable and the coin falls. The same is true of a man standing on one foot.

The expression 'balancing' is used for the process of setting one object on top of another where the available area of support is small compared with the height of the centre of gravity above the support. The result is not necessarily a condition of precarious balance. Consider the example·of a pole balanced on an oil-drum laid on its side (*Figure A1.1*). It is necessary, first, to experiment by trying the pole in various positions in order to determine the 'point of balance' of the pole. Thereafter, the pole will stay in place even though the area of contact is very small. If you now give one end of the pole a little downward push, it will rock up and down like the beam-balance. The mechanics of the two oscillations are, however, quite different.

The beam of the balance is supported at a point *above* its centre of gravity, so it behaves like a pendulum. In contrast, the support for the pole is the area of contact with the drum, which is

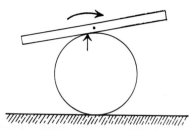

Figure A1.1 *Mechanics of stable equilibrium. Pole balanced on an oil drum. The point of application of the support force moves in such a way as to oppose a tendency to fall over.*

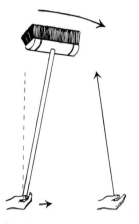

Figure A1.2 *Active preservation of balance. Broom balanced on the end of the handle. The hand has to be moved quickly to provide, in a new position, a support force so directed as to counteract unwanted toppling motion of the broom.*

necessarily *below* the centre of gravity of the pole. The pole is stable because of what happens at the support point. When the pole tilts, it rolls over the surface of the drum. The point of application of the supporting thrust provided by the drum thus changes. The condition is stable so long as, for any displacement, the movement of the point of application of the support thrust is greater than the movement of the centre of gravity of the supported body. When this condition is satisfied, the support thrust always tends to tilt the supported object toward a rest position with its centre of gravity vertically over the point of support.

This is, in fact, a general statement of the condition that obtains also with any object whose centre of gravity is above the support, even where the supporting surface is not relatively restricted. It applies for instance to a rider sitting in the saddle when the horse is stationary. We do not usually observe any rocking, unless parts of the supported structure are relatively springy. Nevertheless, the centre of pressure of the supporting force does move when any attempt is made to displace the supported object. The principle applies to living things, such as our own bodies and the bodies of animals, as well as to inert objects.

Achievement of balance

There is always a certain amount of movement in the body, arising from the activity of the heart and from breathing. The resulting sway needs to be opposed if the body is to avoid falling over. If you stand on one foot you will be able to feel the process in operation. Pay attention to the sensations from your foot. You will be able to feel the way the body makes automatic adjustments to the pressure between the foot and the ground. You will feel the pressure moving between heel and toe, and from side to side of the foot. If you make a deliberate swaying movement, to take your centre of gravity outside the area of the foot, you will start to fall over. When this happens, you will find that your other leg is automatically swung out in the direction of the impending fall and stiffened to catch your weight on the other foot. It is by sequences of movements of this kind that we walk about, run, jump and so on. These reactions are so commonplace that we are usually quite unaware of what is going on.

To get some idea of the nature of this process, consider the task of balancing a broom upside down on your hand. Suppose you have the end of the handle resting on the palm of your hand and the broom-handle upright with the broom-head in the air (*Figure A1.2*). When the broom starts to topple in a particular direction you quickly move your hand in that same direction. Try to move far enough and fast enough to arrest the tilt. The broom-handle will start to tilt in a new direction, calling for a new corrective movement of the hand, and so on. Skill is needed, but this comes with practice. Some people are better at it than others. Eventually, you will be able to manage with quite small movements.

When the broom is tilting over, three things are happening: the falling toward the ground, the horizontal movement, and the tilting over. Each of the movements is affected by a different aspect of the support thrust that you are applying with your hand. The falling is produced by the gravitational attraction of the earth, directed along a radius of the planet, a direction that we can call the 'gravitational vertical'. When the thrust line is at an angle to this direction, we can regard the thrust as made up of two components, an upward one directed along the gravitational vertical, and another at right angles to this. The relative magnitudes of these two components depend on the angle between the thrust line and the gravitational vertical. The vertical component of the support thrust to a greater or lesser extent opposes the tendency of the broom to fall under gravity, and the horizontal component of thrust influences the horizontal movement of the broom. The tilting movement depends on the relationship between the thrust line and the centre of gravity of the broom. The movements of your hand alter the force with which you press up on the handle of the broom. Your strategy for keeping the broom from falling is to keep changing the direction, magnitude, and point of application of the thrust. The vertical and rotational movements occurring in various directions at different times then all eventually cancel one another, leaving only such desired horizontal movement as you decide upon.

Ordinary standing and walking about involve precisely similar adjustments of the direction and point of application of the support thrust provided from the ground. Instead of sliding our feet about, in the way in which we have to move the hand that supports the broom, we just use the two legs in turn, repositioning one leg while the other is supporting the weight. If, for some reason, we have only one leg available, the body has another trick for avoiding falling over. Suppose you are standing on one leg and have lifted the other foot to do something to your shoe. If your raised foot is still trapped when you start to tilt over, you will hop. Your supporting leg suddenly relaxes a little and then straightens strongly. This throws your body up in the air for a moment. The supporting foot is then lifted and moved smartly to a new position where the leg stiffens again to catch the weight of the body and avoid the imminent fall.

A corresponding sequence of tossings and catchings, but using the two legs in turn, forms the basis of what we are doing when we run, where the extra thrust just before take-off is sufficient to allow both feet to be off the ground at the same time. The horse, with four legs available, uses his legs in different combinations for the different gaits, but the principle is the same: he applies a sequence of thrusts against the ground in different directions and at different places for each step.

The horse's movements

When a horse is grazing, he always has at least three feet on the ground. Three legs give a stable support, allowing the horse to move the fourth foot at will. By adjusting his leg thrusts, he can move his centre of gravity over the area of support which, at different times, can be provided by a different set of three legs. At any gait other than the grazing walk, there occur periods, in each cycle of locomotion, during which there are less than three feet on the ground. This leads to a tendency to topple, just like the upside-down broom. Corrections are made by extending different legs in turn in such a way as to provide thrusts in the appropriate directions.

When a horse is carrying a rider, the upthrust force to support the rider's weight is transmitted through the saddle. The movements of the horse cause the saddle to move about in quite complicated ways. It moves up and down, forwards, backwards and sideways, and it also tilts from side to side. Because the saddle is located quite near the horse's centre of gravity, the horse himself is unable to make much of a contribution to the rider's balance except in certain special circumstances. He can, of course, deliberately upset the rider's balance, as by bucking, or by jinking to one side after tossing the rider upward and then lowering one shoulder while the rider is coming down to land again in the saddle. The horse can also be helpful. If the rider is accidentally thrown forward onto the horse's neck, the horse may, if he is in a co-operative mood, catch the weight of the rider on his neck, allowing time for the rider to scramble back into the saddle. Most of the time, however, the rider must look after his own balance.

The force transmitted from the saddle to the rider depends on the rider's reactions. When a moving object pushes against a part of the body, we can adjust our muscles so that we either yield to the imposed pressure, resist it, or actively push back against it. To stay in the saddle, the rider must keep control of the upthrust forces in such a way that his centre of gravity does not get displaced too far from the safe region near the horse's midline.

When the horse is in active motion, the rider's main area of contact with the saddle consists of the inside surfaces of his knees and lower thighs. The seat-bones and stirrups come into the picture only intermittently. The rider corrects any tendency to be thrown to one side by pressing down more with the knee on that side than with the other, keeping his body as near as possible to the horse's midline. Adjustments in the fore-and-aft direction are made by moving the elbows forward or back; the position of the rider's spine will then follow automatically. The exact position of the centre of gravity of a rider depends on the attitudes of his limbs. It is usually not far from his navel. Hence the rule for staying in the saddle is: 'keep your breastbone over the horse's midline', as in the safe position for the beginner explained in Chapter 1.

Problems at the jump

When a horse is taking off for a jump, the whole of the thrust against the ground is provided by the hindlegs in order to launch the combined weight of horse and rider upwards and forwards. At this stage you need to lean well forward, from the hips not from the waist and without rounding your shoulders, with your trunk well forward over your knees, your elbows in front of your knees and your seat-bones out of the saddle, in the jump-seat position. While passing over the jump, the horse's body pitches over from aiming upward to aiming downward, ready for the landing on the forefeet. During the descent you need to unfold at the hips so that your knees can follow the forward tilt of the saddle. You should also push your feet forward. This puts you in a good position to absorb the impact when the horse's forefeet strike the ground.

It is important to keep your heels away from the horse at all times. This helps to press your knees into the saddle so that the saddle cannot stray to one side without your being aware of it. If it were to do so, the next contact would tend to tip you over to the other side. During the descent, you must prepare your body to 'give' so as to make a soft landing in the saddle when the horse lands on the ground, because the forces of impact are large and sudden. It is a mistake to rely on the stirrups for balance at this stage. Either stirrup or leather may break, so that the unbalanced thrust to the other leg would throw you over. If the stirrup accidentally slips back under your foot, the springy shock-absorbing action of the ankle is lost, leading to a jolt which can also be unsettling, particularly if you get more of a jolt on one side than the other. Your aim should be to keep yourself supple enough to be able to 'give' adequately and promptly to allow the saddle to move under you without disturbing the thrust line. If you are not supple enough, you will be in trouble. When the saddle comes up against an unyielding part of your anatomy, the thrust communicated will tend to tip you over. Unskilled and poorly timed adjustments then just make matters worse and over you go.

In all these adjustments, the important direction is that of the thrust line rather than that of the gravitational vertical. This can be seen clearly when a horse is making a sharp turn, and even more so when a racing motorcyclist corners at speed. In each case the area of contact with the ground is well away from a vertical line through the centre of gravity. The rider's body has to be balanced with respect to the thrust line from the ground, not with respect to the gravitational vertical.

Some confusions resolved

The use of the word 'balance' introduces three areas of confusion common in the context of support forces. These areas may be labelled 'stress forces', 'forces in opposition', and 'balance' itself. A full treatment of these topics would call for a whole book devoted to this alone. The explanations given here are accordingly compressed and highly technical. The relations between some of the terms used may be found in the entry under 'momentum' in Appendix 3.

Stress forces

Force is defined as the rate-of-change of momentum and it is measured as the product of the acceleration of a body multiplied by its mass. This definition suggests that force implies movement. Nevertheless, it is quite usual to speak of forces as acting in the absence of movement. The reason for this is that our notions of the measurement of force are derived from observations on collisions, usually without consideration of the deformations occurring in the colliding bodies. Such deformation is always inevitable, even though it may be so small as to escape notice. Any deformation in a solid body is always accompanied by stress, that is to say, by a tendency of the deformed object to return to the original shape. It is the stress occurring in the colliding structures at the impact region that is responsible for the changes in momentum. We come thus to speak of 'stress forces' present in a material by virtue of its deformation. It is natural to extend the usage to cover instances where deformation and stress are present even in the absence of movement. For example, if a weight is supported by a spring balance, we may speak of the deformation of the spring as exerting an upward force on the weight, even though the weight is not moving. The material of the weight is deformed in the same way as the spring, though the deformation is less obvious, and the weight exerts a downward stress force on the pan of the balance. Thus the weight of a rider exerts a downward force on the saddle, while the saddle exerts an upward, supporting, force against the rider's seat.

Stress forces are invariably associated with deformations ('strains') involving changes in the detailed molecular architecture of the structures that are stressed. We are usually paying attention to one particular structure, which is in contact with others which are not themselves the prime object of our attention. We can then distinguish the various contact regions according to the 'work done' in setting up the deformations. Work is measured as the product of the magnitude of the force multiplied by the distance through which the point of application of that force is moved. Work thus has a direction; it can be done *by* a structure (active), or *on* a structure (passive). Where work is done on a structure to which we are paying attention, this is a 'load point'. Where that structure does work on another, this is a 'support' from the point of view of the first structure. Where two structures are in contact and exert stress forces on one another, both structures are deformed and where there is deformation, there is also stress force present.

Forces in opposition

For purposes of calculation in elementary mechanics, it is convenient to lump together the stress forces distributed through the molecular structures at the region of contact and to treat the whole as a single resultant force with a single point of application, and it is this simplification that we are all brought up with. In terms of this simplification, we separate the effects of the stress at the area of contact into two forces: the force exerted by the support on the load and the force exerted by the load on the support.

At this point you might ask whether the support force balances the load or the other way round. But these are not truly separate forces; you can't have one without the other. One might as well ask someone to choose between 'the nose is above the mouth' and 'the mouth is below the nose'. These are not true alternatives; they are different aspects of the same relationship. The two 'forces' are different aspects of the same phenomenon, the presence of the condition of stress. Newton's Third Law is concerned with such pairs of forces, which are always equal in magnitude and opposite in direction, as a simple consequence of the relationship between the simplified scheme and the detailed phenomenon that the scheme describes. The Third Law is really a tautology. The two equal and opposite forces in a Newtonian pair are not 'opposing forces', and they do not 'balance against' one another, because they do not act on the same structure; one acts on the load, the other on the support. There is no 'transmission' of force across the area of contact.

A different situation arises where two independent agents act separately but against one another, as when one person tries to push open a door while another person pushes back to prevent the door from being opened. We then have two separate loads applied to the door. These forces are not necessarily equal; one person may be stronger and force the door open. But where either person pushes against the door, the door itself pushes back against that person, because the material of the door is deformed by the push, just as the body of the pusher is deformed, at the region of contact. So here, at one side of the door, we have two forces that are equal and opposite. Another pair of forces can be distinguished on the other side of the door. There is also a sense in which the force exerted by one person is transmitted through the door to the person opposing him. If the door is at rest (i.e. does not move under the action of all these forces) then the forces exerted by the two people are equal in magnitude and opposite in direction. The stresses are not necessarily the same at the two regions of contact because the areas of contact on the two sides are not necessarily equal. If the door moves, the forces exerted by the two people are necessarily different, since the work done by the winner is spent in two ways: in addition to the work done on the loser, some work is expended in accelerating the mass of the door. It is converted into the kinetic energy of the moving door. Opposing forces are not necessarily equal in magnitude. They are equal only when there are no accelerations.

Thus a rider's weight presses down on the saddle, not only through the rider's seat, but also through his knees and through the tension in the stirrup leathers which pull downward on the stirrup bars. At the same time, the horse's back pushes upward against the saddle with a force that continually varies during the different phases of the locomotor cycle.

When a supported structure is loaded, stresses of different magnitudes occur in different parts of the structure, depending on how the parts of the structure are assembled. If the structure is being accelerated by unequal external stress forces, the local stresses have to provide the accelerations of all the elements of the distributed mass. In these conditions, we may speak of a 'stress gradient', since the local intensity of the stress will depend on how much mass that part of the structure has to accelerate, and this will be different for different parts of the structure.

We can measure accelerations with an 'accelerometer'. This is a device consisting of a frame enclosing a small mass which is tethered to the frame by a springy support. This small mass is otherwise free to move while being at the same time isolated from the rest of the structure by the frame. The indication given by the device depends on the stress gradient across its frame. It measures the strain in the springy support of the tethered mass. When the whole structure is accelerated, the support of the tethered mass is strained by the force needed to keep the mass in place within the frame. The indication is then interpreted in terms of the acceleration of the whole structure to which the device is attached. The balancing organ present in the inner ears, of both horse and rider, functions as such an accelerometer. It plays its part in the process of deciding which is the best direction in which to push against the available supports in order to avoid falling over, since it indicates the relative direction, as well as the magnitude, of the stress gradient in the animal's head, which in turn is related to the support force acting on the head.

Gravity

Newton's genius led him to describe the observed accelerations of unsupported bodies in terms of a hypothetical force that he called 'gravity'. This is a force that is not associated with strain, so an accelerometer tells us nothing about the 'gravitational force' on an unsupported body and it does not indicate the 'acceleration due to gravity'. This has led some to suppose that, in free fall, there is no gravity present. But, of course, the whole idea of introducing the notion of gravity was to be able to hold it to be responsible for the acceleration of bodies in free fall.

To bring his ideas on gravity into line with his other ideas on force, Newton supposed that all bodies exert an attractive force on all other bodies, the magnitude of the effect between two specific bodies being proportional to the product of their masses and inversely proportional to the square of the distance separating them. Thus the force with which the apple is attracted to the earth forms a Newtonian equal-and-opposite pair with the force with which the earth is attracted to the apple. This formulation has had dramatic success in accounting for the observed relative motions of the celestial bodies. (The remaining, very small, discrepancies are dealt with by an alternative, and quite different, scheme of explanation proposed by Einstein. This alternative scheme does not contradict Newton's; it is just another way of describing the same phenomena.)

Unfortunately, the uninitiated majority have mixed up the ideas of gravitational forces with the stress forces acting on bodies supported on the earth's surface. Supported bodies do not accelerate like unsupported bodies, but there is no reason to suppose that the gravitational attraction to the earth is affected by the presence or absence of the supports. The fallacy is to suppose that the gravitational force is the same force as that with which the body presses down on its supports. (Even the space agencies, both of America and of Europe, fall into this trap.) After making this supposition, it is then stated, mistakenly, that the support force acting upward on the supported body is equal and opposite, in the Newtonian sense, to the gravitational force acting downward on the body. However, a very simple experiment demonstrates that this statement cannot be true. All you have to do is to jump in the air. This action can have no conceivable effect on gravity, yet the magnitude of the supporting force is temporarily reduced to zero.

During each unsupported phase in any locomotor cycle, such as at the trot or during a jump, the bodies of horse and rider are in a state of 'free fall', and acquire downward momentum under the unopposed action of gravity. This unsupported phase is often spoken of as a 'period of suspension'. This is an unfortunate usage, since the word 'suspension', in one sense, indicates support by hanging from above and, as we have seen, there is no such support force available during this phase. In fact, the weight of the forequarters of the horse is suspended from the shoulderblades when the forefeet are on the ground, but this suspension is interrupted during the free-fall phase. There is a second sense in which the word 'suspension' is used, namely for the interruption of a process, as work may be suspended during a holiday. These two usages are confused here. It is preferable to keep to the unambiguous expression 'unsupported' for this phase.

The momentum acquired during the period of free fall has to be absorbed by muscular forces during the landing, and a new upward momentum has to be developed during the action of throwing the weight upward for the next phase of the cycle. The required changes of momentum call for the deployment of substantial forces, since the average upthrust over any complete locomotor cycle must, on level ground, be exactly equal to the body weight. If the time available for the action of a support force is restricted, its magnitude must be correspondingly increased to compensate. The shorter the duration of its action, the greater is the thrust required to achieve the same change in momentum.

Part of the upthrust developed by the horse's legs is transmitted to the rider through the saddle. Here again, the intensity of the thrust depends on the time available for its action. All the thrusts are stress forces involving deformation, and the thrust against the rider is no exception. Deformations take time to develop, the rate of deformation depending on the springiness of the material that is to be deformed. It is accordingly an advantage to the rider if he can make his muscles as springy as possible, thus prolonging the deformation process, increasing the time available for the action of the thrust forces, and correspondingly reducing their intensity. In this way he makes use of the 'shock-absorbing' function of the musculature.

During the bouncing motion of a rider on a horse, the supporting thrusts vary considerably in intensity. The skilled rider takes care to ensure that his body is always suitably supple. This means that the various heavy parts of his body are held together by very springy links, in contrast to the beginner whose body tends to be comparatively stiff. The effect of being supple is that, when the rider comes down into the saddle for a bounce, it is at first only those parts of his body that lie close to the saddle that have to have their momentum changed suddenly. The effects on other parts develop gradually a little later, in consequence of the shock-absorbing behaviour of the springy connecting links. As the thrusts on these parts are spread out in time, the intensities of the forces are kept comparatively low, and the ride is correspondingly more comfortable.

Balanced forces

Weight is the stress force with which an object presses down on its supports. If a weight is placed in the scale-pan of a 'balance' it tends to tip the beam over. Two weights are equal if the beam comes to rest in a level position; that is to say, when the two opposing tendencies to tip the beam happen to be equal and opposite (not in the sense of a Newtonian pair). By extension, we say of the two people struggling with the door that their efforts balance one another if the door does not move.

When an object is at rest on the earth's surface, its supports exert a stress force at the area of contact. Stresses also occur throughout the structure of the supported object, but the intensity of these stresses in different places depends, not only on the way the structure is built, but also on how the mass is distributed through the whole. There is thus a stress gradient, measurable with an accelerometer, although the object is at rest and is not accelerating. The indication of an accelerometer in this situation is interpreted as a measure of the intensity of the local gravitational field, though it is the stress gradient that is measured, not the gravitational force itself. There is a sense in which it is reasonable to say that the effect of the stress gradients in the supports 'balances' the effect of the downward gravitational force.

Similarly, for the body of a rider seated in the saddle when the horse is not moving, the stress gradients associated with the pressure against the saddle balance the downward gravitational force on the rider's body. The justification for this statement is that, if either the support thrust or the gravitational force were unopposed, the rider's body would accelerate, as indeed it does if the two forces are unequal. Too large a thrust throws the body upward, and if the support is withdrawn, the body falls.

The task of 'maintaining one's balance' consists in adjusting the stress forces with which we push against the available supports in such a way that the cumulative effects of the support thrusts (accepting that they vary with time, as they inevitably must) will, in the long term, preserve the body roughly in its preferred posture.

APPENDIX 2

Learning and Teaching

When one sets out to acquire a new skill, or to train a horse to perform a new manoeuvre, it helps in the planning if we have some idea of how the learning process works. This is a somewhat confusing topic since many of the words commonly used in discussing it appear to mean different things to different people. In what follows, I explain some of the relevant ideas. Clarification of the terminology of these various reactions, together with consistency in the use of the terms, makes it much easier to understand what is going on in animal behaviour and in the training of animals and people to perform specific tasks. Loose usages all too often produce confusion and can lead to serious failures of communication.

Perception in animals

In considering the learning capability of the horse we should avoid the temptation to suppose that the horse's perceptions resemble our own. The example of the horse Clever Hans should reinforce this point. It was at one time maintained that Clever Hans was able to do simple mental arithmetic. In demonstrations of this ability, an arithmetical problem would be set either by direct question or on a blackboard, and the horse would give the answer by counting out the appropriate number in a sequence of pawing movements, using one foreleg for the tens and the other for the units. It later came to light that it was essential that the questioner should remain within the animal's field of view. The crucial feature in Clever Hans's responses in these demonstration tests was his recognition of eye-movements and subtle body-language signals emitted, quite without realising it, by the questioner. He, of course, was a human familiar with the calculations involved. There was thus no real evidence that the animal could understand the significance of the spoken words in which the arithmetical problem was put to him, or that he could read the blackboard, or that he was able to count. All that was really necessary for the complete performance was that the horse should be able to recognise, from looking at the questioner, when he should start and when he should stop tapping with each foot in turn.

Recognition

There is still a great deal of mystery about what goes on during an act of recognition. Indeed, the elucidation of this mystery may turn out to be the most difficult of all the current problems in neurophysiological enquiry. It is not always appreciated how important a part the act of recognition plays in any stimulus-response situation. Even a coin-operated slot machine has to have a mechanism for 'recognising' that a coin has been inserted and that certain dimensions of that coin fall between prescribed limits. The mechanisms may, for example, incorporate a device for rejecting discs with holes in them (such as washers) if it is intended to be operated only by coins of the realm.

Context is important. We tend to think of our world as made up of discrete objects, each of which is distinguished as separate from the background. We persist in this type of interpretation even when looking at pictures in which the patches of colour contributing to our image of an object are, in themselves, indistinguishable from similar patches of colour 'representing' the background in the same picture. There is no reason to suppose that animals behave similarly to ourselves in separating 'figure' from 'ground'. Thus what we may think of as a familiar object may, to a horse, constitute an alarm signal when it is presented in surroundings where it does not otherwise commonly appear. Any unfamiliar detail in a horse's environment might indicate the approach of a predator – just the sort of warning sign that a potential prey must be continually on the look-out for.

The recognitions performed by a horse may be very different from those performed by a human. If our horse shies it is often very hard to see just what it is that has upset him. I remember a puzzling occasion when my horse refused to walk past a certain point in the road. I eventually concluded that the sticking point occurred in this way. The place in the road past which he would not go was where there was a change in the smoothness of the road surface. The two sections of the roadway had been re-surfaced at different times and the part ahead was much smoother. There had been rain earlier, so the road was wet. It was a bright morning, though lightly overcast. We were going southeast, toward the sun, and the road ahead was reflecting the bright sky. I later discovered that the horse would not step into a puddle, even if it was only a quarter of an inch deep. There was no trouble taking him into a river, and he would splash about there quite happily, but puddles – no way! I imagine that the shiny wet road ahead was taken to be a large puddle. I don't know why he disliked puddles. Perhaps he had had a bad experience at some time in the past, such as stepping into a hole through thin ice.

Conditions for learning

This brings out an important difference between humans and horses in the way they learn things. The difference may reflect a fundamental difference between predator and prey species. A predator is not easily discouraged by failure. The behaviour is characterised by the saying, 'If at first you don't succeed, try, try, try again'. For the prey, on the other hand, it is important for his survival that he should avoid situations in which he has previously had occasion to be alarmed. The relevant saying here is 'Once bitten, twice shy'. Man, being partly a carnivore, counts as a predator, while the horse, which is exclusively herbivorous, belongs to a prey species.

Learning is a process by which behaviour is modified in the light of experience. It happens to be true that any behaviour that is followed by some sort of reward is more likely to be repeated than actions that are not systematically rewarded. The effect is often small, but it is usually cumulative. In man, the effects of a positive reward are often large and dramatic. A single trial may suffice for the solution of a problem, if it succeeds, so that the problem is no longer a problem when it arises again. On the other hand, failures, even painful failures, are often not taken too seriously. The trial may not need to be 'acted out' but only imagined, and it will still be effective. The opposite is true for the horse. Alarm situations are learned, almost indelibly, at a single trial, whereas changes in behaviour induced by positive rewards build up only very slowly.

The context in which learning is to take place is also an important factor. In the horse, there appear to be three main 'states of mind', so to speak. There is the state of 'placidity', in which the horse will graze, sleep, or just stand around; and there is the state of 'alarm' in which the horse lifts his head, pricks his ears and looks around in a highly alert state, ready to take off at once if there is any sign of a predator (from which his best defence is usually flight). In between there is a 'play' state in which he may engage in all sorts of activities with other horses, including chasing games.

A peculiar thing about the domesticated horse, and a feature in which he differs markedly from many other animals, is that he is prepared to allow humans to participate in his games. At all times, however, he has to be ready to change abruptly to the alarm state if he detects something suspicious.

The horse is particularly open to positive reward when he is in the play state. He will accept human caresses, and even a kind word in the right tone of voice, as a positive reward. The reward does not have to be a titbit of food. But the teacher has to have a lot of patience. On the other hand, anything that triggers the alarm state is instantly learned, so that the horse very quickly appreciates the sort of situation in which he is likely to be alarmed. He remembers such situations well, and for a very long time. He does not take any account of the possibility that it was actually some action of his own that set off the trigger. Indeed he seems to have very little idea of what he himself did on any previous occasion and this characteristic no doubt contributes to the slowness with which he learns the new tricks which we try to teach him. The alarm state is not conducive to the acquisition of new skills. Accordingly, if we wish to teach an animal something by the technique of repeated positive reward and reinforcement, it is important to avoid allowing him to slip into the alarm state.

Communication

We tend to take communication between humans very much for granted, and in spite of language barriers we take it that the medium of communication is by speech. There are, however, a number of other ways in which we communicate with one another. In particular, our mood and aspects of our expectations can be conveyed by subtle changes of posture of which we are often unaware, together with variations in tenseness or relaxation as well as by the tone of voice. It is this type of communication that Clever Hans was responding to.

An important feature of communication between individuals is the recognition by one member of a communicating pair of the state of mind of the other. It often happens that the significance of a signal depends on its context, so the interpretation of a particular signal on a specific occasion depends on the conclusions that the receiver has come to about the state of mind of the sender at the moment in question.

Let us take an example. It happens that some of the movements made during play are very similar to movements used in courtship. Now courtship belongs in the domain of 'placidity'. That is to say, the animals must have decided that there is nothing untoward going on, just the ordinary dull routine, and no cause for alarm. Confusions can thus arise between movements made in play and similar movements intended as signals in courtship. Serious misunderstandings and even downright ill-feeling can arise when individuals interact and one partner misclassifies a movement by the other partner, taking it as courtship rather than as play or vice versa.

It remains totally unexplained how it comes about that an individual can recognise some movement of another individual as constituting a significant signal. Nevertheless, we know this to be a fact, and it forms the basis for our attempts to train horses.

In considering how our communication processes are involved in training both the horse and the rider, we need to be a little careful about the terms used. Discourse can become rather precarious unless we can agree on conventions about the meanings of the words. A recurring problem arises when words that have a precise significance in an academic context come to be used much more loosely in common speech.

The meaning of 'reflex'

The word 'reflex' is an important example. It is often used, particularly by sports commentators, to denote any rapid action, including the highly skilled reactions of a competitive sportsman. Strictly speaking, the word denotes a group of simple reactions such as those obtainable even from a decapitated frog, provided that certain parts of the spinal cord remain intact. Rigorous scientific definition to cover all present-day usages can be dauntingly long-winded. The involvement of the nervous system is essential; the responses must be simple, automatic and not voluntary; the triggering conditions have to be specific for individual reflexes; and recognisable repeatability is another essential part of the idea. The original notion that the stimulus was also 'simple' has had to be abandoned, now that it has been discovered that even quite lowly parts of the nervous system can take account of a whole range of aspects of the environmental conditions and will generate different responses to specific stimuli according to the conditions.

For example, the response seen in the knee-jerk reflex when the tendon is tapped by the physician's tendon-hammer in a suitably relaxed and seated subject does not occur when the same tendon is suddenly stretched under the subject's weight when landing after a running step. We must suppose, therefore, that the nervous system is able to make distinctions even without the involvement of consciousness.

The notion of a 'gestalt'

At this point I need to explain what I mean by a 'gestalt'. Let us take first the process of 'gestalt perception' where the use of the term is familiar. When we look at an outline drawing of a face we carry out a number of steps without thinking about them. We first distinguish the page from the rest of what can be seen. Then we notice the markings on the page. Now comes the miraculous part. We suddenly decide that we are looking at the representation of a face. It is this sudden recognition stage that is referred to as 'gestalt perception'. The odd thing about it is that the actual pattern of marks on the page can be altered in all sorts of ways and yet we can still achieve the recognition 'that we are seeing the representation of a face'.

In fact, of course, no real face looks quite like a white patch with black marks on it. What has happened is that we have performed an act of classification, associating certain features of our sensory experience together to form a pattern of a recognised type. All sorts of different patterns, the appearances of different people, different parts of certain pictures, and so on, are all classified together to count as faces. Because patterns that differ so much in their component details are all classified together, it is very hard to specify just what features should be used to define each class, such as the class of faces, or whatever. This difficulty of definition does not, however, hold us back from making the classifications. Indeed, it may be argued that the whole of our experience is made up of such acts of classification, not necessarily involving actual naming.

If it is accepted that the use of the word 'recognition' does not necessarily imply conscious perception, we can extend the idea of the 'gestalt' from the context of perception to other processes of recognition where all that is implied is the performance of some form of discrimination. It is in this sense that I use the term 'gestalt recognition' to refer to the distinguishing of one set of conditions from another, as in the mechanism by which the nervous system sorts out the conditions that are to count as the presence of a particular 'adequate stimulus' from other conditions in which no response is to be generated.

Voluntary action

When we say that an action is performed 'voluntarily', by ourselves or by another, this implies two things. Firstly, that we do not see any particular event that can be singled out as the stimulus for the action; and secondly, that we infer that this action, though performed by another, appears to resemble actions of our own that are accompanied by a feeling that we are doing them spontaneously. The production of a response does not imply the intervention of the will. Many reflex responses can be demonstrated in animals in conditions that preclude any possibility of consciousness or of voluntary activity.

Conditioned reflexes

A 'conditioned reflex' is an ordinary reflex that has been modified, by a special routine, in such a way that the response comes to be produced in a new way. In the example usually quoted, the ordinary reflex is the production of saliva by the presence of meat-juice in a dog's mouth. In the training routine, Pavlov took elaborate precautions to exclude all of the cues normally associated with feeding, in order to avoid any possibility of learning in the normally accepted sense. He arranged to deliver the meat-juice to the dog's mouth through a tube and used another tube to collect the saliva. In this way he ensured that the dog could not see what Pavlov was doing. In the next stage, the delivery of the meat-juice was preceded regularly by the ringing of a bell. Then, after a number of repetitions, he observed that saliva could be produced in response to the ringing of the bell without any meat-juice being given to the dog at the same time, and it is this special kind of link between stimulus and response that is called a conditioned reflex. The response itself, the production of saliva, remains unchanged.

The formation of Pavlovian conditioned reflexes can be readily interpreted in terms of the gestalt-recognition nature of stimulus detection. The training routine has the effect of altering the content of the gestalt that is to act as the trigger for the production of the same reflex response as before.

'Operant conditioning'

Confusion arises because the word 'conditioning' is also used in a quite different context. In what is called 'operant conditioning', an animal discovers that certain of its actions lead to a reward of some kind. Thereafter, such actions tend to be performed more frequently. This is an example of true learning: the modification of behaviour in the light of experience. When we say that an animal learns the significance of a particular signal, this means that the behaviour elicited by that signal will thereafter be different from what it was before. A trainer can make use of the propensity to learn, which all animals possess, by artificially presenting rewards whenever the animal performs some action that the trainer has decided to 'reinforce' — the 'target behaviour'. At a later stage, the trainer can accompany the presentation of the reward with some convenient signal. The animal comes to incorporate the detection of this signal into the gestalt indicating the likelihood of imminent reward. The signal then comes to act as a promise of a reward to be delivered later, and after some repetitions, the signal itself serves as a reinforcement on its own, even if the reward is considerably delayed or even if it is presented only intermittently.

Training to a cue

The trainer can now introduce another signal which is to act as a cue. This cueing signal is presented when the animal is not doing anything particular and the reinforcement of the target behaviour is given only in the presence of the cue. The animal then comes to associate the cue with his expectation of receiving a reward and thereafter produces the target behaviour whenever he detects the cue. After this training routine has been established we reach a stage where the trainer's cueing signal is followed pretty reliably by the animal's performance of the specific action selected. There is a superficial resemblance to the conditioned reflex situation, but there are important differences. The training routine is different. In classical conditioning, the trainer's signal must precede the response, which is always that obtainable in a reflex of the ordinary sort. There is no change in behaviour. In operant conditioning, although the cue precedes the perform-ance, it is the trainer's reinforcing signal on which the training depends, and this has to follow the performance by the animal of the target action. This action is a piece of voluntary behaviour and may bear no resemblance to any response that can be obtained in any ordinary reflex.

One may often read of an animal, or a person, being 'conditioned to behave in a particular way' where all that is intended is that the subject has 'learned to do it'. The usage ignores the fact that conditioning is done by someone other than the subject, while learning is something that the subject does for himself. Furthermore, a good deal of learning takes place without the intervention of any outside party.

'Anticipatory pre-emptive actions'

Indeed there is a very important class of learned actions that closely resemble the responses in certain ordinary reflexes. They are the 'anticipatory pre-emptive actions'. These are performed in situations where the ordinary reflexes are likely to be evoked but the pre-emptive actions are set off by expectations rather than by direct stimuli. The effect is that corrective actions, for example in the avoidance of overbalancing, can be initiated early, before the situation has become so extreme as to trigger off the ordinary reflexes of balance. The advantage of these 'anticipatory pre-emptive actions' is that they avoid the delays that are inevitably incurred in the conduction of nervous messages in the ordinary reflexes. This leads to a much smoother and more secure maintenance of balance. The individual limb movements in locomotion are all pre-emptive, rather than reflex. This allows scope for changes in speed, in gait, or in direction, and even for the aiming of individual footfalls in the avoidance of obstacles.

Habits

The anticipatory pre-emptive actions, once developed, rapidly become habitual; that is to say, the reaction comes to be produced almost automatically whenever the 'trigger gestalt' is detected. The recognition of the triggering gestalt often occurs before one has become aware of the changing situation. That is why we are so seldom able to say what it was that triggered off a particular habitual movement. We just find ourselves performing the habitual action 'without thinking'. It is this feature of habits that makes it so hard to change them. It also highlights the importance of avoiding the development of bad habits during the initial training of both horse and rider.

In the attempt to change a person's habit, two things appear to be essential. The first is an adequate desire to change, and for this the instructor needs to use his ingenuity to build up a suitable degree of motivation in his pupil. The second requirement, and one which is much more difficult to meet, is that the person with the habit has to be brought to a condition in which he is aware of the 'feel' of that changing situation which will eventually produce the habitual action. It is only when he has learned to recognise this crucial moment that he can take effective action to produce an alternative pattern of behaviour.

In the training of the horse, one cannot suggest to the animal that he should watch out for a particular set of conditions. It falls to the trainer to spot the crucial moment at which it might be appropriate to intervene. He needs a finely tuned awareness of what the horse is doing, based on a close attention to the most minute movements made by the horse, so as to be able to anticipate that the horse is about to manifest the habitual behaviour that is to be changed. It is only when he gets the timing right, and intervenes with the appropriate aids, that the trainer has any chance of successfully modifying an established habit. However, if one can avoid the situations in which a bad habit is likely to be performed, the force of that habit will gradually dwindle through lack of the reinforcement of repetition.

Notes on Some Terms in Common Use

with explanations of terms borrowed from mechanics

Additional definitions are given in the body of the book and these may be located through the Index.

Airs above the ground A group of High School movements in which the horse performs, on command, a controlled and limited rearing up onto his hindlegs, with his forelegs curled under his chest. He then either holds this pose, or jumps into the air off his hindlegs.

In the *levade*, the horse performs a controlled, partial, rearing up and sustains this pose, balancing on his hindlegs with deeply bent hocks and with his forefeet tucked well in toward his chest.

In the *ballotade*, the horse performs a controlled rearing up and then jumps upward and forward with hindlegs well flexed but showing the soles of his hindfeet to the rear, and lands on all four feet.

In the *croupade*, the horse performs a controlled rearing up and then jumps vertically upward with forelegs and hindlegs well flexed under the body, to land again on the hind feet.

In the *courbette*, the horse performs a controlled, almost vertical, rearing up and then, maintaining this pose, makes a series of forward jumps on the hindlegs alone.

In the *capriole*, the horse performs a controlled rearing up and then, after balancing for a moment with well flexed hocks, jumps vertically upward, high into the air, at the same time kicking out strongly with the hindlegs before landing on all four feet.

Amble This term was formerly used for a gentle leisurely form of progression, without implying any particular gait. Muybridge, in his pioneering analysis of locomotion, used 'amble' for a four-beat symmetrical running walk which is also referred to as the '*singlefoot*'. This gait combines considerable speed over the ground with a very smooth ride. There is always at least one foot on the ground. Phases of support on a single leg alternate with phases of two-point lateral and two-point diagonal support. Nowadays the term 'amble' is more often used to imply a laterally coupled gait at walk, running walk, or trot, including the two-beat lateral trot used in 'trotting races'. Muybridge called this latter gait the '*rack*', but it is now commonly called a '*pace*', while 'rack' is used for the four-beat running walk. The rack is described as 'smooth and comfortable', reflecting an association with the word 'rock' rather than with 'rack', an instrument of torture.

There remains some further ambiguity in the use of the term 'amble' for the laterally coupled gaits (which are also called 'paces'). Some describe the ride at the 'pace' as 'comfortable', while others speak of it as 'very hard on the rider', resembling the ride on a camel, which commonly uses the lateral trot. The reason for this difference of opinion may be that there are two forms of four-beat lateral trot. The footfalls of the lateral pairs of feet are often spread out in time, rather than precisely synchronised. The gait is then called a 'broken pace'. In one form, the sequence of footfalls is the same as at the grazing walk, namely: left hind, left fore, right hind, right fore. In the other form, which is developed from the two-beat pace, the sequence is: left fore, left hind, right fore, right hind. The difference in footfall sequence is likely to entail marked differences in the motion of the horse's trunk, with consequent differences in the feel of the ride.

Asking with the rein Here 'asking' is used in the sense of a polite request, as in 'asking for' some action. The expression refers to the slow alerting signals sent by the rider through the rein to attract the horse's attention and to tempt him to move his head to one side or the other, or to flex his neck at the poll.

Balance A state in which opposing tendencies are equal. In a balanced posture, there is no preponderating tendency to tip over to one side rather than to another. The horse is also said to be 'balanced' when he appears well placed to initiate a change of course in any direction on command, and is not obviously having to struggle to avoid falling over. (See also under **Centre of gravity**, and Appendix 1.)

Behind the bit A condition in which the horse persistently draws his nose in, allowing the rein to go slack in order to evade those of the rider's commands that are normally transmitted through the bit. This is a fault that is incompatible with the development of impulsion.

Bracing the back The action of a rider, using his back muscles in conjunction with a movement of his pelvis, to drive the saddle forward with the seat-bones. This is the action required in the seat aid, which encourages the horse to go forward with increased vigour.

Cadence An expression indicating the increased liveliness of the lifting and setting down of the feet that accompanies the shortening of the stride during the development of increased collection.

Centre of gravity The point through which the resultant of the supporting forces must act in order to oppose the pull of gravity.

This might seem a simple idea, but it is not easy to explain in simple language. The concept depends on a number of other ideas each of which involves complications which may be unfamiliar. (For definitions of the terms used, see under **Momentum**.)

If the line of action of the resultant of any system of external stress forces passes to one side of the centre of gravity of a body, one action of that system of forces is to produce a rotation. That is to say, it will generate an angular acceleration of the body about its centre of gravity in a direction and of a magnitude that are dependent both on the moment exerted by the applied forces about the centre of gravity and on the moment of inertia of the body. The position of the centre of gravity depends on the geometrical distribution of mass within the body, not on the magnitude of the mass. Gravity does not enter into it, since gravitational forces, of themselves, generate no rotations.

For a rigid structure, the position of the centre of gravity is fixed relative to recognisable reference points on the structure, and its relative position is not affected by movements of the structure as a whole. If the structure is flexible, the position of the centre of gravity at any one time depends on the shape of the structure at that time, and it may shift when the shape of the structure changes. The position of the centre of gravity, within a rigid structure, is determinable by calculation from the results of experiments to find the point of balance in different orientations, where the *point of balance* is the position of a fulcrum through which supporting forces may be applied to a body without a tendency for the body to tip one way or the other under the action of gravity. For the body to be 'in balance', the fulcrum must be placed in the same vertical line as the centre of gravity. Conversely, the position of the centre of gravity may be determined from a set of experiments in which the position of the vertical line through the point of balance is marked on the body in a number of different orientations. The centre of gravity then lies at the intersection of these lines.

This procedure is not directly applicable to a flexible structure. However, some idea of the position of the centre of gravity of a man or of a horse can be arrived at by the following procedure, which has been adopted in calculating the positions indicated in *Photos 2.8* and *2.14*. The body is treated as composed of a number of rigid segments whose individual shapes do not alter when the posture changes. Then, for a particular posture, the positions of the various segments are measured in terms of the appropriate anatomical reference points. From these measurements, the locations within each segment of the centre of gravity of that segment can be worked out with the aid of published tables. Other tables give the relative masses for the individual segments. By combining this information, we can calculate the location of the centre of gravity of the whole body in the chosen posture.

There are some small uncertainties. Very few of the joints in the body really act as simple pivots and there may correspondingly be some doubt about the precise locations of some of the reference points. Furthermore, if the animal's conformation differs from that of the specimens from which the tables were derived, the relative masses of the segments may not correspond with the figures given in the table. Nevertheless, the calculations show that the position of the centre of gravity of the horse is not greatly affected by changes in the attitudes of the head and limbs such as those occurring in the various phases of locomotion. This is partly due to the relatively small masses of the lower parts of the limbs and partly to the fact that, when one part is moving forward, there is usually a compensating simultaneous backward movement of some other part. Extreme postures occur at take-off and landing for a high jump. Even here, the associated shift of the position of the centre of gravity turns out to be limited to, at most, a very few centimetres.

This means that there is no sound basis for statements such as have been published from time to time to the effect that significant changes occur in the position of the horse's centre of gravity.

Centre of mass A point in relation to a body such that any plane passing through that point divides the body into two parts whose masses are equal. It corresponds to the centre of gravity only if the body is of geometrically regular shape and of uniform density.

Centre of motion A point in a body that remains at rest while other parts move around it. If the points P and Q revolve about the point N so that, when P goes up, Q goes down, then N is said to be the centre of motion. It thus corresponds to a point on the axis of rotation. The expression has crept into the equestrian literature without careful attention to this definition and without any alternative definition being specified. For a horse in motion, any foot that is temporarily on the ground would fit this definition, but this is clearly not what is intended in the equestrian context. In the unsupported phases of locomotion, the motion is at a minimum at the centre of gravity, while, in the supported phases, the lines of action of the intermittent upthrusts of the forelegs and hindlegs commonly cross somewhere above the centre of gravity. These thrusts accordingly produce rocking in the fore-and-aft direction, but it is not a simple matter to determine the location of the axis of rotation at any particular instant, and the location of this axis is clearly not constant in relation to the horse's body.

Centrifugal force An illusory 'force' supposedly responsible for objects being flung toward the outside of a curved path. The true situation may be clarified by considering a weight supported by a string and swung in a circle. An *inward* force is required to cause the weight to move along a curved path. This force is provided by the string, which is in tension. The string cannot exert any outward force, or push, on the weight, so there is no outward, or genuinely 'centrifugal', force involved. In the absence of an inward pull, the weight tends to continue in its state of uniform motion in a straight line. Objects that are loose in a container tend to move in a straight line until they collide with the wall of the container if that container is itself moved in a curved path. The objects are not thrown toward the wall of the container. It is the wall of the container that moves toward the objects and collides with them before carrying them round with it by exerting inward thrust against them. See 'Forces in opposition' in Appendix 1.

Collection A controlled, bouncy, condition of the horse in which he gathers his hindlegs forward under his body to take a larger proportion of his weight on the hindlegs with slightly lowered haunches. In forward progression, the strides are markedly shorter than at the corresponding working gait. The horse indicates a high degree of impulsion by the arching of his neck and in the springiness of all his movements. He does not fight the bit or lean on it but maintains a light, steady pressure and is alert to respond to the slightest indication by the rider. Since the same degree of impulsion can also be obtained at the halt, it is appropriate to speak of 'a collected halt'. Extreme collection leads eventually to the levade, in which the whole of the weight is taken on the hindlegs with lowered haunches while the forelegs are lifted from the ground and tucked up under the chest.

Contact Used in the sense of 'the horse taking a contact', it is the horse's indication that he is willing to 'listen' to the rider's signals through the rein. He adjusts the position of his head to play his part in maintaining a light, steady tension in the rein.

Descente de main An expression indicating that the horse is seeking the bit. When the rider's hand moves forward, the horse responds by extending his head and neck forward and downward, thus maintaining a very light tension in the rein and retaining contact between the bit and the rider's hand.

'Easy gaits' A group of running walks that provide the rider with a very comfortable ride, since they lack the bouncing action of the trot and canter. (See under **Amble**.)

Energy The capacity to perform work (see under **Momentum**). The word is also used as though synonymous with 'vigour', to mean 'forcefulness' or 'intensity of activity'.

Engaging the hocks What is usually intended by this expression is that the horse brings his hindfeet nearer to the forefeet to put more weight, proportionally, on the hindlegs. The degree to which he does this is an indication of the degree of impulsion attained.

Extension A vigorous forward progression in which the horse covers as much ground as possible at each stride.

Force See under **Momentum**.

Forehand: 'Going on the forehand' The opposite of 'engaging the hocks'. The horse places proportionally more weight on the forelegs than on the hindlegs.

Foxtrot A gait in which the forelegs trot while the hindlegs walk. One of the 'easy gaits', characteristic of the Missouri Foxtrotter. The gait is often, incorrectly, described as 'walking in front and trotting behind'. But slow-motion cine-photography has revealed: (1) that each forefoot is lifted before the forefoot of the opposite side has touched down, i.e. with a running changeover; and (2) that the changeovers of the hindlegs are executed at the walk or at the race-walk. (For the distinctions between the changeovers, see under **Transitions**.) In the related gait of the Tennessee Walking Horse, an exaggeratedly elevated foreleg action for the show ring is encouraged by training with weighted shoes.

Galt A way of going; a mode of locomotor progression. Different gaits are distinguished according to: (1) the sequence of support patterns; (2) the presence or absence of coupling in the movements of the limbs, as by lateral, diagonal or transverse pairs; and (3) whether the transitions between one foot and the other of a transverse pair are walking, race-walking, running, or leaping. Varieties within each gait are distinguishable by length of stride in relation to the position of the successive footprints, and by the degree of elevation of the feet during the swing phase of the stride. (See also under **Amble**, and under **Foxtrot**.)

Impulse See under **Momentum**.

Impulsion A self-controlled eagerness to go forward, as evidenced by the way the horse surges forward as soon as, but not before, the rider indicates that this is permissible. There is an important distinction to be made between true impulsion, in which the horse controls himself calmly, maintaining a very light tension in the rein, and those states of excitement in which the horse pulls at the bit and has to be restrained quite forcefully to prevent him taking off out of control.

In hand In a routine of 'schooling in hand', the trainer works from the ground rather than from the saddle, standing beside the horse and controlling him with rein, voice, and schooling whip.

Inertia See under **Momentum**.

Inside/outside It is necessary to specify whether these terms are to refer to the relative position in the arena, to the curvature of the path, or to the bend of the horse. Many ambiguities may arise in relation to manoeuvres such as the counter-canter loops along the long side of the arena.

Jog A slow trot with very short unsupported phases, giving a rather jerky ride.

Leaning on the bit The horse's habit of persistently pulling steadily on the rein as though relying on the rider to support the weight of the horse's head. This is a distinct fault, which needs to be remedied by the rider suddenly releasing all tension in the rein and immediately taking up a light tension again. The sudden release signals to the horse that the tension in the rein is not to be relied on for support.

Lightening the forehand This expression is used by some writers to indicate the effect aimed for by raising one hand and moving both hands over to the other side. The object is to persuade the horse to put more weight on one foreleg than on the other, thus freeing that other leg to make an extended stride, as in an emphasised aid for starting the canter. The procedure has the disadvantage that it encourages the wrong bend.

Locomotor cycle, or 'cycle of locomotion' The sequence of movements and events occurring repeatedly during progression, during a period such as from one footfall of a particular foot to the next footfall of the same foot.

Mass See under **Momentum**.

Moment of inertia See under **Momentum**.

Momentum A property that bodies possess by virtue of their movement, as revealed, for example, in a collision.

When two solid bodies collide, both become deformed by the stresses set up at the area of contact. The resulting stress forces alter the motions of both bodies, and we can measure the changes in their velocities. We use the word *velocity* to indicate that we are referring to the direction of motion as well as to the speed. In a series of impacts between the same two bodies, the changes in velocity for the two bodies are always in the same ratio. For a number of bodies taken in pairs, it is thus possible to assign a fixed number to each body such that the change in velocity for the two members of any colliding pair will be in the inverse ratio of the assigned numbers.

Such numbers express the relative resistance to linear acceleration, or the *inertia*, of the bodies. After choosing some arbitrary body as a standard, we can express all the assigned numbers as multiples of this standard unit. A number derived by this procedure is referred to as the *mass* of the relevant body. Thus 'mass' is a measure of relative inertia. The *momentum* of a body is measured as the product of its velocity multiplied by its mass. In a collision, momentum is transferred from one body to another, the total momentum of the two bodies taken together remaining unchanged by the collision.

Force is defined as 'that which produces a change in momentum'. It is measured as the rate-of-change of momentum. In a collision between two bodies, the forces exerted on the two bodies are equal in magnitude and opposite in direction. These forces are associated with the deformation of the colliding bodies at the region of impact. Accordingly, the presence of deformation, even in the absence of movement, also implies the exertion of a force tending to restore the shape to what it was before the deformation occurred. This kind of force is referred to as a 'stress force'. Other kinds of force are recognised in other conditions where there is a tendency to movement. These are distinguished as 'gravitational', 'electrical', 'magnetic', and two kinds of 'nuclear' forces. *Impulse* is the product of the magnitude of a force multiplied by the time for which it acts. It is equal to the change in momentum produced by the force.

When two equal forces act on a particular body in opposite directions along parallel but not co-incident lines of action, their combined effect is to tend to produce a rotation. Such a pair of forces is referred to as a *couple*.

The effect of any combination of similar forces acting on a particular body can be represented as equivalent to the combined action of a single force, called the *resultant*, with a single point of application, together with a couple.

The two forces of a couple are said to exert a 'turning moment', or *torque*, measured as the product of the magnitude of one of the forces multiplied by the offset distance between their parallel lines of action. This measure is the same as the turning effect or *moment* of one of the forces about an axis somewhere on the line of action of the other member of the pair.

The effectiveness of a couple in producing a rotation of a particular body depends on the distribution of mass within the structure of that body and on the offset distance between the axis of rotation and the centre of gravity of the body. This resistance to angular acceleration is referred to as the *moment of inertia* of the body about that axis.

When a force produces a movement, it is said to perform mechanical work. *Mechanical work* is measured as the product of the magnitude of the force multiplied by the distance through which the point of application is moved by that force. It is a measure of the energy transferred from one body to another by the action of the force. *Power* is the rate at which the work is performed. It is the product of the magnitude of the force multiplied by the speed of movement of the point of application of that force. *Energy* is the capacity to perform work. It may be present in a system in various forms, such as electrical, chemical, mechanical etc., where equivalent definitions apply. It may be converted from one form to another, be stored in one system and released later by transfer to another system, but it cannot be created or destroyed.

On the bit A condition in which the horse responds willingly to the signals transmitted by the rider through the reins, and continually adjusts the position of his head to play his part in contributing to the maintenance of a steady light tension in the rein. This is a necessary precondition for the development of impulsion.

On the left/right rein Indicates the direction of proceeding round a circle or around the arena, with the named rein nearer to the centre of the circle or of the arena.

Outline An aspect of the horse's posture that refers particularly to the curvature of the back and the degree of extension of the head and neck, and is usually qualified to indicate the result of comparison with some notion of the 'ideal'.

Pace This has a number of meanings, and it is essential to specify the context. In human locomotion, a 'pace' (noun) is the distance between successive footfalls of a particular foot. There is a generally used sense of 'paces' to mean 'steps at the walk' (in man). In many contexts, 'steps' would be a much better word to use, since no ambiguity is then likely. 'Strides' might do sometimes, apart from the tendency for this word to carry the implication of 'striding out', as in an extended gait. A *step* refers to the movement of a foot from one place to another, without implication about the movements of other parts, whereas *stride* implies continuous progression, and includes the sway of the body during the stance phase as well as the swing of the limb. In quadrupeds, the 'pace' is a specific gait: a laterally-coupled, two-beat, progression, either at walk or, more usually, at trot. This is the 'lateral trot', as in trotting races (see also under **Amble**). 'Pace' is also used in the sense of speed, either over the ground, as in 'setting a spanking pace', a 'funereal pace', or in a temporal sense, as in the 'pace of social change'.

'To pace' (verb) in man, means: (1) to progress with regular, deliberate steps, as in 'pacing to-and-fro'; and (2) to measure out a distance in terms of the number of steps traversed. In quadrupeds, it means 'to progress with lateral-coupled limb-alternation'.

There is a definite ambiguity in the use of the word 'pace' in the context of horse gaits. It is not clear in what sense the BHS is using the word in the Dressage Rules. It may refer to speed over the ground, since 'medium' and 'working' are supposed to involve no change in rhythm. The idea of 'medium', as opposed to 'working', is awkward, since no clear criteria are offered. For the BHS, 'medium' comes 'between working and extended'.

Passada A change of rein through a small half-volte performed in full-pass with haunches well in. The hindlegs move on a somewhat larger circle than they do in a half-pirouette.

Passage A very elevated, collected trot in which the horse appears to dance forward from one diagonal pair of legs to the other, elegantly pointing the feet to the ground during the moment of hesitation when the legs are fully flexed at the top of each unsupported phase.

Phase A region, of time or of space, between changes of conditions. Thus one distinguishes an 'unsupported phase' from the moment of the last lift-off to the moment of the next landing, a region of time during which all four feet are off the ground. One may also distinguish phases of two-point support and the like. The number of phases in a locomotor cycle depends on what conditions are, for the moment, the subject of attention.

Piaffe A very elevated, collected trot on the spot; in some ways similar to a passage performed without forward progression. Some riders attempt to develop the elevation for this movement by training in hand with a schooling whip. This procedure tends to produce merely a form of marking time at the diagonal walk. The result lacks the brilliance of the true piaffe, in that there is no momentary unsupported phase and consequently the horse's body does not bounce to the same extent as it does in the true piaffe.

Point of balance See under **Centre of gravity**.

Position left/right The posture adopted in the saddle by the rider to indicate to the horse the nature of the bend that is to be performed (see page 162).

Power In the sense of 'forcefulness', implies the ability to be both strong and swift. For technical meaning, see under **Momentum**.

Rack See under **Amble**.

Reflex A stereotyped involuntary reaction regularly elicitable through the nervous system by applying the appropriate specific stimulus. For the distinction between 'reflexes' and 'habits' see Appendix 2, 'Learning and Teaching'.

Resultant See under **Momentum**.

Rhythm is the relationship between the successive time-intervals between events in a repeating sequence. It takes emphasis into account where the markers for the events, such as the sounds of the hoofbeats, are not identical in intensity. Thus we speak of rhythm as 'even', 'uneven', 'syncopated', and so on.

Running walk A gait in which the transverse pairs of legs execute 'running transitions', but the movements of the two tranverse pairs are made at different times, so that when both feet of one pair are off the ground, at least one of the feet of the other pair is still on the ground. There is no completely unsupported phase. Consequently, the vertical bouncing movements characteristic of the trot, canter and gallop do not occur, and the gait is correspondingly comfortable for the rider. Such gaits are sometimes referred to collectively as the 'easy gaits'. They include the fast gaits characteristic of the Tennessee Walking Horse, the Missouri Foxtrotter, the Peruvian Paso, and the Icelandic pony. (See also under **Amble**.)

School walk A highly collected, elevated walk in which the legs are moved in diagonal pairs, as in the trot and in the rein-back.

Schooling Causing the horse to perform exercise routines with a view to developing suppleness and obedience to the rider's aids.

Self-carriage An aspect of the horse's posture that refers particularly to the attitude of the head and neck, and which usually implies a favourable comparison with some notional ideal of elegance.

Sequence The order in which events occur, without specification of timing.

'Singlefoot' See under **Amble**.

Spanish walk/trot Extended gaits in which the forelegs are, at each stride, momentarily held out horizontally forward from the shoulder. The foot is then brought to the ground without bending the knee. The horse's head is held high, throwing more weight onto the hindlegs. The special movements of the forelegs in these gaits resemble the 'goose-step' of human military display marching. It is taught in hand, using a gentle touch with a schooling whip to prompt the horse to raise his forelegs one at a time. Tact must be exercised to avoid misunderstanding and to distinguish the desired unilateral movement from the more vigorous rearing action which it partly resembles.

Speed A term used both for the rate of succession of events, as in tempo, and for the rate of progression over the ground. This ambiguity makes it necessary, in the context of horse locomotion, to be careful about specifying which sense is intended.

Step A term signifying a shift of the position of one weight-bearing foot, together with the subsequent weight-transfer. It starts with the discontinuance of weight-bearing and the lifting of a foot. It ends after that foot has touched down and has begun to resume weight-bearing.

Stride A term signifying the set of changes occurring during a single complete locomotor cycle, as from the landing of a particular foot to the next landing of that same foot. It includes the swaying of the body over the feet during the stance phase of a limb as well as the swing phase of that limb.

Suspension To 'suspend' is used in two senses: (1) to hold up by tension from above, as a chandelier is suspended from the ceiling, rather than by thrust from below; and (2) to interrupt the temporal continuity, as in suspending operations for a holiday period. The horse's rib-cage is suspended (sense 1) from the shoulderblades when the forefeet are on the ground. This support is not available when all four feet are off the ground: the support is interrupted, suspended (in sense 2) for a period which many people refer to as the 'moment of suspension'. Since the animal's body is in free fall during this period, the notion that it is 'hanging in the air' is incorrect and to be avoided. It is preferable to use the expression 'the unsupported phase' to describe this period.

Tempo The rate of succession of events, e.g. the number of beats in unit time.

Time (in relation to the gaits of the horse) The number of hoofbeats in a locomotor cycle, as 'two-time' for a trot, 'three-time' for a canter, and 'four-time' for a walk or a gallop.

Torque See under **Momentum**.

Transitions The word is used in different senses: (1) to refer to the change from one gait type to another, as from walk to trot, from canter to halt, from halt to rein-back, and so on; (2) to refer to a change in type of movement, as from shoulder-in to half-pass etc.; or (3) within a specific gait, to refer to the changeover of support from one member of a transverse pair of legs to the other, as from left fore to right fore, or from left hind to right hind. Such transitions may distinguished by comparison with the various gaits of man. Thus they may be (a) *walking*, in which there is always at least one foot of the pair on the ground at all times; (b) *race-walking*, in which the duration of the period of support by both legs of the pair is reduced almost to vanishing point; (c) *running*, where each of the feet of the transverse pair is lifted before the opposite foot has touched down, to leave two unsupported phases in the cycle; or (d) *leaping*, where, after a phase of two-legged support, the two legs of the transverse pair are lifted in turn to throw the quarters, hind or fore, or both, upward for an unsupported phase before either of the feet of that pair touch down again. There is only a single unsupported phase in the cycle.

Virtual action A procedure in which a person rehearses a proposed movement or plan of action in his imagination without overt movement. This enables him to anticipate the 'feel' to be expected when the proposed plan is put into execution, and also to prepare himself for the consequences of his actions. It is remarkable how effective virtual action can be in the development of skilled movements.

Volte A very small circle. In the Dressage Rules, it means a circle of 6 m diameter.

Weight The total stress force needed to prevent a body from falling freely under the action of gravity.

Work See under **Momentum**.

INDEX